Reviews

"This is the inspirational story about a woman who was able to rise above an extremely abusive childhood and later marriage, to learn faith, love, and motherhood from her own son's courageous fight with cancer. It provides an illuminating example of how women who are in physically, mentally and emotionally abusive relationships can successfully escape even in the most challenging of times. It also warns of how the actions of medical professionals can be a soothing balm or a deadly arrow. The story draws the reader into the life of a mother and her wonderful little boy, who is strong beyond his years and who leaves a lasting impression on all who knew him".

~ M. Gielas, *Editor*

"Excellent read. Tragic story of a woman and the abuse she suffered growing up and later in marriage. This book shows the struggles she faced while in an abusive marriage, losing two children, and one child's battle with cancer. She tells of hospital life while sitting by her son's bed and having to be 230 miles away from her other child. And how she finds true love and a man to love, cherish, help her through, and spend the rest of her life with."

~ Janese Base, *RN, BSN*

D1309691

"I read this book after the author appeared on the We Love Memoirs group, Spotlight on Sunday. The story is a very moving account of the author's life and most importantly the story tells of her son Eli who becomes sick with cancer and subsequently dies. The book is in four parts with the third part being told from her journal recounting the months of Eli's illness and his passing away. The first two parts of the book set the scene and show how Sarah's life has been hard with an abusive mother throughout her childhood and then marrying a husband who is also abusive. As I read I felt very much that the mother was a psychopathic narcissist at best and the husband was an abusive alcoholic who had no feeling for his family and his only love being the bottle. Sarah has a very hard road which many of us would not survive I am sure. Her faith though does give her solace and even though it wavered at times in the end does help her through. I admired Sarah's love and devotion to her children and her loving heart comes through. How she managed to cope with the mother's ongoing abuse through her son's illness is beyond belief."

~ **Julie Watson,** *Author*

"Tissues are a must. A true story about pain and suffering, life is not the same for anyone, and in this case, it is so very tragic. A heart-warming story and I don't want to give anything away, but once you sit down to read it, you won't put it down. This is a must-read book and a must share when you are done. I highly recommend When Angels Fly."

~ **Susan Vance, Author,** *Eyes Like Mine*

"This was a heart-wrenching story! The protagonist, Sarah, suffered the type of abuse that no one should ever be subjected to. First, from her mother, Ethel, who seemed to be a mother from hell, and then her husband, Henry, who was a maniac, a sociopath, a psychopath and any other "path" I could find to throw at him! I have read about men who abuse their women, but Henry's form of abuse was extreme. As if that was no enough, life threw Sarah an ugly curve with the scourge of cancer that ravaged her son Eli for several months. I could not put the story down. I just wanted to know what happened with Eli, and how things ended between Sarah and Henry. I also wanted to know what happened to her mother. I was glued to the story until the end. The evil that men do always returns to haunt them."

~ **Joy Nwosu Lo-Bamijoko,** *Author*

"I read your story and came to the conclusion that you are a fighter after my own heart. You fought for your child with every ounce of strength you could muster, and in the end, that's all you can do. You can sleep well knowing that you did all you could do and therefore have no regrets. Be good to yourself and keep moving forward."

~ **Shirley Harris-Slaughter,** *Author*

"So much praise to you for surviving the unthinkable. Thank you so much for sharing your story with the world as inspiration to any other woman who is going through this or has been through this and needs to know they are not alone. "I loved, cried, was saddened, and strengthened by reading When Angels Fly. You both are wonderful and inspirational role models. We each have challenges to face in this lifetime, and I believe they are opportunities to grow and be stronger."

~ **Karen R. Ingalls,** *Author*

"I was fortunate enough to be given this book as a gift, and I am so grateful to my friend for giving me this to read... it was truly inspiring. I can honestly say that no book that I have read in recent times has had the emotional impact on me that this book has had. I rode right alongside this mother from the first diagnosis of her child's illness, right through to the conclusion. Even before her child's illness, I had to keep asking myself; are there really parents out there who treat their children as horrifically as this woman's mother and her family had treated her? She went from an abused child, to a loveless marriage filled with physical, mental and sexual abuse, to losing her first child to a stillborn birth and then finally reaping the rewards with two beautiful young boys. Life was finally looking up for her before little Eli was struck down with cancer. We follow his journey, step by step as the young mother attempts to keep her sanity, split her time between one child in the hospital and one 250 miles away. You can really feel her anguish and pain in every page. All the while, the very people who should have been helping to ease her burden; her mother, her siblings and her soon to be ex-husband were so busy plotting and planning on how they could benefit from this turn of events, she was left to struggle along with support only from some special friends.

This book is a harrowing read, make no mistake, but it is also incredibly rewarding. To anyone who has ever complained about how hard their life is - I say; read "When Angels Fly". To anyone who has ever said their life sucked - I say; read "When Angels Fly". When you have seen the courage, the fortitude and the immense challenges that this woman and her beautiful son faced you can't help but be uplifted and reminded just how much we all have to be grateful for.

This book reveals our indomitable human spirit in such a powerful and uplifting way. The book is in a large part a daily journal of Eli's time in hospital, but I totally understand the need the author felt to document every day - every day with her son was so very precious. This book had a powerful impact on me as a reader. I was truly moved by and genuinely felt everything this poor woman had to endure... mostly alone. There was no way I could not give this book five stars. The memories of Sarah, Noah and Eli will live in my memory well after I've consigned this book to the "read" shelf. I feel privileged to have shared Sarah's harrowing journey. When Angels Fly does exactly what it sets out to do I believe - it reminds us that "There but for the grace of God, go I". I recommend this book to all.... it will make you cry, but it will also uplift you. Well done.

~ **Grant Leishman, Author,** *The Second Coming*

When Angels Fly" by S. Jackson and A. Raymond is a heart-wrenching, powerful story of a woman's suffering, pain, faith, and love, a story that will open a whole new world to most readers, especially those who have never been abused or forsaken. Reading this memoir will open the eyes of readers to the sufferings and struggles experienced by many women silently, their courage, and their silent hopes. Sarah's suffering started early in her childhood with frequent abuse from her mother and the insensitivity of her school friends. "In fifth grade," she writes, "a tumor was found under my left nipple." The benign tumor could not cause so much trouble for her as it was curable. But Sarah will suffer more abuse from a husband and be driven to near insanity by the loss of her two children.

I couldn't help thinking about womanhood while reading "When Angels Fly". As a man and a father, it is hard to imagine the kind of feeling my wife has for our two kids. Many times, I had to stop reading, close my eyes, and ask myself: "Could this be really happening?" I couldn't help but wonder about the stuff of which women are made, because Sarah is a tough woman, sensitive, and rich in her humanity. It is inspiring to see how she gives life and nourishes it. The experience with Eli, her son suffering from cancer, is very touching and one that will inspire many people in the way they relate with their children. S. Jackson and A. Raymond have done a wonderful job in sharing experiences that will offer hope and provoke a silent revolution in the way most of us see women and life. It's a book that every man should read. And I mean every man!

There are some of those books for which we find no words and "When Angels Fly" is one of them. In this memoir, the authors show how a woman can find meaning and survive unimaginable suffering by connecting to her motherhood. It is a story of hope and the power of love and prayer. Although it will draw tears from your eyes as you read, it will inspire hope and courage. I love this book for the deep experience of the narrators and for the powerful lessons it offers".

~Romuald Dzemo for *Readers' Favorite*

Awards

Awards

2016 New Apple Official Selection eBook Award

2016 Circle of Books Ring of Honor Silver 2nd Place Award

2016 Amazon Number One Best Selling Book

2016 McGrath House Indie Book Awards Finalist

2016 Readers Favorite Five Star Book Award

2017 Literary Titan Silver 2nd Place Award

2017 Book Excellence Award Finalist

2018 International Bronze Medalist Reader's Favorite Audio-Book

WHEN ANGELS FLY

WHEN
ANGELS FLY

S. Jackson
& A. Raymond

Fresh Ink Group
Guntersville

When Angels Fly
S. Jackson & A. Raymond

Fresh Ink Group
An Imprint of:
The Fresh Ink Group, LLC
Box 931
Guntersville, AL 35976
info@FreshInkGroup.com
www.FreshInkGroup.com

Edition 1.0   2015
Edition 2.0   2017
Edition 3.0   2019

Book design by Amit Dey
Cover design by Stephen Geez & M. Schmidt/ FIG
Edited by Lauren A. Smith / FIG
Cover art by Anik / FIG
Associate Publisher Lauren A. Smith / FIG
Interior photos by M. Schmidt, S. Jackson, & A. Raymond

BISAC Subject Headings:
BIO026000 BIOGRAPHY & AUTOBIOGRAPHY / Personal Memoirs
REL012030 RELIGION / Christian Living / Family & Relationships
MED062040 MEDICAL / Oncology / Pediatric

Library of Congress Control Number: 2019904004
ISBN-13: 978-1-947867-53-6 Papercover
ISBN-13: 978-1-947867-54-3 Hardcover
ISBN-13: 978-1-947867-55-0 Ebook

Table of Contents

Dedication

Always to Eli and Joshua who taught us so much about life, and showed us that a baby and a five-year-old can be wiser beyond their brief time on Earth;

Always to Noah, our son, who we cherish so much, and has been so very wise beyond his years during this traumatic time in his young life;

Always to Matthew, my beloved husband, partner, and best friend in the entire world;

Always to Sarah, my beloved wife, partner, and best friend in the entire world, thank you for allowing the use of your journals to write this book. This project has been so difficult for you and I love you for opening your heart to millions of other people allowing them to know there is always hope in life no matter the circumstance.

Always to Ardy who proved just how great a child care provider she was and is to this day. You remained steadfast throughout this period of time, no matter what was thrown your way; you went above and beyond to protect our son.

Always to Casey Hunter, you took the time to always stop by and say hello to Eli and Sarah when delivering medications to the pediatric unit, and PICU; your visits made home seem like it wasn't quite so far away.

Lastly to Carola, on Earth and in Heaven, you took the time to comfort Sarah after the shock of your untimely death and you made it possible for Sarah to know that Eli and Joshua are cuddled under your wing as only a mother can do.

PART ONE

My Life Before Eli

Chapter One

I want to believe that I was once an angel; a gift that my mother had held in her strong arms. I looked down on my own arms and they were normal, the usual two long pale stretches of muscles and bones God had blessed me with. But in these arms, I held my angels also, and for that I send Him my gratitude.

But before I met any of my beautiful angels, when I was the one flying, hovering on earth all innocent and full of hopes and dreams like an angel, I became aware that there were bad things in the world. In fifth grade, a tumor was found under my left nipple. The good thing was that it was benign. My wings were clipped a few inches, but with a great zest for life, I still fluttered around. In eighth grade, another tumor which turned out to be nothing to worry about was found in my upper left arm. Though it was removed, the incident had managed to break my fragile wings. I became more aware of life, seeing it unfold before my young eyes.

I had become accustomed to hospitals, doctors, and to them saying that everything was going to be all right. In the end though, good news wasn't always to be had. And cancer, no matter how much I battled it, would come and go in my life. Tormenting me about how beautiful life could be.

Little girls have the wings of angels, and so do little boys. But as they grow, challenges would be hurled at them like a shuttlecock at a badminton game. Like the sport, if they are facing veteran players, the shuttlecock would shoot toward them rapidly; and more often than not, the feathered, conical birdie would land on the wooden badminton court.

My mother Ethel perhaps underwent a lot of stress and pressures too when I was growing up, because instead of remembering her affection toward me, all that flashed in my memory were the strong unyielding hands that dragged me by my hair across our house. During those times, I would scream, curse, and beg her to release me. But when her hands loosened my hair, her feet would then find their way to my stomach. More often than not, they would land on my head too, and I would howl in agony. How could a mother act with such hatred toward her daughter?

I really have no idea why she was never affectionate toward me or any of my siblings. I suppose she may have grown up without hugs or family affection herself in Oklahoma. Loving warmth was never learned. As a child, I would try to pull my siblings next to me in photos.

When I see families who truly love and care for each other, it is the most beautiful thing. I had that with my father, but sadly, not with my mother or siblings. Most of my siblings were estranged from her. On Matt's side though, some of his siblings consider me their sister, and I feel the same way. To have a man who truly loves you is most precious. I am thankful that Matt is in my life. I am thankful to have had my boys on Earth for the time the Lord let me have them, and I am thankful Matt's sister, Jolana, has shown me what being sisters really mean. I am just thankful.

Peas have Vitamin C, E, and Zinc. Because of that, I have to agree that they were indeed nutritious. For that reason, I shouldn't have felt Mother was punishing me for giving me peas. But, when peas were being served to me most of the time, and I was forced to finish what she packed me for lunch, which was more than any five-year-old could eat, I knew what she was doing was not a manifestation of her love. She force-fed me, mostly with peas, and there were many instances I threw up. I kept on begging her to make me peanut butter sandwiches instead, which I would have gladly eaten, but she never did. My food was not open for discussion. I never had the option…aside from peas.

At school, when I was beyond her peripheral vision, Mother would tell my teachers and friends to make sure I ate the lunch she packed for me. The food she forced me to eat at the school lunches, such as cooked spinach and cheese, were foods that made me sick to my stomach and caused me to throw up. I had to stay in the lunchroom for hours. I would sit there alone, feeling horrible and bad about myself. Was I being a disobedient child?

At such an early age, I missed classes because of the horrid reason that I had to finish the food my mother insisted I eat, whether I liked it or not. When I finally finished my lunch—either by downing the food or by dumping the remainder of my meal in the trash bins—I would stand up, clean up the table I used, and alternately walk and run back to my classroom. It was a long journey because lunches were in the old junior high basement in Golden, Colorado, where I went to school, and a good two blocks separated it from the grade school building.

In the 1960s, there were only a few channels on television. The meager variety of shows being offered made me interested in other types of media, such as books and magazines. One day, as I was browsing *McCall's* magazine, I came across an article that featured scrawny, malnourished kids. I stared at their pitiful bodies which were mostly bones covered with a thin coating of skin and told myself that maybe my mother didn't want me to be like these children. But when day after day, she would repeatedly serve me large quantities of food that I hated, I realized that it was the opposite. Mother wanted to punish me. She literally spoon-fed me. If ever there was a reason for that, I never knew what it was.

In high school, I would invite some of my friends over to my house, and they would stare at me and my mother with horrified expressions, as soon as Mother became shrouded with her usual coat of hostility toward me. Sometimes, it was just a wrong word I'd said, or a smile that she believed was not right at a particular moment, and without hesitation, she would grab me by my hair and start dragging me into the house, unmindful that my friends were gathered around watching us.

When tears rolled down my face, my friends would stand one by one, as though they knew the tears were the cue for them to leave. They did leave me. I watched sadly as their backs turned on me, and prayed that the following day in school I would receive comfort from them. And always, my friends' eyes would acknowledge me with understanding, and they would talk to me as though they had not experienced Mother's tumultuous outbreak. They knew that I did not want to discuss the incident. The friendly smiles on their faces and the gentle pats of their comforting hands were all I needed.

My mother scared our neighbors as well. On many occasions, they heard her wrath, usually directed towards my stepfather Paul or me. I never understood why we were the "chosen ones" for her wrath during my teenage years.

Later in life, after most of my siblings had been estranged from her, she chose to pick on my mentally ill younger sister, Ella. Even on the phone in another state, I could hear her in the background, mentally and emotionally abusing Ella. I saw Mother more than once drag Ella around by the hair, but I never was able to rescue her. My little sister had to endure my mother's wrath until my mother died. When I heard my mother yell and scream and abuse my sister, it brought back everything she had done to me in years past. Even in her early eighties, she had remained abusive. That was why I kept a "Protection from Abuse" court order on her, so she could not contact me, email me, write me letters, or go through Ella to get to me.

I had three stepbrothers, Levi, Isaac, and Wyatt Hunter. My mother treated them better as they were larger, stronger men and she did not beat on them. However, she also did not really want them in the home she now shared with my stepfather, Paul Hunter. My mother and Paul really weren't together very long, and the day Levi turned eighteen-years-old she banged on his bedroom door and ordered him to "pack up and leave!" Levi was forced to leave then and there. Isaac already was living out in the country with another family per his choice and that left only Wyatt at home. Wyatt eventually left as well, and he moved in with his mother.

As I grew more mature, I became stronger and more open-minded and there were even moments when I felt like I could handle any challenge that might come my way. And maybe in a way, I did. Because after the devastation that came with each blow, I stood up more limber and suppler, ready to bend and play along the hurdles of life.

Chapter Two

I got married when I was twenty years old with only one goal in mind—to escape my mother's clutches.

When I was younger, I didn't know that there were really evil mothers. In a way, *Cinderella* became an inspiration to me because of the hardships that she had to endure from her stepmother. Because I understood her so well, what being berated and hurt physically meant, I was happy when I met Henry in 1979 at a Kremson, CO bar. He had dark brown hair and brown eyes, and although he wasn't the "prince" a *Cinderella* would have swooned over, I didn't dismiss him. I was young, but I was far from idealistic.

Henry and I went out on several dates, and for most of them, he was drunk. Because I knew life wasn't perfect, I didn't mind.

We'd been seeing each other for six months, sharing a cabin in Kiowa, and I thought our union would be my salvation. Little did I know how harsh the reality would become.

I admitted to myself that in a way he scared me. He was far from perfect. He was a drunk, an alcoholic even, but I wanted to believe that he was a good man. That beyond his layers of roughness and callousness, perhaps waiting for me to discover, was his heart.

And because of my strong faith in myself, that I never wanted to be someone like my mother, I thought that some of the good vibes I had about the union would rub off on Henry.

The way things were with my mother, I didn't think life for me could get any worse. But our union was doomed from the start. I should have known that a union that started without the typical consensual agreement between two adults would only end in disaster. How was I to know that a fairy tale with him was never to be had?

When I was younger, playing with my dolls, and beginning to get familiar with stories, I believed that when I become a lady, someone would claim my hand in marriage and we would have beautiful babies together. We would fly on the back of unicorns in search for a palace where I would be queen, and the man in his shining brass armor would be my king. The moment that I took the vow which sealed my marriage to Henry, I thought it was the start of my very own fairy tale. One that would be read to little girls someday, and inspire them into believing the magic that comes with love.

I also thought of what I would become as I got older. I knew I would be either a secretary or a nurse. When I was young, I played with a black "Julia" doll. "Julia" was like Barbie, one who had her own world and dominated it. In Julia's world, she was a nurse. In my world, I was able to do both. "Julia" was my inspiration. I never thought that my role model would be a lifeless doll, and not my own mother. Henry was a violent husband. He was rough, rowdy, and a difficult man to live with. He had many "edges" that made us fight most of the time; I thought I could change this man into a better person. I wondered then, what does it take to make a marriage work? Of course, there's love. At the very core though, there had to be respect.

So, when Henry was having one of his "rough" days, and I became the subject of his crudeness, I would shut my eyes tightly, pray, and cry silently. Things happened for a reason, I told myself. And this man was given to me by God. I had to trust Him and believe that something good would come out of our marriage.

It was just another day, one where I prayed I wouldn't do anything wrong to make Henry angry enough to hurt me. Oh, how I prayed.

Henry drank in the mornings and the evenings. In fact, most of my memories of him consisted of the stench of alcohol coming from his mouth, his coarse, callused hands that very often found their way to hurt me, and his curses. He was creative, when it came to physically and emotionally hurting me. At first, I tried to make him stop binge drinking because I noticed that he hurt me only when he was drunk.

But as the months dragged, he hit me even when completely sober.

"Who's that guy you were talking to?" he snarled.

"That's just the postman."

"Don't talk to him again! If he drops by, call me." "He's just delivering bills," I argued.

He turned his back on me, picked up the recently delivered bills, still unopened, and slapped me with the envelopes. My face grew hot from anger, but he was so much bigger than I.

"Call me. Or I will kill you. Don't talk to any other man, you bitch," he yelled.

"Please stop with your accusations!"

He moved toward me rapidly and pointed his finger at me. "You are mine. No one else will have you! You are sealed to me in marriage. I will have you and no other will!"

Then he lifted me by gripping my upper arms tightly and he was so harsh that my eyes started to water. I wanted to cry, but I bit my lower lip to fight it. I prepared myself for what was coming next.

Then I felt my body hurled against the wall.

I screamed.

"Bitch!" he shouted. He kicked me in the stomach. I couldn't control it anymore. I sobbed raggedly, fighting for my breath.

"Stop, please," I begged.

He kicked me again, and this time, I pretended to pass out. Because if I didn't move and he thought I was unconscious, he would stop hurting me.

This was my first traumatic brain injury, but I did not know that at the time. I went to the doctor and he found both ear drums punctured and bleeding. The police took photos and I filed charges, but in the end, I dropped them out of fear.

He left me lying there, bleeding and bruised. He didn't even look back. The thing with him was that he would hurt me for no reason at all. He would come home drunk, and he would unleash his wrath on me. But why did he do that? I didn't know. It's as though he was cut out that way.

When he left, I slowly sat up and dried my tears. I looked at my gnarled hands. I would leave him, I told myself. I was afraid to be on my own, but I had to do something about our situation.

So, with my body aching all over, I gathered my strength and walked inside the bedroom.

I had told a friend of mine about my situation with Henry. Anna told me that I had to make a decision, perhaps leave Henry while I still could. She said that I was still young, and surely, I could find another man - someone worthy of my love. There was no family to save since we didn't have any child yet.

I opened the dresser and started packing some clothes. With trembling fingers, I zipped the luggage that I would take with me. To my horror, Henry entered the room and caught me.

My throat constricted in fear.

"What are you doing?" he asked brusquely.

"Nothing," I said softly, scared and wondering where a bruise would appear on my body this time.

"Fuck you! If you are planning on leaving me, I tell you—you're gonna die! I'm gonna fucking slit your throat!" he shouted, his brown eyes angry slits.

I collapsed onto the bed because my knees shook so badly. I didn't want him to see how scared I was, but my shaking hands gave me away.

He moved toward me and hit me across the face. That was when I started crying again.

He punched me in the stomach and I curled up in the bed in pain. Then, he walked out and slammed the door.

That night, I put my clothes back in the dresser. In my head, I kept on repeating, *our marriage could still work*. Maybe there was still some hope.

I prayed fervently for a baby. Someone I could love with all my heart, and who would be capable of loving me back.

Chapter Three

It was late in the evening in the winter of 1982, and, as usual Henry was already passed out drunk. The doorbell rang, and I ran to see who it was. I saw Ethel's face through the peephole.

"It's a little late already. What's up?" I said.

Ethel smiled, which she seldom did. I was surprised to find her in such a good mood. The world must be playing tricks on me. First Henry, and now, my mother stopping by – but why? Something was up for sure.

"Can't I visit my daughter?" Ethel asked.

I nodded, a cloud of doubt still hanging in my head. I opened the door wider to let her in. I was still dumbfounded. Why would Mother visit me now?

After a while, the doubts were removed from my head. We sat down and shared coffee and leftover bread from breakfast, the conversation flowing between us almost naturally.

It was one of those rare moments when Ethel opened up to me, and I, the daughter who always craved for her love, basked in what I believed was a reconciliation.

"Something's bothering me," Ethel said.

I paused. *Something's always bothering you*, I wanted to say. But feeling that the barrier was broken somehow by the evening's conversation, I said instead,

"What?"

"Paul." Ethel stopped laughing. She was telling me a funny incident earlier, and when she shifted the topic to her husband, her facial expression immediately changed.

"What about him?" I asked.

The wrinkles in the corners of her eyes deepened as she smirked. When she spoke, I thought I caught a hint of concern in her voice. I wasn't sure though.

"Do you think people are really capable of suicide?" she asked.

I looked at her, surprised. If anybody were to ask me if I'll ever commit suicide, the answer would be a resounding no. True, there were a lot of challenges that I experienced in the past and the woman in front of me was one of the reasons the challenges and problems occurred. And yet—I didn't think I would ever be capable of committing such a selfish act.

"There's news about suicides every day," I said. In my head, I found it hard to understand them though. Life was so wonderful. Why would anybody want to take his or her life if tomorrow holds a promise of something better that could come along? It was daunting though, not knowing. "Why? How's Paul?"

Ethel shook her head. Her expression brightened once again. "I think he wants to take his life."

"That's preposterous!" I burst out. I didn't know if my outburst was because I couldn't believe Paul would take his life, or because Ethel didn't show any compassion. I continued, "Why? He doesn't strike me as the type."

"He's been depressed these past days. I'm worried about him," she said, averting her gaze.

I didn't know if it was because Mother had been so hard on me that I found it hard to believe she would worry over someone so deeply. Besides, she seemed very buoyant that night.

"Do you know what his problem is?"

"I don't know. But he seems really depressed. Then she laughed loudly. "Enough about that; this time is for us." She pointed her finger to herself and then to me.

"Let's forget about Paul and just go back to other more meaningful discussions."

I frowned, but for the first time, I felt a step closer to her. Maybe there was still a bridge that could connect us. Maybe, just maybe, this broken fence could be mended.

So, for that night, I sat across from her, exchanging laughter and jokes that felt as much a stranger to me as the person I was sharing them with.

Paul was forgotten.

When the following day came, I woke up to such horrible news. Ethel found Paul with a gunshot wound in his upper abdomen outside the house they lived in.

My earlier trips to hospitals when I was young came back to me. The feeling of fear, of whether there would still be tomorrow, taunted me. My heart clenched thinking about poor Paul and his wound.

He was brought to a hospital to undergo surgery, mostly to repair the internal organs torn by the bullet. The procedure was successful, and I was finally able to breathe in relief.

I was afraid of Ethel, so I never had the courage to visit Paul in the hospital. What was relayed to me was that Paul lay in his bed and he was very pale. His eyes were listless as though he had lost the will to live.

My conversation with Ethel came to mind, and I remembered her telling me that Paul was depressed.

Police officers came in to talk to Paul. They wanted to talk to him alone, but Ethel never left his side.

Was it possible for Ethel to transform into someone so caring overnight, for her to not want to leave Paul's side? Or was there another reason she didn't want to leave him alone?

When asked where Ethel was the night before the incident occurred, Ethel said that she was with me. It was true, but it horrified me because in a way, I felt used. I WAS her alibi–she did use me.

Paul was confined in the hospital for two weeks. The town's folk, my siblings, and I, blamed Mother for the incident.

Two things played in our minds.

First, Ethel shot Paul. But if she did, why would Paul not tell the police about it? Was he scared? Was Mother the kind of woman that even her husband would fear? I pushed the thought away because inside of me boiled an answer I knew for certain—yes. She was that and more. Paul was a scared man. Most people feared my mother in one way or another.

Second, on the premise that Ethel might have loved Paul too at one point in their marriage, then maybe she didn't shoot him. Other things did figuratively. Like the way Ethel always nagged him, or fought with him, or made him feel as worthless as Mother once made me feel. Each and every day of Paul's life, my mother emotionally abused him, blaming him for one thing or another. She blamed him for things that were never his fault. She blamed him for Gabriel having Down syndrome, even though they had both been advised not to have children. Paul carried a bad gene as he had a little girl with hydrocephalus, and my mother was in menopause. Enough for him to pull the trigger!

Either way, Mother would carry the burden of Paul's condition.

Paul was a decent man — that much I can vouch for. And though we were not affiliated by blood, the knowledge that he had been living a life with Mother made me empathize with him. I knew exactly what he must have gone through with her.

Up until now, when I heard a loud voice cursing or yelling, or the sound of feet stomping, or running, or of doors slamming loudly, my heart would start beating rapidly, and I would become conscious of my long, blond hair. Afraid that from out of nowhere, Ethel would material-ize, grab my hair, and drag me all over the house again.

Though the surgery was successful, the doctors told us that Paul had to fight for his life. There was still the danger of infection developing in his wound. Should it fester, he could still die.

The doctors urged Paul to cough, to let the phlegm and secretions out. But, he refused to do so.

Then one day, the veil of depression lifted slightly, and Paul's eyes became determined as he fought his way out of the pneumonia that had started to render him sicker. He coughed as advised by the doctors. In one coughing fit though, he did it so hard that his abdominal incisions tore, and his internal organs came spilling out.

It was unexpected that Paul would require another surgery to repair and mend the same wounds that almost ended his life. His pneumonia didn't give the wound a chance to heal though.

Sadly, he didn't make it. I've referred to him as poor Paul since then. Ethel, on the other hand, became known as the Black Widow.

Later on, when I visited with Levi one day, he told me of a time before his father's death, when Paul was leaned over a steering wheel in their truck. My mother became enraged and she up and bit him hard on his back near his spine! The wound became badly infected and stayed that way until the moment he passed away. I have never known any parent that resembled anywhere close to how my mother was with people.

Chapter Four

S o, I was right. Something good would turn out from my marriage with Henry.

I looked outside the window of the house we rented and saw that the sun was already up. Wisps of clouds adorned the blue sky.

I smiled.

I opened the drapes in the living room and let the sunlight in. Then, I sat on the couch and watched eagerly for the result of the pregnancy test.

I tapped my right foot in excitement. I was almost sure that I was pregnant because I'd been having morning sickness since last week. Initially, I thought that it was because Henry struck me so hard in the head. But, when the succeeding days still found me nauseated, I felt hope that it could be the blessing I was waiting for.

I peered at the plastic strip again. This time, the result stared me in the face.

I was definitely pregnant.

If the baby wouldn't have been endangered if I jumped up and down, I would have. Even though the baby was nothing but a speck inside my uterus, the feeling of a budding mother overwhelmed me, and I was instinctively protective already.

I touched my belly and smiled. Finally, it happened to me—to us. Henry and I would be having a baby. Two years into marriage, and we would be blessed with a child.

"Henry?" I called out.

Henry lay stretched on the sofa. His arms were thrown upward, and he was snoring slightly.

"Henry," I said again. My aura reeked of happiness.

"Huh?" he stirred. His brown eyes gazed at me sleepily.

"We're going to have a baby," I said.

"Fuck! You had to wake up a tired man from sleep just to share your crappy news. Women!" he shouted and turned his back to me. In a few seconds, he was snoring again.

Even that didn't dampen my mood. Our baby would not know a difficult life, a life where love was difficult to come by; I would make sure of that.

I would be nothing but a loving, doting mother to our baby.

I left the living room. Already, my head was flying.

I picked up the phone and dialed a number I knew by heart. I waited for a few seconds for someone to pick up.

"Anna?" I said over the phone.

"Yes?"

"Sarah here," I said cheerily.

"Spill it now!" Perhaps she sensed in my voice that there was something very important and good that I wanted to share with her.

"I'm pregnant." I smiled.

"Congratulations," she said in a rush. From the sound of her voice, I could tell she was smiling too.

At last, there was someone who shared my happiness. "What do I do?"

"Get a good obstetrician. You need to have regular consultations to make sure that the baby will grow as expected."

"Is there anybody you could recommend?" I asked. This was all new to me. The joys of being a mother were there within my reach, and it was impossible for me to stop smiling.

Obstetrician, check! Consultations, check, good healthy diet, check and double check!

I would follow what every good pregnant woman did. I would have my baby. I smiled to myself as I put the phone down in its cradle.

A lovely thought crossed my mind. In nine months, I would have a beautiful baby in my arms.

I looked expectantly at the face of Dr. Nicholas, my obstetrician in Silverthorne, Colorado.

"Can we do it today?" I asked.

He smiled at me. "Yes. You're five months along and we can already see its gender."

He put gel on my belly and I watched the monitor. He paused and asked, "Can you see it?"

I stared at the monitor and shook my head.

"Here. Look at this. There's a small protrusion." He paused and looked at me. "It means you're having a boy." My heart became warm with joy. *A boy!*

"Do you already have a name?"

"Yes," I said. "Joshua."

"Joshua's a good name for a baby boy," he said.

"Yes," I whispered, a smile still frozen on my lips. "My baby's name will be Joshua."

When it was over, I went home feeling light-headed. Only four more months of waiting and my baby and I would get the chance to meet. I couldn't wait.

I started buying some clothes for Joshua. Feeding bottles in light blue shades already lined the counter in the kitchen. I wanted Joshua to feel loved.

I made sure that I didn't skip any scheduled consultations with my obstetrician. I took care of my health. Everywhere I went; I tried to be more positive and smiled at everyone because I was told that the baby would feel my emotions too. And unborn yet, I didn't want him to feel sad.

Henry never went with me to the obstetrician though. He always had a reason. He was busy. Or he was far too drunk to stand up. Or sometimes, the reason was that he just didn't want to.

When he declined going with me several times, I stopped asking. He may not be the ideal father, but he had some good sense somehow because all throughout my pregnancy, he refrained from hitting me in the stomach.

That was not something that should be said proudly by any wife because nobody deserved to be hit by her husband. Regardless, I was thankful for it. His hands flew to my head and face instead.

One day, I got the feeling that something was terribly wrong with my baby. I touched my belly, in the usual spot where I most often felt my baby kick at me. I waited seconds, then minutes, but there was no movement.

I called a friend and asked for advice. What should I do? I shouted over the phone in panic.

Eat chocolates, each of my friends would say.

So, I did.

They said that if I ingested a high level of sugar, the baby would be very energetic and would start moving again.

I lay down on the sofa in the living room, staring at my belly, willing it to move.

Sadly though, the baby inside of me remained still.

I laid in bed restlessly that night, wondering if something happened to my baby.

I carefully went through the past days, analyzing if I did things that could have put my baby in danger. But nothing came to mind. Were there visits to the obstetrician that I missed? I jumped out of bed and checked my notebook. There — every appointment was checked. I did go to all of them.

Did I consume alcohol during the pregnancy? I paused, racking my brain really hard if indeed, there was a miss on my part. Nothing came to mind; not even one drop of alcohol.

The following days, I walked around the house like a zombie. I couldn't sleep well. I ate food high in sugar to be sure that the baby would get a lot of energy. But night came soon and still, the baby inside of me did not move.

I did what I usually do when I have a problem. I picked up the phone and dialed Anna's number.

"Hey," I said.

Her familiar voice greeted me.

"I'm scared," I said weakly. "The baby still hasn't moved."

There was a pause from the other line. "How long has it been?"

I closed my eyes, trying to remember when it was that I felt my baby kick me. "Two days, I think."

"Consult with your obstetrician. I'm sure there's nothing to worry about. But just so you can sleep peacefully at night, it's better to have your check-up." I nodded, though I knew she couldn't see me. "Thanks, Anna," I said, feeling better already.

I checked my reflection in the mirror. I put my hand around my belly as though to assure my baby that it was going to be all right. Then, I walked out of the house and locked the door.

Lying in bed at my obstetrician's clinic, I stared at his face. He was smiling when he put the gel on my belly.

But as soon as he started moving the plastic contraption over my belly, his smile disappeared. He put on his stethoscope and listened for the baby's heartbeat.

Fear rendered me frozen.

"What's wrong?" I asked worriedly.

He stared at me with a blank expression on his face.

"There's no heartbeat," he said.

I felt my face drain. I was losing color. "What do you mean?" "I'm sorry," he said. "But there's no heartbeat. The baby's gone." "That can't happen!" I said.

The obstetrician checked the image again and this time, he pointed out something to me. All around my baby's neck was what appeared to be his umbilical cord.

I gasped. "Oh no, no, no, this just can't be happening!!"

"The baby was not able to breathe. I'm so sorry."

I wailed and cried.

"Is there anyone you want me to contact?"

I shook my head. Henry wouldn't care. And Ethel was sure to find some harsh words to throw at me at this inopportune time.

I was grateful when the obstetrician left me for a while. I needed to be alone with my thoughts. This would take some time to sink in.

When he came back, he told me that he was referring me to the hospital that was across from the clinic.

I nodded to his suggestion, although what he said never registered with me. I was even surprised to find myself a few hours later, already inside the hospital, wearing a hospital gown.

"You're not going to take away my baby!" I shouted at the doctor. "This baby is all that's good in my life—nobody has the right to take him from me." The doctor gazed at me concernedly. "Listen to me carefully," he said.

I averted my eyes. I didn't want to listen to him.

"If you keep the baby longer in your system, you could die," he said. "Your baby has started decomposing inside your uterus and he will poison your blood supply through the umbilical cord." The obstetrician didn't mean to be that harsh to me, but at that moment, I felt like he was the enemy.

"Please," he urged. "The baby has to come out."

With my face in my hands, I spoke softly. "Can I keep him for a little while?"

It took him a while to respond to me. "Of course," he said. "But only for a little while. I'll be back to check on you later." I heard the door to the room close. I was left with my baby — a baby that would never get the chance to know his mother.

Maybe I was wrong. Nothing good could ever come out of my marriage to Henry.

I shed tears for my unborn baby, and through the hospital gown that I was already wearing, I caressed him, unmindful that he could no longer feel my affection.

"I love you, Joshua," I whispered. "Mama's sorry you had to leave so soon."

The anesthesiologist injected me, and I was asleep immediately. I found comfort in the numbness, in the feeling of escaping the world. It wasn't my nature though, to run away from my hurdles. I was a warrior, a survivor.

Labor was induced and after nine hours, I gave birth to Joshua. The procedure was not finished. The doctor had to ensure that I underwent dilation and curettage. This was a process to clean out the remnants of blood and tissue after birth, which ordinarily, had I given birth to a live, healthy child, would not be necessary.

I woke up to the dim lights of the hospital. I was back in my room, and IVs were inserted in my right wrist.

I pressed the button that would make the nurse come to me and, I waited. After a few seconds, she hustled in, a sad expression on her face.

"Can I see my baby?" I asked tearfully.

The nurse shook her head. "I'm sorry, Sarah. Your baby is going to be incinerated."

"But you can't—" I protested.

The nurse became pale. Then she left.

I made a call immediately and searched for a funeral home. My request was to get my baby for me, so he wouldn't be incinerated. I was too weak though, physically and emotionally, to handle this alone, and so I had to ask Ethel to help me. Mother proved to be very helpful at this time. She was able to contact a funeral home in Silverthorne, CO, and they were able to get Joshua from the hospital. Thanks to them, we took my baby home.

It was a very trying time. I was still weak from giving birth to a son, and yet here I was, standing bravely to hold a simple funeral for that same son.

I looked at Joshua. He was so tiny. This was supposed to be a happy moment. What did I ever do wrong?

His eyes, the nurse from the hospital told me, were blue like mine. My baby still had no hair. Tears rolled down my cheeks upon realizing that I would never get to know if his hair would be brown like Henry's or blond like mine.

His tiny hands would never get the chance to hold a basketball, or a football. His feet would never be able to pedal on a bike. His mouth would never open to utter that he loved me.

I could though, so I did. "I love you, Joshua," I told him. Although his ears would never hear my words, I prayed that keeping him safe inside my belly for as long as I could, let Joshua know I meant the words I said.

Afterward, I leaned over a special baby wooden container and put Joshua inside.

It was not a real funeral. There were very few guests, just family—Ethel, my sister, and myself. I looked around, wondering if Henry would come. But why would he? When Joshua was alive inside my belly, he hardly cared. Why would I think that he would grace the occasion now?

While we were burying Joshua, Henry was probably doing the only three things that he was good at—drinking, driving a dump truck loaded with salt or cheating on me.

Chapter Five

The apple pie that Anna baked was still untouched. The tea that I boiled had gone cold. There seemed to be no point in talking. I found no comfort in losing my baby.

"Why don't you go to a fertility clinic?" Anna suggested.

I leaned forward in my seat. Since losing Joshua, that seemed to be the only topic that got me interested.

"Do you think I should?" I asked, hopeful that she would answer positively.

"Of course, you should. Your chances of getting pregnant will improve. I have friends who could never get pregnant, but after going to fertility clinics, were blessed with child," she said.

Her eyes were shining as though her words were a promise I could hold on to.

"I will visit one," I said. The determination to have children pulsing inside my chest. I knew I would make a good mother.

That night as I lay in the bed, I had a dream. It was a picture of a beautiful family. A man was holding a little boy in his hands. I asked the man what the boy's name was, and he just smiled at me. He had kind eyes.

Even dreaming, a terrible sense of loss ate at my heart. When I turned to leave the boy spoke, although at his size it would've been impossible for him to speak up.

"Mommy," he said in a voice that was so innocent and pure.

I looked at the boy and the man, but before I could go back to the baby and hold him in my arms, he was gone.

I woke up sobbing against the pillows. My cries echoed in the night and it meshed with Henry's snores. How very ironic that the sounds he made while he rested fell in a rhythmic pattern against the sounds I made when my heart was breaking.

In the stillness of the night, I watched Henry's chest rise and fall as he slept fitfully. I paused for a moment, wondering if it would be all right to squeeze myself against his body and seek comfort from my husband. After all, he was my husband. I couldn't do it and instead, I turned my back on him and cried myself to sleep.

Upon awakening the next morning, I wondered if my obstetrician, Dr. Nicholas, could help me with the medication. I closed the book and looked away. My gaze fell upon Joshua's sonogram. I must have left it lying on the coffee table.

My hand started to tremble as I moved to pick up the picture. As I gazed into the image, my chest felt as though it were being ripped apart. I realized that I was clenching the edge of the picture too tightly because the picture folded and my knuckles were turning white. My chin quivered, and I was angry again. I was so angry at my husband, at my mother, and at God.

Why would Joshua be taken away from me? If I were being punished for something I had done in the past, couldn't the punishment just be the brutalities I received from Henry? Surely Joshua could have been spared this unfortunate demise. And yet, I still hoped.

I clutched my chest because I had difficulty breathing. I prayed again and again. Please Dear God, please let there be another child. You knew the deepest yearnings of my heart, and I would make you proud. I would be a good mother, I promise.

Then tears fell from my eyes.

I took a cigarette from my pack and went outside the house. I puffed and inhaled the ghastly scent. Its stench was horrible, and I coughed slightly. But this stick became my companion when I was recovering from Joshua's loss. In effect, this cigarette substituted for Henry's absence. The comfort that my husband couldn't offer me, I got from this stick. And for that I forgave myself for smoking several packs.

As I tossed the cigarette butt though, the pain of Joshua's loss would come back. Nothing could make me forget the loss.

That was when I decided that I should have another consultation with Dr. Nicholas immediately and seek advice about fertility pills.

I thought that all my prayers were in vain because I had been on the fertility pills for six months already and still, I had not become pregnant.

Maybe it was my body. Maybe my husband's and my genes were not a good match. Maybe Ethel was right when she didn't believe that I could carry a child until birth. There were a lot of maybes, and truth be told, my faith was wavering at this point.

I stopped taking the pills. If I was never to become a mother, then no number of pills could make me one.

A month later, I found out that I was pregnant again.

I stared in disbelief at the plastic strip that revealed my condition. I was about to have another child.

It was true—that God has three answers to any prayer, namely: yes, no, or wait.

And in my hands right now was the proof that my prayer was answered in the affirmative.

Tears streaked my face once more. I was happy and sad at the same time. I was scared, too. It was a delicious mix of emotions. I was so happy because I would get the chance to become a mother again. I was sad because I remembered how it ended with Joshua. Scared because being pregnant was not an assurance that I would be successful delivering a baby into this world.

But for the moment, I felt my chest bursting with hope. God is good. He gave me what I needed at the time. He knew I wouldn't be able to take it if He had said 'no.'

Like in the past, Henry did not care that I was pregnant. He had no reaction when I told him. Well, except for a slight disappointment because he could only hit me again on the head for the next nine months.

Ethel learned about my pregnancy, but her face held the knowing look that told me she doubted if I'd ever make it past the pregnancy. Why was I surrounded with these people?

At least when I called Anna, she sounded genuinely happy for me.

I prayed and waited for the baby to come.

Chapter Six

The months passed by quickly. I guess when there's so much to look forward to, time does fly.

The last time I was in a delivery birthing room, it was right before Joshua was born.

This time, I laid in bed waiting for my cervix to dilate. And this time too, I was expecting a healthy baby boy.

I wasn't completely over the last birthing incident and I had to remind myself every minute or so that this time, I would be successful in giving birth.

The nurse came in again and peered under my gown. She checked my cervix, gave me a smile, and told me that I wasn't fully dilated yet. It could go on for hours, and it did…for about thirty hours.

I felt a strong contraction and I winced in pain. It stopped after five seconds. It meant that the baby was not yet ready to come out.

I closed my eyes and prayed that the baby would come out healthy. That the first time I would hold him in my arms, his chest would rise and fall softly like a gentle mimic of my own chest's heaving.

My left leg kicked involuntarily as a pressure against my lower back started to build up. It wasn't exactly painful, but it was very unsettling. I twisted in the bed, but there was no lying position that made me feel better.

The pain then became horrendous. My mother was there, and she said to me that she had never seen someone in so much pain while laboring to give birth. I was so very tired. The pains kept up for a minute or so and then started yet again. Finally, an anesthesiologist came in and he gave me an epidural to help with the pain. He was new, and the epidural did not make it to where it really needed to be.

I had another contraction, and this time, I was no longer able to keep count of the number of seconds before the contraction was gone. I was breathing hard, almost panting.

I decided to call the nurse. She bent in front of me and when I met her eyes, she told me that I was ready.

I was brought to the delivery room with the obstetrician and several nurses. This time, the pain had grown too strong, and I wanted so much for the baby to be brought out into the world.

When the doctor told me to push, I did. When the nurses took turns holding my hands, or asked me to push, or coached me to breathe properly, I followed their instructions to the letter. Labor was painful, but I wanted to hold my baby in my arms so badly, so I did what was expected of an obedient mother-to-be. Henry was in the room with me, but all he did was joke with the hospital staff; and there were no words of encouragement for me.

"Ok, push harder this time," the doctor said.

I swallowed. I wanted to tell him that I had been pushing with all my might already. But he meant well, so I obliged.

The sweat on the doctor's face told me that either it was hot inside the room, or something was wrong. *Please don't let it be the latter*, I prayed.

He shook his head and looked at the nurses. They whispered something. Then, the doctor removed the mask on his mouth and leaned closer to me. "You have to push really, really hard. Do you understand that?" I nodded; I was too tired to object.

"Your pelvic bones are too small, so you have to give it all you've got because your baby is stuck, and it's too late to take him out any other way. Push really, really hard, OK?" he repeated.

I nodded. "OK," I whispered. I shut my eyes tightly and breathed through my mouth. I pushed.

The doctor's eyes seemed distressed.

"Forceps," he said.

The nurse handed it to him. I gasped as I wondered what the doctor could be doing. I prayed that this ordeal would be over soon.

I pushed harder until my baby was out of me. Drenched in sweat, I craned my neck to see my baby.

The nurses were crowding over my baby. *Move closer*, I urged inside my head, *move closer so I can see my baby.*

One of the nurses moved slightly and I caught a glimpse of my boy, who was turning blue. Tears started to slide down my cheeks.

The doctor and nurses worked on my baby. Their movements were hurried and yet precise, until one by one, they moved away from my baby. And also, one by one, they removed the masks covering their mouths. That was the only time I saw the smiles on their faces.

It was enough to let me know my baby was safe. I broke into a huge smile too. This time, motherhood welcomed me sweetly, as I listened to my baby's cries.

On December 12, 1983, I gave birth to Noah. My baby was seven pounds and fourteen ounces, twenty inches long—a healthy boy. After my son was cleaned up and breathing normally, the nurse laid him on my right breast. I cuddled him, wrapped in baby blankets, as my bed was wheeled out into the hall towards the mother/baby unit down the hall. My mother and a couple siblings were in the hall and they took some photos before my son and I were delivered to my new room.

I looked at the face of my son and tears started rolling down my cheeks again. It was a different feeling, a delicious mix of sorts. On the one hand, I was bursting with pride—this beautiful boy was mine. I would nurse him and care for him and love him dearly. On the other hand, there was a tinge of sadness because somehow, a part of me was telling me that this baby would have loved to play with Joshua.

I pushed Joshua away and told myself that someday, they'd have a chance to meet each other. In the meantime, it was I who got lucky enough to hold my baby. I glanced at the tag on my baby's wrist. It simply read "Baby Boy."

A smile formed on my lips as I racked my brain for a good name.

The following day, I looked at my baby who would now be known as Noah.

In *Romeo and Juliet*, when Juliet questioned the Capulet and Montague's feud, she asked, "What's in a name?" I never appreciated her words. As I looked at the lovely blue eyes of my son, I realized how very significant Juliet's question was. For truly, how important is a name when the person it belongs to is the person you love the most in the world?

"Noah," I whispered to my boy before kissing him on the forehead. Then I froze when realization hit me, that it was the only time I spoke that name with such reverence and love.

When the time came to leave the hospital and take Noah home, Henry arrived drunk. He had brought hamburgers and French fries for all the nursing staff, but nothing for me. That was another jab in my gut. He was making the car swerve so bad that I had to take over driving us home the entire forty miles. Noah started crying and there was nothing I could do to help him while my hands were on the steering wheel.

Henry simply did nothing at all. I did not want to stop on the highway to see what I could do for Noah as it was a cold day in winter with record breaking temperatures.

Finally, I managed to reach home safely through all the snow. After pulling up in the driveway, I ignored Henry and took Noah inside to get warm. The house in Everton was cold. I worked on the thermostat while Henry did nothing. Then, I was able to get enough heat to change my newborn baby's diaper. After that, I put my baby to my breast to get nourishment.

While Noah was suckling, I heard a loud commotion in the kitchen. Henry's father Carter was in the kitchen with Henry. They were in a loud fight and they even threw a couple of punches. I am not sure now how I managed to finally get Carter to leave, but I did persevere in getting him out of my house.

Carter's presence didn't bring comfort to us. He came not because he wanted to see his grandson. He didn't even ask about him although he knew we had just come from the hospital.

I managed to get Henry onto the sofa and he passed out while I was in the master bedroom feeding Noah again. I sat in my rocking chair cradling my son and loved my baby with my whole heart. The Lord had been so good to me.

PART TWO

My Baby Eli

Chapter Seven

I was busy with motherhood. Everything became different. The dishes that piled in the sink were now joined with Noah's feeding bottles.

Henry's clothes which usually stank with a mix of stale cigarette smoke and alcohol were now washed together with Noah's baby clothes. Of course, I had to segregate them and do the laundry in batches. The chores doubled, especially since Henry didn't offer any help in the house. But truth be told, my body didn't complain at all for the extra chores it had to do. Life became so much more meaningful with my son in the house.

My ordinary day would turn bright once I held my son in my arms. I was not yet over the euphoric state of having Noah in my life when I learned that I was pregnant again.

I could hardly believe it. Noah was barely seven months old. I was twenty-three years old and pregnant for the third time. Who would have thought that after an unsuccessful first birthing experience, God would immediately give me two babies? It didn't make me forget the loss of Joshua, but being pregnant a second time reminded me of God's greatness. On this planet, there may be very few people who loved me sincerely, and yet out there, God cared so much to give me the gift of a second child.

On April 6, 1985, I gave birth to another healthy baby boy and I named him Eli. He weighed 7 pounds 6 ½ ounces and was 21 inches long. Henry almost missed Eli's birth as he was drunk, and I had to drive us both to the hospital. My obstetrician worked on putting coffee into Henry until he finally woke up enough to see his son born.

When I held Eli in my arms the first time, I felt really blessed. I had two beautiful boys in my life.

I had to leave Noah with my friend and babysitter, Ardy, while I was in the hospital. It was nice to have Ardy around because after giving birth to Eli, I had to stay for another day at the hospital due to the tubal ligation Henry forced me to have.

I grew worried thinking about how Noah would react when I brought home another baby in the house. Noah was still so young, and I was sure that most toddlers wouldn't want their mothers to pay attention to other kids.

Contrary to what I was expecting, when I showed Eli to Noah, my darling boy took to Eli instantly. Noah held out his hand to his brother. I still remember that wonderful day because at the moment Noah reached out to touch Eli, they both smiled. And the smiles were enough to bind them for the rest of their childhood days together.

The years flew, and Noah was already four and Eli three.

I pushed the door open and the two boys raced toward me.

"Did you miss Mom?" I asked.

Noah nodded vigorously, and Eli smiled at me. I kissed their lips alternately and wondered how happy they would become once they opened my gifts to them.

I carried both of them in my arms and put them to bed.

The following day, I got up more excited than my boys and went to the living room to fetch the identical packages.

I placed them side by side, and once I removed the plastic covering the seats, I stood up. I went to the bedroom and kissed their tiny noses. Noah opened his eyes lazily and instantly, an impish smile flashed.

"Wake up, Hun," I said.

Eli lay with his hands and legs cuddling a pillow. His blond hair fell across his forehead and his mouth was slightly parted.

I bent down and kissed him again. His lips curled as though he was tickled and brushed my head away. I laughed and kissed him again. Then he woke up.

I carried him and bent down to take Noah in my arms, too.

The three of us went to the living room. The boys were still sleepy, but when they caught sight of the red 3-wheelers, both leaped from my arms and ran toward them.

"Careful," I shouted, but no one paid attention to me anymore. They were giggling in delight.

"Wait," I yelled. Then I picked up both and put them in the garage.

There, the boys raced round and round, and when they felt ready to explore, they headed out of the garage.

I called out to them and immediately, they rode back inside the garage. It was only for the meantime though, before both of them rode in and out of the garage again.

What do kids love the most? My two boys loved candies! And one Easter Sunday morning, we woke up to the sun creeping inside the bedroom windows. My boys and I got up and went to the living room. When we looked outside, our lawn was littered with candy.

Noah ran toward the door and pushed it wide open. Eli peered from his brother's back. Angelic smiles were pasted on their beautiful faces at the sight of something so extraordinary. They ran to the lawn, hopping and skipping gaily. Seeing my two boys as they happily gathered the candies made me bless our neighbor Jacob. God bless this sweet man for keeping his tradition of making children happy on Easter Sunday.

When the room was dark, when it's just a few minutes before I get up from bed, I usually take my time to go over the things that happened in my life. My childhood was not exactly one I was very fond of remembering, and growing up was not any better. Adulthood, which I believe started for me when I lived with Henry and married him, didn't turn out too well either. Still, in bed, as I gazed at the dark room and I would hear the soft breathing of my two little boys, I would realize that life was just starting to get better.

I enrolled in Foxwoods University to study nursing. This may be a little late already, but my sons gave me the inspiration I didn't realize I was trying so hard to get from my mother and my husband. This inspiration made me dream bigger so that I could provide better for my children.

I could compare this stage of my life to dawn, when it was still dark and yet I know that any moment now, things could turn around for me, and the brightness of a future I had not gleaned in the past would just come to take me in.

In these few minutes that I spent in bed dreaming, I would create beautiful images in my head. One where I would receive my nursing degree, my boys would start schooling, and together, we would face life's challenges with broad smiles and determination.

Little did I know that the challenges that had come my way in the past were only preparing me to be strong because somewhere along the road, another much bigger, more painful trial would be thrown my way!

Chapter Eight

I thought that with two kids running in the house and with the great weight of love now circulating inside our household, Henry would somehow change some of his ways. It was wishful thinking on my part I guess, because I had always been optimistic. I believe in the value of families—and though I never admitted that I wanted to work on our marriage, Henry made it difficult. If his harsh, mean ways were kept between us, I could have tolerated them. But then, he started hitting the kids for the little things that they did.

Sometimes, the boys being boys would be running around and shouting. Or at times, they would bicker and fight the way it's customary for kids their ages do. Still, Henry would snap as though the kids were spawned by the devil himself—no pun intended on that.

Today was no different.

In the distance, I could hear Noah crying. His father raised a hand on him for not cleaning up his toys. Eli was beside Noah, holding his brother's hand. I could tell that he was on the verge of crying too.

I stood up, ready to fight my husband.

My husband Henry was at the front door, holding a beer in his hand. He was drunk as usual and I could smell him.

"He's just a boy," I muttered.

Henry glanced at me. "What did you say?"

I wondered if my body could tolerate bruises that he would undoubtedly give me if I got him cross. "Nothing," I said and picked up Noah and Eli. Then I locked the door inside the bedroom.

For young boys, Noah and Eli seemed to know more about life than my husband. They were sensible enough to know that I was sad. Maybe it was the tears on my cheeks or the trace of sadness in my eyes that made my boys behave and race toward me.

Noah and Eli climbed to my lap. Then they were clutching my body, their little hands making me feel better. Eli took my head in his soft little hands and held my face.

"Don't cry, Mommy," Eli said.

The effect of his words on me was the opposite. I sobbed. Eli kept his hands on my face. Noah was concerned, too, and he squeezed his head under the curve of my bosom. To this day Noah remembers seeing his mother thrown into the kitchen wall putting a hole in it.

I pulled both of them closer and lay down in bed. Noah and Eli squeezed against my chest, and when they fell asleep, I felt peace I had not had in a long time. And that was when I fell asleep too.

Something had to be done about our living condition. I prayed that Henry would change his ways so that we could stick together as a family. But if he ever lifted a hand again to hurt either of my boys, I vowed I would find a way to leave him.

Chapter Nine

June 1989

I finally had the courage to leave Henry and get a restraining order of protection against him. There were things I did in the past that admittedly, were results of my being impulsive at times. But leaving Henry was not one of those.

Throughout our marriage, I always gave him the benefit of the doubt. After all, no one's really perfect. And sometimes, we had to get by and make do with who God gave us to spend our lives with.

I could find a place in my heart to forgive Henry for not being a good husband, but I could never find that same spot to forgive him for being an even worse father. I could not find any place in my heart to forgive any of the abuse he inflicted on my children.

There were three incidents that really made me realize that I had to leave and file for divorce. First, Eli started a new antibiotic, Bactrim, for his upper respiratory infection and I had given him his initial dose at home before I left for work. When I got home, I found Henry drunk on the couch with Eli next to him. Eli was hardly breathing and had a raised red rash all over his little body. I wrapped him in a blanket and took him straight out to the car along with Noah and drove as fast as I could five miles to the local hospital praying I would get there in time to save Eli from complete anaphylaxis and death.

Eli was given epinephrine immediately. The doctors took one look at him and they worked with his breathing. As I clutched Noah to my chest, I watched my other baby as the medical team tried to save him. I prayed to God and to angels, and I hoped that Eli would get through this incident that was definitely the result of his father's reckless actions. My shoulders loosened in relief as the doctor told me that Eli was safe, but he would be admitted overnight for observation. Eli was placed in a hospital crib and since it was already 1:30 a.m., I just stayed in a rocking chair and held Noah while we all went to sleep.

Second, on another day I arrived home from work to find Henry passed out on the couch. There was nothing new in that. But when I called for my boys, I found that they were fully dressed and soaking wet lying on the carpet sound asleep. The bath tub was full of water and broken glass littered the bathroom. My boys had been playing with no adult supervision while Henry was passed out. As I bent to gather the broken pieces of glass and put them inside the trash bin, I realized that the broken pieces resembled my marriage. They were shattered into so many pieces already that it would be impossible now to repair it at this point.

What worried me most was that my boys could have cut themselves badly or drowned. While I was busily cleaning up the bathroom and changing the boys into comfortable dry clothes, Henry never had the decency to wake up and help out—but then he was passed out from all the alcohol.

The last straw came when Henry pulled into the driveway about thirty minutes after I arrived home from work. He was driving drunk with both boys in the back seat. When I went to the car, I noted that they were not wearing seatbelts nor were the child seats strapped in the backseat. But that wasn't all. Imagine my horror when I looked at the backseat once more and found a shotgun in the back-window area behind my boys.

Henry argued that he had unloaded the gun. I was frustrated and angry, so I took the gun and looked. It was fully loaded. I took the shells out and leaned in to carry my boys out of the car.

As I walked toward the house, my mind was racing. I knew right then that I had to leave Henry. Our marriage had collapsed a long time ago and if there was something that could still be done about it, it had to be an effort from Henry and me. The problem was that he never tried. And this time, I didn't care about a marriage that could end up hurting or killing my boys.

I left at the end of June 1989 and moved into an apartment in Durango, CO. Henry and I were not divorced but we were truly separated. I filed for the protection order and separation which Henry fought me on.

In November 1989, I dated Matt twice. I met Matt in 1987 at work and we were just friends then. When Henry learned that I dated Matt, he blew his lid and verbally and emotionally abused me. He came over to the place I rented and kept yelling outside. He was drunk, so he kept calling me and harassing me outside my home. I wasn't a bad woman. I never dated when I was still with Henry and I dated Matt three months after filing for separation.

True, I was still married at that time, but I never once felt that way with all the horrid treatment Henry gave me.

One day, Matt became a close friend when he gave me a tender hug, and we had broken through the barrier of being mere acquaintances.

Fall and Winter of 1989

Eli was four when I noticed that he had a pattern of illnesses starting early in the fall of 1989. I took him to see Dr. Owens, a general practitioner and to Dr. Brown, a pediatrician.

In September, Eli was diagnosed with sinusitis and mononucleosis. His diagnoses consisted of middle ear infection and upper respiratory diseases. Eli and I were in and out of the hospital starting September all throughout December of 1989.

Eli was able to attend pre-school. He loved seeing the children there and Mrs. Parker.

Dusty was the student Eli liked the most and when Eli's brother Noah would talk about one of his friend's Eli would butt right in and start talking about Dusty. There was competition between my boys, but it was all healthy as they loved each other dearly.

On Thanksgiving, I noticed a tiny nodule on the back-right side of Eli's neck. It was quite small, and Eli had mononucleosis, so this gave me reason to believe it was a full lymph node. Eli played with his cousins and happily ate his turkey dinner. My brother Caleb, who was older than me by eight years, and his wife Nina, together with their boys Connor and Ryan, my younger sister Riley and younger brother Gavin, joined us in celebrating Thanksgiving at my apartment. No one noticed anything unusual with Eli while celebrating Thanksgiving.

By the following Monday, the nodule was gone, and Eli had no swelling of any sort.

At this time, Eli was still sick with upper respiratory disorders, but no one felt like there was anything seriously wrong with him. Both Eli and Noah wore pilgrim hats they had made in preschool and kindergarten. Everyone was smiling for the pictures taken that day.

In December, I knew something was wrong with me. I felt a grueling pain stretching across the lower portion of my stomach. It started out as something tolerable, until the pain made it difficult for me to stand upright and more so, to take the walks I usually did around the neighborhood.

The ambulance brought me to a hospital to undergo emergency surgery for a total hysterectomy and my younger sister Riley was with me.

Due to the urgency of the situation, I had to leave the boys with Henry while I was in the hospital even though we were already separated at that time. I did not remember much as some was such a blur to me with the pain and being so sick. I was bleeding internally throughout the journey from Durango for the medical exams and to Silverthorne for the surgery. I remembered nothing about the long ride except for what I felt. It was fear of the unknown—of what could happen to me during the surgery that remained vivid in my mind.

I tasted the sweet temptation of escaping all the pain in my body when I was sedated and on the operating table. I never knew the surgeon's procedures. It was then I realized then the value of faith; of believing in something greater than myself, because right before I lost consciousness, I uttered a fervent prayer, which was mostly a plea...that everything would be all right.

And then it was over. The cancerous tumor that had started inside my uterus was removed. I believed my prayer was heard—because after the operation, I was informed that no further treatment was needed.

I was grateful that I was out of the hospital and I was home again in time for the holidays.

I decided to put up a Christmas tree in the living room of our apartment; and when I turned on the dancing lights, Eli was in awe. He hopped and skipped and played all around the tree with his brother Noah. The smiles both boys wore as they gazed at the tree spoke volumes; and my effort for buying a tree, decorating it with lights, balls, and homemade decorations that both boys made in school, paid off.

Eli still had mononucleosis at this time, so he had to take a lot of antibiotics. The doctor said that Eli's resistance was low, so my little boy had to take refuge in antibiotics to help him get better faster.

At the end of December 1989, Eli saw Dr. Noonan in Silverthorne, CO. He was an Ear, Nose, and Throat specialist. He stated that Eli would need tubes placed in his ears for proper drainage of the fluids that built up in his middle ears and so the procedure was scheduled for January 1990.

PART THREE

Living It One Day
at a Time

Chapter Ten

At this time, I was growing more concerned. The year had turned, and Eli was still constantly sick. There were good days, but the days that I became overwhelmed with worries were more numerous.

Call it a mother's hunch, but from this point, I documented every little thing that Eli went through. I knew I had to take care of him more, if that was even possible, because I had always been giving him more than any good mother could.

The journals are all I have now—the journals and my memories. This is like my diary of all the significant events in 1990. I will lay them all down as far as I can remember because each one of them was significant in Eli's life. Each one reverberates with pain and joy, with frustration and belief, with weakness and strength, with desperation and hope—opposing emotions that rattled my family at this most trying time.

Chapter Eleven

January 10, Wednesday

I took Eli to see Dr. Owens at 9:00 a.m. Dr. Owens said Eli had an inner ear infection and he was given yet another antibiotic.

January 12, Friday

At 7:30 a.m., I attended Noah's kindergarten school conference. It went well. I was very proud of my son as he received many reading kudos and I was so happy for him.

January 15, Monday

Ardy watched Noah and Eli while I attended night school, so I could earn my nursing degree. Ardy was the best child care provider I knew.

January 19, Friday

Eli was seen by Dr. Owens at 9:30 a.m. Eli still had a middle ear infection and ran temperatures up to 102 degrees.

January 21, Sunday

I took Eli to the Durango Hospital Emergency Room because Eli had a fever and I was worried. Dr. Owens said Eli had sinusitis and gave him a new antibiotic. I was torn up and so worried about Eli.

By now, Eli had seen three different doctors, a pediatrician, an ear, nose and throat specialist, and a general practitioner. Scans were made of his head and neck and when the results were out, the radiologist read the scans as normal for a child Eli's age. The doctor went over the radiologist's reading and didn't look at the scan himself. Little did we know that the radiologist tragically misread the scan and that there was a mass the size of my fist inside Eli's head! This mass was very close to his brain. I did try to file a lawsuit through my divorce attorney months later; and he sent the scans and records to a lawyer in Gunnison, CO. Ultimately, that lawyer decided that the outcome may have been the same, so I no longer proceeded with the lawsuit. Had they done the scans in late November or early December, Eli could have lived, and a lawsuit could have worked. As it was, the pediatrician, Brown and the ENT doctor, Noonan, both left their jobs and the state toward the end of 1990.

January 22, Monday

I took Eli to the Emergency Room at the Avon Hospital in Silverthorne as he was still not getting better. Eli was diagnosed with a positive mono-spot, which meant that he was infected with Epstein-Barr virus (EBV). This was nothing new though.

January 24, Wednesday

Eli saw Dr. Owens again today. By now, both Dr. Owens and Dr. James were at odds over what was going on with Eli. They kept on bickering and I sensed that they didn't really like each other. I wanted to yell at them and tell them how disappointed in them I was. To me, doctors should help patients, and any animosity between them should be kept separate from their professions.

It seemed to me that although the desire of both doctors to help my son was there, he wasn't their priority. What was more important to them was the bickering.

I was angry at them, but there was little I could do because they were the only doctors here in the clinic in Durango.

January 25, Thursday

Eli saw Dr. Noonan in Silverthorne today. This was his last visit before the tubes were placed in his ears to help drain the infection he had.

January 30, Tuesday

I took Eli to Avon Hospital to have lab work drawn. The next day, the tubes were placed in his ears.

January 31, Wednesday

Eli was taken to surgery at Avon Hospital. Dr. Noonan had trouble getting the tube in the right ear to stay in, but he never took the time to find out why this was. Had he done so, he might have seen the large cancer mass in Eli's right neck and head area.

Instead, Dr. Noonan said he was done, and the tubes were both properly placed. I had no way of verifying it though, so I just relied on the doctor's words.

Chapter Twelve

February 1990

February 8, Thursday

I took Eli to Silverthorne to see Dr. Noonan at 10:30 a.m. for follow-up after having the tubes placed. Dr. Noonan said he could not see a tube in Eli's right ear and he ordered more antibiotics for Eli to take. I was so very worried for Eli. Would my son ever get better?

February 12, Monday

I took Eli to see Dr. Owens at the Durango Hospital Emergency Room as Eli's temperature was hanging around 102 degrees. Dr. Owens elected not to change Eli's antibiotics at this time.

February 15, Thursday

I took Eli to Silverthorne to see Dr. Noonan for follow-up. Still, Dr. Noonan made no changes on Eli's care.

February 17, Saturday

Henry and Mother both called Ardy and harassed her over the phone. Mother was jealous because she believed that it was her right to have my sons with her when I worked, but knowing how Mother cared for me when I was little made me reluctant to turn over the boys' care to her. There was no way I would allow Mother or Henry to watch over my boys for reasons that Mother was too abusive, and Henry was dangerous.

February 18, Sunday

Henry phoned Ardy several times to harass her while she babysat my boys.

In the afternoon, I took Eli to see Dr. Owens as the right side of Eli's face was drooping and I was terrified of what was happening to him. Dr. Owens didn't seem concerned about it. On the other hand, Dr. James said Eli had Bell's palsy. Then the doctors bickered yet again.

February 19, Monday (4 p.m.)

I took Eli to his pediatrician in Silverthorne because he was still sick. Mother followed me and harassed me at Dr. Brown's office.

Eli had a Computerized Tomography (CT) scan of his head at Avon Hospital. The radiologist reading the scan of Eli's right head and neck area missed seeing the tumor that was as big as my fist. Dr. Brown did not even look at the scan himself and relied solely on the radiologist's reading.

It was a busy day for Eli and me as I had to take him to Dr. James in Durango, too.

February 20, Tuesday

I filed the divorce papers today. Attorney Troy did this for me. Henry was livid upon receiving the documents. At this time, I still had my protection order on Henry.

February 21, Wednesday

At 7:00 pm, my mother continually harassed Matt by driving in and out of his driveway. Afterwards, she went to my place and harassed me instead by yelling outside my door. Her actions terrified my boys.

February 23, Friday

Mother was terribly jealous of Ardy for being allowed to care for my boys while I worked, or when I took some time off to spend with my friends. Her jealousy was driving me insane.

At this point, I sought the help of Sergeant Fritz Adams to protect my kids and me from Mother's harassment.

But nothing could stop Mother. She traveled ten miles to get to the place I was renting. Then, she went to the club and kept yelling curses at me, telling me that I should let her care for her grandsons.

Anna owned the club and was with me at the time, and my friend simply shook her head unbelievingly at the stupid things my mother raged about.

At around 10-10:30 in the evening, Mother pulled into Matt's driveway several times. Then, when Matt didn't pay her any mind, Mother climbed out of the vehicle and banged on the door once.

I was thankful that my lawyer, Troy, had suggested that I write down everything that transpired after I filed for divorce. Without the journals, I would have had difficulty recalling the events and places during the months Mother and Henry were behaving irrationally.

February 24, Saturday

Between 7:00 to 7:30 a.m., my mother pulled into Matt's driveway and honked repeatedly. Matt beat me to the police station to report on Mother's actions. When I reached the police station, I filed my complaint too. Up until now, Matt had been a saint to put up with my mother's bull crap.

At 6:45 in the evening, Mother cornered me at 8th Street and Douglas Avenue while I was with Anna's husband Spencer, who happened to be Matt's best friend. In the parking lot, Mother continued to harass me outside the Quik Shop. My youngest stepbrother, Wyatt, took on my mother verbally and he got into an argument with her. He repeatedly told her to leave me alone. While Mother was occupied bickering with Wyatt, I got the chance to escape from her.

Like me and my other siblings Wyatt blamed his father, Paul's, death on my mother, too. Wyatt hated the fact that his father was not alive to see him get married and have children. This saddened me, too. Paul missed out on so much in life, but he had wings of gossamer in Heaven.

February 25, Sunday

Noah was playing "King of the Mountain," a game where he and the other kids climb up a dirt pile and try to race each other to the top. The one who got to the top first was hailed king of the mountain. Noah and the neighbor's kids played on this dirt pile often. Unfortunately, Noah slipped and slid down the pile of dirt and into a small sharp rock, cutting him in the process.

I immediately cleaned the wound and took my son to the hospital. Dr. Owens closed the wound with four stitches. My son was current on his immunizations, so a tetanus vaccine wasn't given.

The incident did not escape my mother's criticisms and she went on a tirade over the accident.

It was something unforeseen—that's why it was called an accident. My son was simply playing and there was no danger in what he was doing. Still, Mother blew it out of proportion. I wondered if she ever rationalized that she herself was a good mother when I, at age seven, fell off a car's back trunk in our driveway in Golden, CO. Because of the fall, my missing teeth created a hole in my mouth, which Dr. Nolan had to close with four stitches.

I also wondered if she remembered that in 1961, at age one, I munched on a few glass Christmas tree lights, out of curiosity, behind a gas stove at our small house in Golden. My stomach required pumping. I wondered if she rationalized that during this time, she was a good mother too, but accidents were bound to happen.

But Mother was only using the accident with Noah to blame me for letting Ardy remain in-charge of my boys. This was the whole point of her ruckus. The concern over what happened to Noah was to me just pretense. Mother would use any excuse to make me relinquish Ardy's care of the boys in her favor.

February 26, Monday

Mother must be getting frustrated at this point because she could not make Matt flare up and fight her. This time, she harassed Matt's neighbors. She was desperate for any information she could get about him. To her dismay though, all she heard were good things about Matt—that he was a kind-hearted man, a passionate worker, and a reliable member of his church and community.

February 27, Tuesday

Henry talked to me over the phone today and kept on disturbing me at work. He called me at around 4:30 p.m., and then placed another call at 4:45 p.m.

He asked me to let him have the boys for a while, and I finally relented because I did not want him to tell the court that I was keeping our sons from him and vice versa.

While I was in night class, Mother showed up at Henry's house and took photos of Noah's leg with the wound that was obtained the other day while playing "King of the Mountain."

Similarly, Mother took photos of the right side of Eli's droopy face.

It never occurred to me that this was the reason Henry asked to have the boys for the evening. Had I known their foul plans, I would never have permitted my sons to go to their father's house.

Later that night, I found out from Eli that my mother made him cry so his face would be scrunched up. Then she took pictures of Eli's puffy and paralyzed face. It was as though she arranged for a pictorial of my sons to use as evidence against me and Ardy.

Mother didn't stop there. She taunted the boys with leading questions, questions that upset both boys, and then taped the conversations.

I never understood why my mother had to do all these things. It's as though she was derailed, a sick person who wallows and finds satisfaction in creating drama. She simply thrived on drama.

Chapter Thirteen

March 1990

March 3, 1990 - Saturday

I had to go with Henry to Durango and file taxes for 1989. I joined him in the car.

When we were driving, I told Henry about a funny feeling I had about Eli, but he ignored me. I didn't know that he was taping the entire conversation we had during the trip.

At around 7:30 p.m. to 8:15 p.m., my mother went to Henry's place and made Eli cry again. While she was harassing him, she taped the conversation yet again. Later that night, Mother showed me the cassette.

I wanted to tear out my hair in frustration because I never understood her reasons. Why would she keep on doing this? She literally taped Eli's voice as he cried. Then she would hold the tape in front of my face to taunt me about it.

I gave up trying to understand why she had to do this. All I knew was that she thrived on drama.

March 4, 1990 – Sunday

I noticed that Eli had lost the peripheral vision in his right eye, so I took him straight to the emergency room in Durango, CO.

Upon arrival, it enraged me that Dr. Owens summoned the emergency room nurse to come into the examining room. He told her to look at Eli, and then he said in these exact words, "You will never see this again." Conferring further he went on to tell her that Eli's physical condition was caused by a tumor.

I was furious at the lack of professionalism he displayed. I was standing right there, and worse, Eli heard Dr. Owens's words too. As a mother, I always wanted to protect my son and this doctor went on blathering about my son's condition as though we weren't there. He should have spoken to me first.

Anna drove Eli and me to Frisco in Silverthorne. The medical team did a spinal tap on Eli and gave him some pain medications. Henry went to Frisco, too, in a separate vehicle. At the hospital, he refused to leave so I decided he could stay the night and I would be back early morning.

March 5, 1990 – Monday

It's almost six months now since Eli started to become sick. It started with the sinusitis that later on turned out to be cancer. All these months, I had no source of support but Anna.

Today, at 5:00 a.m., I decided to see Matt. He used to only be an acquaintance, but as the days turned into months, and Eli's condition kept worsening, Matt's presence in my life became a source of strength.

I told him why I was worried about Eli and we talked for about thirty minutes. It was funny how a good conversation with him lifted my spirits.

At 6:20 a.m., I was in Eli's room at Frisco. Eli was asleep. He had a CT scan of his head and neck areas done at St. Peter's hospital.

The results came by soon enough and while I was going through the radiologist's reading, my world stopped turning. The scans revealed that Eli had a soft tissue mass—a pharyngeal tumor extending up through the cerebral fossa into the brain cavity.

My mother showed up in Eli's room after the scan. She became angry at me and told me I was a worthless piece of shit. The nursing staff called security and Mother was ordered out of Eli's room twice. While this was ongoing, Mother had the gall to bring out her cassette recorder and begin taping everything again. She taped my precious boys crying at what

Grandma was doing and they were afraid of my mother. Eli kept begging me, "Make her go away, make her go away."

Some may think "too much information" and some may realize some things just need to be said. For twenty-three years, I waited in gut wrenching sorrow to hear Eli's voice (my youngest child who died from complications of chemotherapy at age five years). My mother held his cassette taped voice over my head for twenty-two of those years, using it as just one more way to abuse me. It took forever (it seemed) to obtain some of those cassette tapes from her estate after her death in November 2012. In listening to one of them after Eli was in his room at Frisco Hospital following biopsy surgery, my mother was in the doorway giving me hell and calling me names and more. All the while little Eli who needed his mommy was begging me to make her leave/make her go away. My voice is heard telling her, "Eli wants you to leave," yet she relentlessly went on and on. I have not played any other part of the tapes as they are fragile. Now, I have given those tapes to Leo and Layla Cooper of Cooper Audio Visual to turn them into discs. Having known them and their work since 1995, I have full faith in their ability to do this task.

Thank you, Layla and Leo, I know you will do this in the best way possible. Please try to ignore the evil in those tapes, and the ignorance. Thank you very much. Maybe someday I will be able to forgive her fifty-three years of abuse to me. Time will tell.

My world was in shambles. The findings about Eli were getting clearer and although it didn't comfort me knowing his true condition, at least now I knew that indeed there was a tumor. I prayed that the detailed findings would come soon enough so we'd finally know what we'd be fighting against.

Noah and I stayed the night with Eli. Noah was only six at this time, and he might not have comprehended what was going on around him except that his dear brother was very sick.

I held Noah close and I reached out to touch Eli's hand. We were in this together. We're a family. We'd fight this.

Henry made so much noise that night and he would keep on pestering Eli. I knew this wasn't helping Eli at all, so I asked Henry to leave.

When I was alone with my sons, I cried once more. The tumor still had to be analyzed further. All the events in the past months came back to me in a rush. The initial scans Eli had and the misreading of the scans. If the tumor was found then, would it have made a difference?

But more significant issues were cropping up now. Where would Eli have the treatment? How would I be able to take him to the specialists if I had a job and night class to attend to? Would I be missing out on a lot of events in Noah's life as I tended to Eli?

There were so many things that kept haunting me as I sat by Eli's bed. On my lap, Noah was curled up.

My heart broke for my two boys, and when I thought the tears had dried up, a new batch would gush forth.

March 6, 1990 – Tuesday

Eli's pediatrician, Dr. Brown, asked me if I wanted Eli to be at Everton University Medical Center (EU) or Winter Park for treatment. I chose EU.

Dr. Noonan took Eli into the operating room for a biopsy of the mass. Eli had a Magnetic Resonance Imaging (MRI) done today.

Dr. Brown and Dr. Noonan said Eli would sleep all night with the medications on board and that Eli was recovering very nicely. With this information, I decided to take Noah back home.

I immediately spoke with Ardy to discuss the necessity to have Noah under her care twenty-four hours a day while I was with Eli at EU. Ardy said she would gladly provide the necessary care. Ardy was a renowned child care provider in Durango.

I went home with Noah feeling as though a burden was lifted from my shoulders. At least, I wouldn't have to worry about Noah while I was away caring for Eli.

Upon entering the house, I called the Frisco hospital. The nurse told me that Eli had a respiratory spasm. Eli's air passages had narrowed and constricted unusually, but it was gone now. When Henry heard this, he told Mother that Eli had a respiratory arrest. I vehemently disagreed and told him that it wasn't true.

The emotional battles with Henry and my mother were bringing me down. I called Anna because I knew she would be supportive about it. After having a brief conversation with her, I called Frisco again and checked on Eli. The nurse assured me that Eli was sleeping.

I exhaled heavily and my fingers automatically dialed Matt's number. He was kind to offer me consoling words, and after I hung up on him, I felt better.

But the day wasn't over yet. Mother showed up with the police. Mother began relaying false information like Eli had coded.

March 7, 1990 – Wednesday

I went to Frisco early to see Eli. Upon seeing that he was sleeping and receiving pain medication, I decided to head to Durango.

As a mother, I had to make sure that Noah received proper care, too. Every time I was away, I went to the Social Rehabilitative Services (SRS), and made arrangements for Noah to be cared for by Ardy. The secretary Nora knew my history with Henry and Mother.

After that, I went to the grade school and spoke with the principal and Noah's teacher. The school would not allow anyone other than Ardy to pick up Noah from school. Henry did not care about this arrangement, but my mother became livid and started yelling upon learning this. Then like what she did in the past, she taped the whole time she was having her tirade. She never even bothered to hide her cassette tape recorder. At one point, mother threatened that she "had papers to take Noah from Ardy before I could get back home from EU." This never, ever came to pass though–she could talk about it, but no lawyer would help her as my son, Noah, was receiving excellent care from Ardy.

When everything about Noah's care was straightened out, I went back to Frisco in Silverthorne and stayed with Eli. Dr. Noonan and Dr. Brown came in and said that the biopsy showed Rhabdomyosarcoma. It sounded Greek to me, so I researched this tumor and found out many things.

First, it was not hereditary. Second, it was very fast growing and would outgrow itself and its blood supply, so that a part of the tumor dies, breaks off and becomes necrotic which will start ear infections, sinusitis, anorexia, mood swings and changes. Third, it was inoperable. Radiation could be used for medication and chemotherapy would have to be instituted for at least fifteen months. After these treatments, Eli could only be declared cured if he showed no signs of cancer for at least five years.

Dr. Landon, who came from Cornell, and Dr. Mason, a resident in-charge who schooled at the University of Everton, were Eli's oncologists at EU.

I barely slept because I was very, very scared for Eli.

March 8, 1990 – Thursday

Anna came to Silverthorne to drive me to EU. I was shaken inside, but I never let the fear show because Eli needed me to be strong. And though I was crumbling inside, I steadied my hands. I had a chance to speak with Matt on the phone before leaving and his voice comforted me.

At the hospital in Silverthorne before leaving for EU, Henry told me mean things. One, he said that I wanted to bring Eli home in a casket like my mother did with Gabriel. Two, he said I wanted to screw around town like Anna. Three, I wanted to be a guinea pig like Anna.

I never comprehended what he meant with the last one and neither did Anna. Anna and I had to be rational about it and shrugged off Henry's comments no matter how hurtful they were.

Anna and I followed the ambulance's dancing lights all the way to the hospital.

March 9, 1990 – Friday

Eli had a urinalysis, full blood work, full skeletal x-rays, a CT scan of his chest, bone marrow scan, an echocardiogram, and a spinal tap.

All throughout these procedures, Anna stayed at EU to support me and I was overwhelmed with gratitude toward her. She left at around 7:00 p.m. when all of Eli's tests were done.

Eli was so tired, and sleep was fast consuming him. Before his eyelids closed fully, he smiled at me. My hunch was that the smile was because he knew I would be staying there to care for him. He fell asleep quickly.

It was a blessing that Henry did not go to EU as Eli and I felt less stressed.

Instead, Henry and my brother, Gavin, were staying at the Ronald McDonald House across the street.

Before the day was over, I spoke with Noah on the phone. He said he missed us, but he said school was fun.

I put the phone down, terribly missing Noah. Right now, though, I knew I needed to stay with Eli.

Halfway through the night, Eli became restless due to a lot of pain. For that, he received IV morphine.

March 10, 1990 – Saturday

Henry and Gavin popped in at 8:00 a.m. for a couple of minutes then they left for Durango. I was relieved when they left.

I chatted with Eli and tried to get him to smile and he did every now and then, although there were instances when his tiny eyes would shut tightly, and he would complain about the pain.

Dr. Landon dropped by this morning and he said that there were two metastases spots on Eli's lungs, one on each lobe.

Eli had an IV pump and was receiving IV morphine. It amused me when Eli named his IV pump "Herman." I wasn't sure where Eli borrowed that name from, but heard the nurses refer to another child's IV pump as "Herman." I think Eli liked the name.

I gave Eli a sponge bath, and when he was ready (wearing a dress robe) I put him in a wheelchair, unplugged "Herman," and went for a walk. I showed Eli the cafeterias, the escalators, and the gift shop over in Boone.

At one point Eli said, "Mom, I think you're lost."

"No, I'm not."

"I think you're lost," Eli repeated.

I told Eli that this place was so big and that might be the reason he thought I was lost—because we kept on walking in circles. The first day we were here, I was compelled to learn the layout of the hospital fast, so I wouldn't get lost when I took him on a tour.

We went for strolls twice this morning and Eli liked them. Not having Henry peering over our shoulders made us relax and surprisingly, even with the worries I had for Eli, we enjoyed the stroll. Eli didn't say it, but as I looked into his eyes and the way he was looking at the other little boys in the hospital, I knew he was missing Noah as much as I did.

At noon, Eli went to lie down and take a nap. Then suddenly, he burst out, "Mom, my head don't hurt no more." He touched his head as though amused by the thought and added, "Mom, my neck doesn't hurt no more."

My eyes moistened, but I blinked back my tears.

Then, Eli said, "Mom, sometimes when I got up in the night and went to your bed, I was not scared, but I had a big head hurt."

I was shocked. I bent toward my baby and asked him why he didn't tell me this before. He did not answer me directly. He just said his head didn't hurt now.

At 7:45 p.m. Henry showed up at EU. Instead of asking me how Eli was, he accused me that my car was not where I had left it, and therefore, I must have gone off to Durango in secret. This was not true, and I told him he should quit messing with my life.

Eli noted the sudden change in the atmosphere and asked his father to leave four times. Young as he was, Eli courageously told his father to leave the room. He confirmed this to the nurse. My son was indeed wise beyond his years.

Upon hearing this, the nurse asked Henry to leave the room and sent him to the Ronald McDonald House, which provided housing for families of ill children in Denver. This housing facility was a huge help to families of ill children as the room rates were on a sliding scale, and many didn't have to pay anything at all. Food and laundry can be done there for free. The facility used to be an old mortuary but was converted into a Ronald McDonald House. As for me, I stayed by Eli's side even though it meant sleeping in a chair and dealing with sore muscles the following day.

I thought the ruckus was over. But after a few minutes, the EU police showed up. According to them, Henry and my mother reported that I had a concealed weapon in my purse, a .38 special.

My face was drained of its color and I was livid. "Go ahead and look," I said.

The police did, and they found no gun.

I heaved a sigh of relief, hoping that the troubles Henry and mother planned on throwing my way were over. I collapsed on the chair and watched Eli in his bed.

As I fell asleep, a thought haunted me. There would be no getting away from Mother or Henry while Eli and I were staying at EU.

In the middle of the night, Eli became restless and he twisted and kept moving in his bed. At that moment, I decided to climb in the bed with my baby and cuddled him for a while. After a while, he stopped thrashing in bed. It was like magic. Maybe it's because he knew that with me, he was safe.

March 11, 1990 – Sunday

Dr. Landon came in at 8:45 a.m. All of Eli's tumor biopsy slides were sent by express mail to the Mayo Clinic in Rochester, MN. There, studies would be performed to conclude what type of cancer was ailing Eli. From here, treatment would be initiated.

At 9:30 a.m., Henry came and like yesterday, he started harassing me again. I didn't understand why he had so much hatred in his heart. Surely, he couldn't be blaming me for our failed marriage. While it is true that it takes two to tango, I made an effort to somehow save our marriage. He never did.

Henry had these facial "expressions" that scared the people around him. Even though we were no longer living together under the same roof, the way his eyes would burn with hatred as he gazed at me still elicited fear inside me.

Eli had not taken anything by mouth since noon yesterday due to his irritated throat. This bothered me a lot and I had to have another good cry with Matt and Anna. They gave me support where no one in my family had. Henry, along with my brother Gavin, and sisters Riley and Lily, hung out together this afternoon and all evening.

It's trifling the way they find it easier to give support to Henry when clearly this man doesn't even care what happens to Eli. Henry did this out of jealousy for my leaving him, and also my mother was trying to help him get Noah although in the end my mother wanted Noah for herself and the money the state would pay her to raise him. None of this ever happened as I was a good mother and everyone in our small town knew Henry and my mother.

As the days passed by, it became clearer that I needed to temporarily file for a leave of absence from all my nursing classes. I wondered if Eli could go into kindergarten this fall given his condition.

Eli and I saw a little boy today with no hair and it made me think of how my son would look, but I said nothing to Eli. I just couldn't.

A little boy who had cerebral palsy was three doors down from Eli. He moaned all the time as he suffered from horrid pain. This little boy was in a body cast and his mother was there all the time. She was constantly telling him to "shut up" and to "stop making noise." My heart went out to the little boy. He had been suffering too much, and the last thing he needed was his own mother losing her patience on him.

March 12, 1990 – Monday

Eli awoke in pain at 1:00 a.m. I told his nurse and she gave him some IV morphine.

At 4:00 a.m., they had a hell-of-a-time getting blood drawn from a vein. Eli hurt badly from all the attempts.

At 9:00 a.m., Eli was given pentobarbital and then we went to hematology for a bone marrow aspiration procedure. I was there the entire time.

The medical staff had to drill through the ileac crest of Eli's hip bone four times and it took three of us to hold Eli down. It broke my heart to see Eli hurting, but I knew that the test had to be done.

I asked for more anesthesia to be administered to Eli, but the doctor refused. They went through the iliac crest to get the bone marrow. Once the sample was retrieved, it was tested for cancer cells.

Afterward, we went to radiation and oncology. This was at around 11:15 a.m. Eli's doctor there was Susan Thomas and she was assisted by Dr. Nigh. Dr. Goodman discussed with me how Eli's radiation treatment would go. Eli was to receive external beam radiation on his entire brain and neck. The radiation treatment would be for six weeks. Chemotherapy would have to be administered, too, and this would last for at least fifteen months. The short-term and long-term side effects of these treatments were discussed, such as radiation burns inside and outside the body, inability to father a child when older as the process kills sperm cells, hair loss, and decreased appetite. Chemotherapy had the same effects save for the inability to father a child. Also, the treatments would bring in much nausea, vomiting, and kidney damage. Worse, chemotherapy kills all cancer and non-cancerous cells; which would eventually lead to low blood counts. Once this happens, patients become more susceptible to infection.

Eli would require dental care – excellent dental care —as his protocol was very aggressive.

Eli hated the table in Radiation oncology as he had to wear a plaster fitted head and neck mask so the fields to receive radiation therapy could be platted (marked out precisely), and it took 100 mg pentobarbital and 1 mg morphine to sedate Eli. Only then was the platting of his head and neck done.

Afterward, Eli had spleen and liver scans.

At around 1:00 p.m., Henry started causing trouble again.

Later the same day, I met with the cardiology doctor who would place a Hickman catheter in Eli tomorrow. My son needed one with multiple ports so that he could have IV chemo, IV antibiotics, etc. The Hickman would run into the superior vena cava.

The doctor told me that the surgery would take two and a half hours. It would start at 8:00 a.m. tomorrow. I spoke with the anesthetist and he explained why the procedure would take so long. He said it was because Eli has asthma and he had a bronchospasm at Frisco. In addition to this, the anesthetist would also give Eli a bronchodilator.

The procedure sounded too much for a four-year-old to take so I called my family and friends for support. I spoke with Anna, Ardy, Noah, Matt, Lucy Owens (Dr. Owens's wife), Lisa, my mother, Mrs. Parker (Eli's preschool teacher), and Nora at SRS. Matt asked me to call him again on Wednesday with an update.

March 13, 1990 – Tuesday

I try to do all of Eli's personal physical care because I love Eli so very much.

Today, I just finished giving him his pre-op bath.

Eli was taken down to the holding room at 6:30 a.m. and he was brought to surgery for the placement of his Hickman catheter, which was scheduled at 8:00 a.m.

I worried about my baby so much. He had lost weight and when I held him in my arms, he was so light.

At 8:45 a.m., Henry still had not shown up.

At 9:40 a.m., Eli was taken to the recovery room. The doctor said that Eli did very well, that the bronchodilator helped, and Eli had no bronchospasm during or after the surgery. I was relieved and thanked God for this good news.

Eli had no problems during recovery. At 10:30 a.m., he was brought back to his room.

At 11:00 a.m., Dr. Landon, his residents, and his medical students arrived at Eli's room bearing bad news.

Dr. Landon said that Eli's cancer was Stage IV since it had metastasized to both lungs. Dr. Landon was coordinating with Dr. Roan (Dr. Brown's partner), and they would have a meeting this afternoon to discuss Eli's condition.

At 12:30 p.m., Henry finally showed his face. The first thing he did was call my mother on the phone inside Eli's room. It was only after the call that he asked how Eli's procedure went and how he was dealing with recovery from the procedure.

The day ended with the final results handed to me.

Final results on lumbar puncture – no cancer!

Final results on bone marrow biopsy – no cancer!

I closed my eyes and thanked God as these results were good. That left me with rhabdomyosarcoma. I walked over to Duke Library and researched all I could on this vicious type of cancer.

At 3:30 p.m., more good news came. Dr. Landon said that Eli's liver and spleen were cancer free.

Hallelujah.

In the evening though, my spirits dampened again, and I had to call Anna for moral support. She was hooked on the phone with me for a long time, telling me words of encouragement that I so badly needed at this time.

Even with her parting words though, I still had a restless night, so I stood up from the chair and made myself useful. With regret, I took Eli's stash of snacks from his bedside table. He never really ate them, but there were instances that he would suck on the potato chips just to get a taste of the flavor.

March 14, 1990 – Wednesday

Eli was NPO (nothing by mouth) again today and it made me really worried.

At around 8:45 a.m., I met with Dr. Landon. He told me that Eli would be on a 49 - week therapy and he would be on a pilot study with a very aggressive protocol.

Eli had an electrocardiogram (EKG) this morning too.

When I gave Eli a sponge bath this afternoon I removed the surgical tape from his wrist and found chemical burns where his old IV had been. The chemical burns were really bad, and I called Eli's nurse, Rita, to quickly come to his room. We cleaned the area, applied Silvadene cream, and did sterile dressing each day so that the burns could start healing. It took me five hours to get a senior resident to come and see Eli's chemical burn and I was so pissed. The chemical burn was caused by his IV site extravasation.

Radiation treatment would start tomorrow, and then Eli's regular schedule would be Monday through Friday at 7:30 a.m. and 1:30 p.m. Damn.

At midnight—this to me was very ridiculous—the medical staff decided to do a lumbar puncture on Eli.

Eli was brought to the procedure room on the pediatric nursing unit and I came in with him, leaving Henry and Gavin in Eli's room. I helped the nurses hold Eli down while the doctor performed the lumbar puncture, and chemo was inserted through it.

When I came back to Eli's room, I found Henry going through my brown pocket planner and reading my notes. Gavin was also in the room.

I learned later on that it was Gavin who took the pocket planner from my purse. He read it and when he was done, he gave it to Henry. Damn them both!

Whatever happened to the concept of privacy?

What struck me as really surprising was how they seemed to dislike the notations I made on each and every doctor's visit in 1989 through 1990. I think they wanted to destroy my proof of all the things I did for Eli – everything that a good mother would do. They focused on the doctor visits and what transpired during those visits. They were so keen on getting the information about the details of doctors' consultations that they neglected the most important reason I kept writing in the journal — that each word I wrote there bled with my love to my darling Eli.

Henry and my mother did not want anyone to know the detailed visits during Eli's entire illness from 1989 to the present as that showed I was taking care of my children very well; and it would reflect badly on Henry.

I didn't know why Mother was so concerned about Henry. Later on, I found out that Mother had a "thing" for Henry and they were messing around at Bow Mar. Talk about betrayal. The funny thing was… I didn't care! If I could only put Henry inside a box and mail him back to Bow

Mar, I would have. I'd rather that he was far away from me and Eli, so that I could concentrate on taking care of my son.

March 15, 1990 – Thursday

Eli was up every hour last night and he was really tired.

At 6:00 a.m. the nurses checked his blood sugar as Eli was receiving Total Parental Nutrition (TPN). The reading was high at 220 so the nurse gave him insulin.

I took Eli in a wheelchair down to radiation oncology for his morning treatment. Then he stayed in recovery for one hour afterwards. It pained me that Eli had two identified treatment fields that would undergo 29 and 28 treatments respectively.

Back in Eli's room, the nurse came in to do a Complete Blood Count (CBC). Eli cried while the nurse inserted the needles on Eli's vein to draw out blood. I was very, very upset at her, but there was nothing I could do but comfort my son.

While Eli braved the procedures and the recovery, Henry stayed at the Ronald McDonald House. I don't know what he did during the time that he wasn't with Eli, but I didn't care. We were better off this way. I suppose Henry got to rest a lot, and conversely, Eli and I were also more relaxed without him around.

When Dr. Mason came in this morning, I told him what I thought of them doing the lumbar puncture at midnight. I also let him know that I was familiar with signs of infection and could put two and two together and come up with four.

Eli's poor chemically-burnt wrist would finally be treated appropriately. Precious, a stuffed bear was with Eli during the treatment.

At 1:30 p.m., Eli took Precious with him to his second radiation treatment. This was followed by another hour spent in the recovery room.

When Eli woke up, Precious was the first thing Eli laid eyes on. I liked to think that this gave him immense comfort, which was similar to the comfort I got whenever I confided to Anna.

Eli required sedation for the first two weeks of the radiation treatment to keep his head and body immobile during the procedures.

At 2:30 p.m., Henry left the hospital.

At 3:30 p.m., Eli started regular chemo sessions. One hour later, Eli was forcefully vomiting old blood despite being given medication, so he would not get sick to his stomach. The emesis was brown and thick, and there was a lot of it. They checked the emesis for blood at the nurse's station and the result was positive.

Eli's doctor stopped by to see Eli and his nurse Rita. Just this afternoon alone, I had to change the bed sheets three times because of all the vomiting Eli did.

Henry came back to the hospital at 9:00 p.m. I informed him how Eli's day had gone and of course, he just stared at me blankly as though I had not said anything significant. He didn't offer any words that could somehow make the situation better.

Instead, Henry looked directly at me and said, "God punishes those who sin, which includes you." When he had nothing more to say, he went back to the Ronald McDonald House. I thought this comment of Henry was rather bizarre. The man did not believe in God and he refused to let me take my boys to the Catholic Church.

His words clawed at me like they were made of sharp metals. What he meant was that I was being punished for moving out on him, leaving him, filing for divorce, and then ultimately seeing Matt on a few occasions. But, I wouldn't let myself be affected by his words anymore. Not after what we had been through together; the endless days of him beating me up whether he was drunk or not, and his incessant curses that were thrown to my face as though I wasn't the mother of his children.

I pushed all the bad memories away. Henry was no longer in my life, and I was moving on. I prayed that Eli would get better so the three of us, Noah, Eli and I, could start anew.

Eli had a rough night again. He was up three times during the night while I had to be up five times to check on him.

March 16, 1990 – Friday

At 6:00 a.m., his blood sugar was 186.

We went down early for the first radiation treatment and Eli was in recovery for two hours this time. Henry finally showed at the hospital at 10:30 a.m. Henry's aunt, Naomi, stopped by briefly.

All hell broke loose after I spoke to Nora with SRS on the phone. I went to put something in my purse and found my brown monthly planner gone!

It could only be Henry who took the brown planner. There were folded papers inserted in the planner, but these were returned to my purse, leaving only the brown planner missing.

Henry and I had a confrontation of sorts, but he kept on denying that he took the planner. I never believed him because I vividly recalled that time I saw him and Gavin going over my notes the other day.

I was so pissed off that I kept cursing him quietly.

How could my younger brother and Henry connive against me when I was in the procedure room holding Eli, while he was being given a spinal tap? The least they could do was offer moral support to Eli. They knew how important the planner was to me. That's why they took it.

Then, Henry sexually harassed me.

"You just want to suck on my peter," he said. Then, he reached out to grapple at my breast. "You want it in the rear, don't you?" he said through gritted teeth.

I was panicking, and I wanted to defend myself and slap Henry, but at the same time, I didn't want to cause a commotion and upset Eli.

My lawyer, Atty. Troy, worked with the EU police to get Henry to stop. It was a good thing that I memorized the telephone extension "3050" by heart, as though I knew Henry would do something horrendous in the hospital.

Eli had been given Compazine and Thorazine before his 1:30 p.m. radiation treatment. Eli was sleepy enough that he did not require anesthesia at this time.

After radiation we went back to his room and then chemo started again.

At 4:30 p.m., Henry showed up and he had more trouble up his sleeve. He started harassing me yet again, and he spoke vile and dirty words that made me cringe.

A social worker intervened. Henry was very angry at the intrusion; on the other hand, I was relieved. The social worker made separate visitation times for Henry and me.

I thought this was a good idea, but when the social worker gave the schedules she came up with, I was disappointed. My time with Eli would be from 10:00 p.m. to 9:30 a.m. and Henry's would be the daytime hours. I found it unacceptable and I demanded an administrator to settle the dispute.

I told the social worker that there was absolutely no way that I could be away from Eli for that long. She finally changed the times. I had Eli from 8:00 p.m. to 8:00 a.m. and noon to 4:00 p.m. Henry had Eli from 8:00 a.m. to noon and 4:00 p.m. to 8:00 p.m.

The hours were much better than the initial, but I still hated the fact that Henry would have Eli until 8:00 p.m. when I know that he wouldn't even lift a finger to change Eli's sheets in case he vomited. But I had to live with the schedule.

The doctor prescribed medicine for Eli's eyes earlier this morning, but the medicine finally arrived from the pharmacy to Eli's room at 6:00 p.m.

Eli woke with his right eye matted shut. I had to get his nurse and ask her to administer the eye drops.

Later that same day, I was on the phone with Brody (a friend and Matt's first cousin) talking about my car's mechanical issues. From beside me, Eli vomited bright red blood at 7:30 p.m. I was so concerned.

He vomited again at 8:00 p.m. and 9:00 p.m.

I ran my fingers through my hair in frustration as I waited for the damn Ear, Nose and Throat (ENT) and Gastroenterology (GI) doctors, who were supposed to check on Eli and the results of the procedures he underwent today. But neither of the two doctors came.

I was very upset because it was the life of my son that was on the line here.

At 10:00 p.m. Eli vomited yet again. I felt hollow inside.

Eli was given a new bag of TPN.

At 3:00 a.m., Anna called me to see how Eli was doing. I was grateful for the concern. It was what I needed at that time, a comforting voice to help me ease the pain of seeing my son suffer. The comforting call did not last long though because after about two minutes, Eli again threw up bright red blood.

At 4:00 a.m. Eli was no longer able to sleep. I stayed up with him. I wondered if he felt as scared as I felt then.

March 17, 1990 - Saturday

Eli's glucose was 230 at 6:00 a.m.

After taking a quick rinse off in Eli's shower in his room, two medical students came in. I told them about Eli's bright red blood in his emeses yesterday and last night.

At 8:00 a.m., I waited for Henry to arrive as it was already his shift time. I still found it ridiculous that he had to be alone with Eli for a long time, when I knew that he couldn't even begin to give Eli the care I had given him; and most definitely not every day!

I decided to stay with Eli until his father arrived - should he actually come to Eli's room – he did not get to carry over his time with Eli just because he was late!

At 9:10 a.m., Henry walked in and I left the room. I wandered and walked the hospital a lot. I prayed in the chapel for some time. I asked God to heal Eli and to take me instead.

At 10:25 a.m. I called Eli's nursing unit (5D) to see if Eli was alone and he was not. Lord, I was so worried. The pain hurt so badly. I just wanted to go up and see and be with Eli so badly, but I couldn't - it was Henry's time.

I wanted to know where the bright red fresh blood in Eli's vomit came from, and I just wanted to see him. It wasn't fair! Maybe Henry had to prove he was Eli's daddy (wishful thinking on my part). Damn.

I walked to the EU bookstore which was part of the hospital and saw a Jayhawks baseball cap. Eli would like that as he was into the Kansas Jayhawks and this was a teaching hospital for EU.

I went to Eli's room at noon. Henry said the ENT doctor was there and that when Eli was "knocked out" for radiation, he would take a look at Eli's nasal and throat passages. Then, Henry said if I wanted to know more "just ask the nurse."

I asked Eli's nurse, Emily. She looked in Eli's chart and nothing was charted yet. Emily also said that it was not right for Henry to withhold information. Emily was correct. Henry did not have that right to withhold information about Eli. I would have to wait until Dr. Mason showed up now.

At 2:30 p.m., Matt came up with Spencer (a friend). Matt gave me a hug and we talked for a long time while Eli slept.

Gavin appeared around 3:40 p.m. and Henry finally showed up at 4:30 p.m., so I left per the EU social worker's visit agreement.

I called Matt and Spencer and then I just talked and cried a lot. I needed to let it all out and I did let some of it out. Finally, the time came for me to be back with Eli and so I went to his room. Henry had already left.

March 18, 1990 – Sunday

Eli's glucose was 196 this morning and he was up five times during the night to go to the bathroom.

I gave Eli his bath and he was alert, so we talked a lot.

Henry showed up at 8:45 a.m. with Gavin arriving somewhat earlier.

I spoke with Dr. Landon and also the ENT doctor two times. While with his father and Uncle Gavin, Eli came out in a jogging suit and walked the halls some.

I went for a drive to clear my head and drove through different parts of the city, being careful to stay in safe areas and near parks.

I walked back into Eli's room at noon and he was ready for another walk. So, Eli, Herman, and I went walking. We went over to A-Building (Murphy) and then back to his room. Eli was then ill and threw up before his chemo started at 2:30 p.m. Eli's protocol was different from the other boy who had rhabdomyosarcoma as he has it in his bladder.

Amazingly Henry showed up on time for once and I spoke with Gavin for a minute then left. While out on "my time" I went and walked through Southwest Mall. In 1990 this was a nice Mall.

At 6:00 p.m. I called 5D to see if Henry was still there and to ask how Eli was doing.

Then at 8:00 p.m. I walked into Eli's room as this was my time with Eli. After Eli fell asleep, I went down to 1F cafeteria. Henry found me and started hitting me up, asking if I would move back in with him. Then, he had the gall to tell me I had a "dying son." I so hated this asshole of a man – to me he was not a man at all.

March 19, 1990 – Monday

Eli was up four times during the night for the bathroom.

At 7:20 a.m., I took Eli down to radiation. I stayed in the waiting area while Eli had his procedure, so I would be immediately notified once the process was finished, and I could attend to my son in case something untoward came up.

At 8:30 a.m., Eli was taken to the recovery room. The ENT doctor came while Eli was in recovery. The doctor did not realize that Eli was receiving a fast-acting anesthetic so he wasn't able to check on Eli's condition. He said he'd come back at 1:30 p.m. Before he left, he told me that he could see Eli's tumor through the back of his throat and through the lining at the back of his nose.

I was horrified. How could so many doctors miss this if the tumor was that visible? It was mind-boggling. I couldn't say it was incompetence on the side of the radiologist who misread the CT scans, or the doctors who no longer reviewed the scans themselves, but what was I to think?

I just bawled while Eli slept. When he was awake, I did my best to hide my emotions because I had to be strong for him and I couldn't let Eli see me cry.

At 9:45 a.m., we were back in Eli's room. Once we were settled, Eli had a nose bleed. Henry was in the room at this time.

I knew I had to see my lawyer and speak with SRS and see Noah, so I left for Durango at noon after I had a discussion with Eli's nurses and the hospital social workers. They were going to monitor Henry and his activities. I first went to see Atty. Troy, and we worked out more of what we needed to do on the divorce papers.

At the SRS, I gave them a full update on Henry's asinine ways.

When my business with Atty. Troy and the SRS was done, I went to Ardy's to pick up Noah. I had to do this last because I didn't want him to hear my discussion with them. My son and I dined out since the food in my refrigerator had gone bad. We talked a lot. Sitting beside him and talking about his activities at school, and his stay with Ardy, made my eyes water because I really missed my Noah so much. I wish I could take him with me to visit Eli, but he had to attend school. Aside from that, I didn't want Noah to see Eli's suffering. I knew Eli's condition would break his heart, the way it broke mine.

At 7:00 p.m. I called EU and I was glad to hear that Eli was doing well. Due to the nose bleed and low counts, Eli received 160 ml. of packed red blood cells. I had previously approved this. Eli's blood type was O- and his father's was O+. I wished for the hundredth time Eli had my blood type A positive, as I would donate without hesitation should Eli need it. I doubted Henry would do so, if it came to that.

March 20, 1990 – Tuesday

At 8:00 a.m. I called EU to see how Eli was. They told me Eli was okay and in recovery.

After feeding Noah breakfast, I took him to school. I dropped by the SRS and by Atty. Troy's office.

At 10:45 a.m. I called EU again to check on Eli. The nurse told me that Eli was okay, but they had to put an elbow restraint on him as he pulled on the lines.

In the afternoon, I saw Matt. After a brief meeting with him, I saw Anna and we had a late lunch together. Then I left for EU.

Being away from Eli tormented me regardless of the assurances that I received over the phone that he was doing well. I had to see it for myself.

Eli was talking with his grandfather Carter when I arrived at EU. Carter left five minutes after I arrived.

At this time, Eli's glucose was 164.

I took Eli to the ophthalmologist. After checking up on Eli's eye, the doctor said that two stitches would be placed in Eli's right eye tomorrow.

After the procedure, the eye would be given a chance to heal. Earlier in the morning, Eli scratched his right eye because he was not able to see from this eye. When this happened, Henry did nothing. Eli's nurse Rita found Eli crying after the incident, and it was only through Rita that a doctor was called in to check on Eli.

I could feel Rita's affection toward my son and I guess Eli felt it too.

Throughout Eli's stay at the EU, Rita has become Eli's favorite nurse.

Eli slept most of the night even though a new lubricating eye ointment was applied to his eye every two hours. As for the sterile Hickman dressing changes, I managed to administer them while the nurses did Eli's chemo, TPN, and IV antibiotics.

Eli's blood sugar was within normal range at this time. I found Eli's Hickman TPN tubing had come away from the white port on his Hickman. The nurse said she did not tape it up well enough to keep them from coming apart. In 1990, large bore needles were still used to access ports with and it had slipped out. With luck, we were able to keep the Hickman from clotting off.

March 21, 1990 – Wednesday

During radiation this morning no anesthetic was needed. I gave Eli a bath after arriving back to his room. Then Eli had his usual treatments.

I took him out in a wheelchair to the main outside entrance as Eli had not breathed in fresh air since arriving at EU. We went over the walkway above Cambridge Street and Eli thought that it was really cool.

After arriving back to his room, the blue team, which consisted of Dr. Landon and his contingent of other resident doctors and medical students, came in to see Eli.

Eli told me he wanted to take a walk again and so we did. We roamed around 5D and I showed him the school classroom and toys, the nurse's station, the elevator, and the medication room. Then I wheeled him by the newborn nursery over in Boone and Eli told me, "I want to take the babies home with me when I get to leave and go back home." I told Eli, "Babies go home with their mommies", and Eli seemed satisfied with my answer.

Much later in the afternoon, Eli saw his ophthalmologist.

Henry showed up in the afternoon and started yelling about my trip overnight to Durango. He became relentless in his verbal abuse and the nursing staff and EU police forced him to leave the unit. Henry was furious that I saw my lawyer, the SRS, and Noah.

March 22, 1990 – Thursday

Eli had not received morphine since last Friday and still had not required anesthetic for radiation either. The plaster face mask with the platted places for the radiation was okay with Eli now. Both of these were positive signs. In addition to these, Eli's glucose was at 145.

Feeling hopeful and happy this morning, Eli and I took a walk again. This time, Eli was not in his wheelchair. My chest was beaming with happiness to see Eli improving.

After Eli became tired, I carried him in my arms and continued to walk around.

Radiation went well this morning and things were looking very positive and I thanked the Lord for these blessings.

Then, shit hit the fan and all hell broke loose with Henry big time! I had to call Atty. Troy three times, but he was unable to answer my calls. He returned my call afterward. There would be a hearing on the fifth of April.

I spoke with Ardy, Anna and Zoe Penson at SRS. I also managed to convince Denise Simms, nurse for Dr. Landon, to send a letter to the court. Lucy Stone and Sandi Tyler, both social workers at EU, saw first-hand how Henry tried to manipulate my mind. That was why I thought they would be able to help me in my divorce proceedings.

As expected, Eli received two stitches in his right eyelids to keep them partially sealed so that the ulceration on his eye could heal. I could still medicate this eye with the ointment.

I grew tired of Henry's and Mother's harassment, so I applied to have my phone number changed. Today, I was provided my new number.

EU social services told Henry he had to vacate the Ronald McDonald House when Eli's status became outpatient. Sandi Tyler said that even if I allowed Henry to stay with us, SRS would object and so would the hospital. I had no problem with that, because I never wanted Henry anywhere near Eli or myself. It only saddened Eli, and he cried whenever he saw and heard his father's antics, or my mother's. I'd been away from work for much too long, and I had to file my resignation a few weeks ago. Anna said she would talk to my old boss about my last pay check, and once my papers were cleared, she would deliver the pay check to me.

I was able to speak with Noah, Ardy, and Matt. Eli's spirits lifted when he spoke with Noah and Ardy. I saw a smile flash in his angelic face.

Ardy kept us posted about another child she was caring for—Oriana, who had started to crawl and scoot.

When the conversations ended and Eli was asleep, I curled up in the chair bed next to him.

Eli was up four times during the night. He vomited a large amount all over the bed once. It consisted of phlegm and clear liquid with bright red blood. I feel like Eli's treatment was killing him and I hated to see him this way. It was a sad closure to a day that began so beautifully.

March 23, 1990 – Friday

Eli and I walked down to radiation oncology. Eli carried a large syringe filled with water, but it had no needle. When we arrived in oncology, Eli started "shooting" everyone. The medical staff was surprised, and they laughed. Eli was in good spirits after he soaked the medical staff with water. I laughed, too, because I missed this mischievous yet endearing side of Eli. How I wished there would be more days like this one.

After radiation, we walked to the EU post office to mail off packages. I had an initial interview with Social Security Administration today regarding Eli and his needs and illness. Eli qualified since he fitted in the "illness lasting more than one year or illness that will kill him" category.

After that, Eli and I went to the dentist. Here, things went rather bad as Eli had personality changes brought about by the main tumor mass. Because of Eli's foul mood, the dentist was not able to attend to him.

We went to the eye clinic next so the doctor could remedy the one stitch in Eli's right eye, which was not placed properly.

After Eli's 1:30 radiation treatment, his eye was freshly stitched.

I spoke with Ardy, Noah, Anna, and Matt on the phone again. At this time, Matt and I had become really great friends although given the circumstances I was not expecting it to happen.

Eli was tired, but he still talked to Noah for a few minutes. While Eli was on the phone, he started to doze off, so I took the phone from him.

Two letters came in the mail today: one from Atty. Troy and the other from Zoe Green of the SRS in Durango. It was snowing here now, and I had to wait in the cafeteria in 1F until I received a phone call saying I could go back to Eli's room.

At 8:00 p.m. I was able to go back up to 5D and to Eli. Eli had to have a chest X-ray and I had to wear a lead shield and hold Eli in place. It dawned on me that Henry had never once gone to any treatment or appointment of Eli's. That jerk really did not care if Eli lived or died. He was so self-centered.

Later, Henry called three times about his room at the Ronald McDonald House and all the stuff he left there. Not once did he ask how Eli was doing.

As Eli went to sleep, I was once again alone. I decided to read up on the home TPN orders so I would be prepared to give Eli the best care a mom can give to her sick child.

On the same night, Henry left for Durango.

Eli woke up three times during the night and I assisted him each time. I seemed to be losing weight now. I was down to 114 pounds, as opposed to my 119 pounds when I first arrived at EU. I needed to take care of myself, too, because I had to be strong for Eli. I decided to eat more nutritious food.

Similarly, Eli had also lost a lot of weight. Even though he was on TPN with lipids.

March 24, 1990 – Saturday

Eli had two more X-rays this morning: one of his chest and another Pan-orex of his teeth and jaw. He was crying due to the pain from his upper back and right neck areas. I spoke with Dr. Mason and the blue team about it, and Eli received pain medication.

At 11:45 a.m., I filed a theft report, Case #6752, with Officer Knight of the EU police. The details included: Brown pocket planner with my name on it, for years 1989 - 1990.

I bought a new blue pocket planner for years 1990 – 1991 at the EU gift shop today, and I used journals to fill in the first months of 1990.

It snowed 7-9 inches last night until this morning. March in Colorado could be very unpredictable.

Henry's aunt Emma called me to see how Eli was. My relationship with Emma was firmed up by past experiences, back to those days when I used to fetch her mother from the nursing home and bring her to my house for Thanksgiving and Christmas holidays. My knowledge of trans-ferring people in and out of vehicles and wheelchairs was what gave me the privilege to attend to the task.

Emma loved the fact that I gave her mother so much good care, and that her mother did not have to be alone during the holidays. Oftentimes, Emma and her daughter Stacy would come to my house for the holidays, too.

Emma knew me as deeply as she knew Henry. Thus, Emma was on my side, supporting me through Eli's hospitalization period and we still remained connected afterward.

Henry hated that Emma knew I was being a good mother to Eli and Noah, and that she also knew about Henry's alcohol and temper problems.

Things had changed yet again at EU regarding who could see and visit Eli. Henry and I were the only visitors Eli was allowed to see now. This came about because of Henry's actions on March 22.

I spoke with New England Critical Care regarding home TPN, and I spoke with Ardy and Noah on the phone. I read that I had been calling Noah daily since Eli and I had been at EU. This made me happy because although it was only through phone calls, I still managed to always care for my Noah.

Henry popped in at around 8:00 p.m., he kept on talking about his drinking buddy Maxie, and little or no words were uttered at all regarding Eli.

After Eli fell asleep, I scooted in the chair bed, too.

At around 3:00 a.m., I spoke with Matt as I could not sleep. He told me he had called twice yesterday, and he said the phone was busy the first time he called, and then the phone went unanswered the second time.

After the call, I lay in the chair bed still wide awake. I was worried because Eli's white blood count (WBC) was very low at 1100. I figured his absolute neutrophil count (ANC) was also low. I feared what may be coming next — isolation.

March 25, 1990 – Sunday

Eli's ANC was 400 this morning and true to my prediction, Eli was placed in isolation, in the same room, to protect him from picking up germs that could kill him.

I wore a mask in the room while I did Eli's sterile dressing change to his right eye and his sterile Hickman. Sores started in Eli's mouth and there was a string of them on his body too. Nystatin was started on both areas.

As if that wasn't enough, we found out Eli had shingles, too. This left him in pain. Eli's resistance was impaired by his low white blood count. He cried out in pain when his skin was touched, so I had to be careful while attending to his needs. It hurt me deeply to see him this way and I cried inside again. I bottled up all the pain until Eli was sleeping, so he wouldn't see the pain I was also feeling.

Henry arrived around 10:30 a.m., but he did not stay long, which was all for the better. With him around, all I felt was pure revulsion.

Matt told me he called twice today, and it was Henry who answered. I'm sure the conversation did not go well. I wasn't in the room at that time, but I can only imagine how it went.

Matt was soothing and supportive on the phone with me and I cherished that. His tender ways were new to me as all my life I was abused by people around me. This time, it was different with Matt. An odd yet welcome thought crossed my mind—I think I am falling in love with him.

Eli was hungry, and he sucked the juice out of one orange section today. It must have given his taste buds a good shock because he had not eaten anything in so long. Eli though, had always loved food and flavors so much.

I phoned Anna and she said she got my letter and would make my deposit for me with my final pay check from work.

Today, the ENT doctor tightened the stitch in Eli's right eyelid.

In the evening, Henry made sexual advances toward me for the millionth time since coming to EU and for the tenth time today alone. I called the EU police as I was just utterly sick of Henry's actions and I filed a complaint. I wish there was a way to make Henry stop saying foul things, harassing, and trying to touch me.

March 26, 1990 – Monday

Radiation was not given today as Eli's ANC was only 300.

Eli's new wheelchair – a size to fit just him – arrived this morning. It was on loan to Eli so that I would have one to wheel him around at EU and something I could use at home when the time came that I bring my son home.

I drove north to downtown Denver and to the Denver courthouse for a peace bond on Henry, but since we did not live together (at Ronald McDonald House) I wasn't able to obtain one. Justice just does not always prevail in the right way sometimes.

Eli's red blood count (HGB) was 8.5.

Henry came in at 10:00 a.m. and he refused to use aseptic techniques and wear a mask. This would bring so much risk for Eli.

I told Rita about this and she talked with Henry immediately, but it did no good.

Then Henry told me he has told a lot of people in Durango that Eli was dying and had two weeks to live. My face literally lost its color. The bastard was so similar to my mother in many ways. I'm pretty sure he told the people about Eli to get attention with his drama. I was still trembling with rage when I left him with Eli.

I went to the Lost and Found section in the hospital to see if my brown planner was there, but it wasn't. I knew Henry was holding onto it, or he gave it to my mother. Either way, I'm pretty sure I will never get it back.

Dr. Benjamin, a pediatric hematologist and oncologist, told me that he would be Eli's doctor in April. The rotation of the doctors in the hospital was due to the large population of pediatric cancer patients and that the three main pediatric doctors were also teaching the residents and medical students.

Dr. Benjamin, although he was still not officially Eli's doctor yet, visited Eli. The doctor seemed really nice and Eli liked him a lot.

At 6:00 p.m., Henry came but only stayed briefly.

Today, Eli received a University of Kansas baseball cap in the mail today from his great aunt Emma and he beamed. He really liked the Jayhawk embroidered on it.

I called Ardy and spoke with Noah for a while. I missed my darling Noah so much. Afterward, I spoke with Anna and Matt and gave them updates on Eli's condition. As usual, they offered me comfort and with that, my strength was somehow renewed.

March 27, 1990 – Tuesday

When I woke up this morning Eli was still asleep. I found his beautiful blond hair all over his pillow and bedding. I simply bawled for a long time. Then, I cleaned up most of his hair and threw it away, forgetting to keep a lock. I wanted to clean up all the hair before Eli woke up and saw all of it spread out on his pillow.

After Eli woke up, I combed his hair and most of whatever was left fell out. I clipped the remaining hairs on his head, but there were so few I doubt counting them would give me a number close to thirty.

Eli's ANC was 300 this morning and his total Segs and Bands multiplied by the white blood cell count left an ANC that was very low. Due to this, Eli received no morning radiation treatment. This also meant that Eli could not place a sticker of his choice on the chart I made him, which was similar to a calendar. Every day, when Eli successfully went through his treatments, he would choose a sticker and stick it on the chart that held the date. This way, he was encouraged to be strong during the treatments. It was an interactive way I devised for Eli to learn about the days of the week, too.

Eli's skin was peeling off, so I gingerly did his right eye care, his Hickman dressing change, and his bed bath. I loved my time with Eli. So far, Henry had not done any of these cares for Eli and he never would have done them to my satisfaction anyway, so that was just as well. Looking back, I realized that Henry had never given Noah or Eli a bath – ever!

My friend Stella called this morning and we spoke for some time. I knew that she could help little Noah with his feelings during this period.

After picking up today's mail, I found out I had to go to Durango again and check my safe deposit box. I left EU in the evening and I was excited to see Noah.

Upon arrival to Durango, I called EU to check on Eli. His temperature was 100.9, and so Eli was started on antibiotics IV as this was what must be done when a person gets a germ while on chemo and radiation. The immune system was compromised because of this.

I spoke on the phone with Matt and it was such a comfort to hear his voice.

Sadly though, I wasn't able to take Noah home with me because I arrived in Durango at 10:45 p.m. I did not want to wake him up.

I called EU a second time to check on Eli. His nurse Mitch said that Eli was getting a chest X-ray in his room, and that he was placed on two antibiotics.

March 28, 1990 – Wednesday

I called EU and spoke with Eli's nurse, Jackie. She told me Eli's condition was the same, and that his ANC had gone up to 800. Eli had his radiation today.

I went to my divorce lawyer and gave him updates on Henry. Then, I did the same at the SRS office.

After going to the bank, I went to the grade school and waited until Noah's class was dismissed, surprising him with my visit. We went out for lunch and it was so sweet to see my son.

When I headed back to EU, I noted that my mother was tailing me from highway 111 to Old 40. I found it ridiculous that she was following me. I considered this action on her part as harassment.

After I arrived at EU, I spoke with Henry at about 5:45 p.m. He said that I "abandoned Eli last night." What a crock of BS! Henry knew that my car, bags, and makeup bag were gone from Eli's room.

At 8:00 p.m. my time with Eli commenced. I talked to my baby and reassured him how much I loved him. Then, Eli told me that his "daddy said and did things I did not like while you were gone." I asked Eli what his father told him, but my son wouldn't tell me what they were. I can only imagine that Henry told Eli things such as: "Your mommy's never coming back" or that "Your mommy doesn't love you." I was so angry at that bastard Henry. I hated him for what he said and did to Eli because clearly, those words bothered my dear son.

March 29, 1990 – Thursday

Eli woke up at 6:00 a.m. today vomiting and in pain. He was given 1 mg. of morphine, and he was strong enough to have his radiation today.

I spoke with chief resident Dr. Mason this morning about Henry not washing his hands or wearing a mask. Dr. Mason said he would explain to Henry about "proper hand washing and the use of a mask to protect Eli."

At 9:10 a.m., Henry arrived. Clearly, he was late again, and I wondered why he never arrived on time based on the arrangements made by the social workers at EU.

I talked with social worker Lucy Stone in her office and updated her about how Henry never seemed to care about Eli's treatment, and the way he wouldn't obey proper hand washing techniques, and how he never wore a mask whenever he entered the room to protect Eli from infection.

After that, I went back to Eli's room. I found out that Henry had opened my mail and Eli's mail while I was gone, even the letters from Dr. Cameron and Lucy Owens.

Volunteer Services violated the hospital protocol because they were not supposed to deliver mail to the room if I was not there. Now I wondered what else Eli and I had been missing from the mail.

I was so upset I told Lucy Stone about the incident. She then had a talk with Henry, but I didn't find out the result of their discussion as yet.

My "time" with Eli went very well. Then, Dr. Benjamin's nurse practitioner, Denise Simms, held a meeting with me and Henry. I could tell she was smitten with Henry because she kept on looking at him while practically ignoring me. She kept smiling at Henry, but not at me. I wondered what she saw in him. I found this especially odd because Henry had always been so racist in the past and because told me more than once that he was a member of the Ku Klux Klan. I never saw a membership card and I don't even know if a person receives a membership card for that matter. All I know is that he said he was a member and that he owned a hat of sorts with bones and things attached to it. It was Henry's time to be with Eli when Denise left, and Henry then left also. This showed how little he cared for Eli.

Although I was pissed off, Henry's leaving also meant that I would have more time with my son. For that I was thankful.

Henry came back to Eli's room at 6:30 p.m., and then he had to leave again for a smoke. Henry came back to Eli's room at 7:00 p.m. and left at 8:00 p.m. I am not sure what he did to fill his time, but I treasured my time with Eli.

March 30, 1990 – Friday

Eli was sick last night off and on. They wouldn't give Eli anything for the emesis or the dry heaves, and I didn't understand why. I knew it was too soon medication wise, but there were other medications they could obtain an order for.

At 1:15 a.m. I went down to 1F for a smoke as Eli was sleeping peacefully. I was so very tired. I went straight back up to Eli's room and lay myself down on the chair bed.

Around 3:30 a.m. Eli started vomiting yet again and this time it was bloody red, and suction was used. Eli received morphine and I was thankful. I was so afraid for Eli. How could this four-year-old little boy be so very strong?

After the morphine was given I changed all of Eli's dressings as they were covered in bloody red emeses. Eli then settled back down, and I called Anna at 4:00 a.m. We talked for some time and then when Eli woke up around 6:00 a.m. I gave him his sponge bath. I also did his ointments and nystatin oral care each morning. After the TPN finished, I saline flushed, and heparin locked Eli's Hickman. I did so much of Eli's care now. I had to learn all the procedures, so I could do them for him when we went home. This was just fine with me. I had more quality time with Eli.

Henry showed up at 9:10 a.m. so I left and went down to the hospital's post office and sent off a package for Noah and a letter to Matt.

Noon came, and I went straight to Eli's room. Eli's ANC was 1150. Eli was slowly climbing back up.

I placed a mask on Eli and then took him down to the gift shop as Ardy, her husband Max, her granddaughter Mia, and Noah had sent him a birthday card with $10 in it.

Eli took his time looking around in the gift shop and he found a couple toys and some stickers, and he spent $9.57. It was such a delight to watch as Eli looked around and decided what to buy.

I did Eli's IV medications today and took Eli down to X-ray at 2:00 p.m. for an esophageal X-ray and tape.

Henry finally arrived at 4:30 pm and then he wanted to leave at 6:00 p.m. until 6:45 p.m. I gladly relieved him.

After I left at 6:45 p.m., I called my friend Lisa and asked her if she and Alice could give their signed statements, attesting to how I have taken care of my boys. They did this gladly, as they knew the kind of mother I was.

Eli was in pain again at 8:00 p.m. and he had also wet the bed when I arrived back at my designated time. To my horror, Henry had only "covered the urine up" with a blue disposable Chux under pad. I would have changed the bed covers and Eli's hospital gown if I had been there, but it was not my time.

I mailed off a lot of things to my lawyer today. I called Ardy around 8:30 p.m. to talk with her and with Noah before he went to bed for the night. Eli received more morphine for pain.

March 31, 1990 – Saturday

I was up as usual by 6:00 a.m. so I could give cares to my son. I drew Eli's lab work from his Hickman and CBC with differential (it measures the numbers of the five different white blood cell types).

Dr. Benjamin and Dr. Mason came in with the blue team. Dr. Benjamin told me the esophageal X-ray and tape showed that Eli's throat did not function properly and that there may be more nerve damage than previously thought. Then, he said that TPN was needed for long-term use. Eli may benefit from a nasogastric (NG) tube or gastrostomy tube. I had reservations on these options as Eli was still throwing up, and with tube feeds, Eli could take the increased emeses into his lungs and die. Because of that, I said no to both options.

Eli and I took two walks and Henry showed up at 10:30 a.m. At noon, I went in to see Eli. Gavin was in the room and apparently, Henry had let him in. What happened to the "no visitors" agreement?

Perhaps sensing my disapproval of what happened, Henry and Gavin immediately left.

Later, I spoke with Ardy, Noah and Anna. Matt called and explained about some of the things that were happening back in Durango. Anna said she had received a letter from my lawyer, Atty. Troy, requesting any information that she had, which could be used against Henry.

At 4:30 p.m. Henry and Gavin arrived and then Henry asked for me to relieve him at 6:00 p.m.

When I returned at 6:00 p.m., Henry and Gavin left in a hurry. As I took Eli for a walk I wondered why Henry never did the same.

Back in Eli's room, I completed his treatments, then flushed both ports, heparinized the red port and connected Eli to his TPN with the white port.

Afterward, Eli immediately crashed and fell asleep.

Chapter Fourteen

April 1990

April 1, 1990 – Sunday (April Fool's Day)

I could not sleep with everything running through my head and Eli was sound asleep, so I went down to the 1F cafeteria at 1:00 a.m. for a smoke. I went back to Eli's room after 30 minutes and ended up staying awake until 4:00 a.m.; and then I woke up again at 6:30 a.m. DST (Daylight Savings Time) begins today.

I gave Eli his Tagamet medicine. Eli's eye doctor came in and cultured Eli's eye drainage. Dr. Benjamin was right behind him. My hunch was that Eli would need a nasogastric tube.

At 11:30 a.m. both Gavin and Henry showed up, so I left to give way to Henry's schedule with our son.

I called Ardy and spoke with her and Noah before going back up for my allotted time with Eli.

I found Eli wide awake in his room. To make the most of my time with him, I decided to take him around the hospital. He got into his wheelchair and the change in the surroundings was welcome.

Outside, I saw that Eli was looking at the cars.

"Mom, do you think we can buy one of these? Who do they belong to?" he asked.

"What's your favorite color for a car?"

Eli looked thoughtful for a moment and then his face broke into a smile. I wished I could see his right eye as a flash of excitement showed in his left. It was all too much for a mother to take in.

"Blue," he said, "like the color of our eyes."

With all the medical bills piling up, I knew that I couldn't afford a car then. But if this simple wish, uttered in all innocence, would make my boy smile, I would seriously consider taking a loan and buying one. Of course, it was only a consideration, because my priorities right then involved only Eli's medications.

"Get better, Hun. Then, we'll get one."

Eli's smile grew even wider. Then, we discussed what's under the hood of cars. I got excited because it was something I was familiar with. The alternators, water pumps, and timing belts were a few of the things I told him about. It was a good thing that I had worked at an auto parts store. My son's face wrinkled in amusement, and his eyes lit up even more.

In the afternoon, I drove around and searched for a grocery store while Henry was in with Eli. I was successful in finding one not too far away so now I could buy non - perishable food for myself, which was much cheaper than what the EU cafeteria charged.

At 8:00 p.m. I walked back into Eli's room and Henry had already left. Once again, I wished that I knew when he would leave ahead of time, so that I could come back and be with Eli. My son should never be left alone.

After Eli went to sleep, I called Anna and we chatted about Eli and if my mother was up to anything new. Then, I spoke with Matt and he told me my letters to him always came at the perfect moment. We had not spoken about the love that we knew was starting to spring in our hearts, so he only told me that my letters were always such a sweet surprise. I didn't ask him to explain further because I knew exactly what he meant.

Early on, we had decided to remain good friends and not get involved romantically, but no matter how much I tried to stay true to our agreement, there was something inside of me that told me how helplessly I was beginning to fall in love with this man, in a way that I had never dreamed possible for me.

April 2, 1990 – Monday

I was up at 6:00 a.m. as usual. I wore a mask and took care of Eli's Hickman dressing site using sterile technique. The blue team changed today so now it was Dr. Benjamin as the head, a third-year senior resident-in-charge, and other residents and medical students.

At 9:30 a.m. Henry "popped in" and all he did was take a shower in Eli's bathroom. This seemed odd to me as there were showers at the Ronald McDonald House. Henry then left for Durango at 9:50 a.m. Intuition told me that he and my mother were up to something yet again. Maybe if he had not drunk beer, he could have woken up earlier and taken a shower at the Ronald McDonald House. But then, even the simplest things seemed too much to ask from him, which only proved how much of a jerk he was.

I was afraid of what Henry planned to do in Durango, but at the same time I was excited to have the whole day with Eli.

Eli and I walked and played much of the day. When he got tired, I got a VCR and Eli fell asleep watching *Ghost Busters*.

Eli's eye doctor and his ENT doctor saw him later in the day. Since his ANC was very good, he was able to resume radiation. After that, we went back to watching *Ghost Busters* again.

After Eli went to sleep tonight, I called Ardy and spoke with her and Noah. Later on, I spoke with Anna and she told me that the club had been taking donations to help with medical and other expenses, and that $226 had been raised. *God bless these nice people!*

Eli had a donation account at Citizens State Bank in Durango, so all the money went into this account to which I submitted bills, and the bank then paid those bills for Eli.

In the evening, Henry never once called to see how Eli was doing so I was quite sure he was typically drunk, and maybe even close to passing out. Some father he was! Eli and Noah needed a man's influence in their lives. I was sure their father wasn't the one who could provide what my boys needed.

April 3, 1990 – Tuesday

I was up early and took Eli down to radiation oncology, and afterward we went to the eye clinic. We passed through the halls and during our walk, many people greeted Eli and me by name. I found it heart-warming and disconcerting at the same time to know that we had been here long enough for people to recognize both Eli and me and call us by our first names. No child should be in a hospital long enough for the employees to know the parents.

Eli had his suture on his right eye lid removed, and then we went back up to 5D Delp Pavilion, and from there we called Ardy. Eli and I took turns talking to Ardy and Noah. Noah said that he did not care if his father and my brother Gavin showed up at Ardy's or not, because he did not want to see them. Noah turned six in December 1989 and he was wise for his years. I distinctly remember him telling me that he could still picture the incident when his father threw me into a kitchen wall, the one where my sore body and head put a hole into the wall. My ears bled from the inside and I think that was the first traumatic brain injury I received.

While Eli napped, I went to the EU bookstore and bought him a small version of the red and blue basketball with a Jayhawk on it. Eli would adore receiving one for his birthday, which was to come in a few days. My son would be five.

Eli was awake when I walked back into his room and he insisted on looking inside the plastic bag I carried, which had a Jayhawk printed on it, so I gave the bag to him. His face broke out in such a huge smile. He played with the basketball all day long and when he was done playing, he hugged the ball to his chest.

Dr. Jordan of pediatric neurology saw Eli in the afternoon, and after an exam, the doctor said that he might only be able to see light in his right eye now. The doctor was not 100 percent sure, but he said that definitely, 99 percent of what Eli would see would only be light.

As a mother, I was deeply saddened by this new information. With my burdened heart, I took Eli down to radiation oncology for his second treatment of the day, and I kept on praying to the Lord for Eli to be able to see — not just light for Christ's sake — but for my son to see once again the palette of colors God showered upon this world.

In the evening, after Eli had gone to bed, I phoned Dr. Cameron, and Lucy Owens (with whom I took college classes.) We talked for a long time. I was ambivalent toward Dr. Owens even though I talked with him in detail about Eli's condition because in my heart, I also blamed him for not diagnosing my son correctly for so long. Dr. & Mrs. Owens's insisted that I call my lawyer, Atty. Troy, in the morning. After that, I called my friends Ardy and Matt, who had become my rock throughout this period. They told me they had heard from someone that Henry had received another Driving Under the Influence (DUI) ticket earlier in the evening. I groaned upon hearing that information, wondering if he would ever change his ways.

At 1:00 a.m. Henry called Eli's room and needless to say, he was very drunk. I did what I had to do — I took the phone off the hook.

April 4, 1990 – Wednesday

Eli was wide awake at 3:00 a.m. and no amount of persuasion would convince him to close his eyes. So, I went ahead and gave him his bath.

Later on, Eli and I went down for the morning radiation which went very well. I was so happy that Eli, with his stuffed bear Precious at his side, could still do radiation without sedation. When we arrived in his room, I did the sterile dressing change on his Hickman.

Henry phoned Eli's room twice and sounded like his usual self—full of verbal abuse and complaints; he never even bothered to ask how his son was.

True to the information relayed to me by Matt and Ardy, Henry indeed received a DUI yesterday evening. I think this is his twenty-third DUI in ten years, not that I was really keeping count. It just bothered me that having received so many in the past years, he was still allowed to drive. DUI is very dangerous not only to the person charged with it, but also to the pedestrians and other motorists. Surely, the laws must be stiffer.

I played with Eli the rest of the morning until Dr. Benjamin came in to see Eli. Dr. Benjamin was not so worried about Eli's right eye and rightly so because the cancer was more worrisome. Like me, the doctor did not want Eli to swallow anything at all as he believed it would go down Eli's wind pipe and into his lungs. Eli now had a Yankauer suction at his side all the time, and he used it himself to clean up his own oral secretions. Any mother would be proud to see her little boy growing up responsibly. I just hoped it didn't have to be in this manner. I would give anything to instead see Eli grown up enough to make his own bed, instead of cleaning up after his secretions.

I looked at the stand beside Eli's bed and my gaze fell upon the stock of food Eli had been hoarding these past days.

"When will we know if Eli can eat something safely?" I asked, afraid of the doctor's response.

Dr. Benjamin was concerned as he said, "We'll have to see after his second round of chemo if your boy will be able to swallow safely."

I welled up inside. My poor little Eli. It broke my heart to know that my boy wanted to taste the food he'd been saving, and yet to allow him to do so could be a significant risk to his health. I was torn up, but I had to keep my tears inside and remain strong for Eli.

I called Dr. Owens and he informed me that Atty. Troy had not called him as of 2:30 p.m. I needed them to speak with each other so that we could be ready for court in our hearing with Henry.

As usual, I phoned Ardy so Eli and I could speak with Noah for a while. Missing Noah was the biggest drawback of staying at EU. It hurt me that I couldn't be with him, and my only consolation was that I knew he was safe under Ardy's care.

Lucy Stone, a social worker at EU, stopped by to see me. She said, "Do not go to Durango for the hearing."

I raised my eyebrows as though to ask her why and she continued informing me that my mother had called oncology last Monday and said I was an unfit mother.

I had tried for so long to not hate my mother, but this was the final straw. The list came rushing to me—her awful torture of me and my boys, her lies, her abusive behavior—I now hated her. She never was a real mother to me, and never would be.

Later, Henry called and started yelling at me so I had to hang up on him. It bothered me that Henry and my mother, the two people I expected to receive support from the most, kept on harassing me. Both had no place in my life anymore, and they could go kiss each other's ass for all I cared.

Eli and I went to his second radiation treatment again; afterward, I took him back to his room. In the evening, I got lost driving as I looked for an Express Mail box. I ended up in Asher Park instead. There, I found an Express Mail so now I could send the documents to my lawyer.

Back at EU, Eli's Aunt Grace called and spoke with Eli and then she hung up rather quickly. Grace was Henry's little sister. I wasn't quite sure why she called because up until now, she had not shown any real affection toward Eli. Immediately after Grace ended the call, Henry called and started bitching — again, totally forgetting to ask how Eli was doing. It was a relief when the conversation was over.

As part of my daily cares to Eli, I flushed both of his lines, then I heparin locked his red port and started the TPN in the white port.

When my son was sleeping, I collapsed on the chair and started to compose a letter to Matt, in between attempting to connect to Durango, but all the circuits were busy. The hearings for divorce, and Noah's primary caregiver/residential parent was tomorrow at 10:00 a.m. in Durango and I would not be there per the advice of Lucy Stone. My absence would also be supported by Dr. Owens's letter stating the need for me to stay with Eli.

April 5, 1990 – Thursday

After waking up at 1:00 a.m., I called the club and talked with another one of my friends, Pippa. Then Anna called me twice at 3:00 a.m. telling me she had left more information with my lawyer earlier yesterday. I was still awake at 4:00 a.m. and felt so nervous knowing I would not be in

Durango for court. I went down to 1F for a smoke, and I poured more of my thoughts and fears in my letter to Matt. After that, I decided to write a letter for Noah.

After going back up to Eli, I found he had been incontinent. I was appalled—my son, who had been potty-trained, had lost the ability to retain bodily discharges.

This tore me to shreds. I gave Eli a bath, changed his bedding, and gown. This time, I had to make Eli wear the smallest sized adult diaper. My son didn't complain about it.

Eli was back in bed by 5:30 a.m. just to rest.

Henry called at 6:30 a.m. and started yelling at me and saying I would be held in contempt of court if I did not show up for the hearing. Then, he started bitching, so I had no recourse but to hang up on him. He kept on calling even though he knew that with all the things he threw over the phone, I would just repeatedly cut the conversation short. I guess he just wanted to inflict upon me all the hurtful jabs he could throw. After flushing and heparin locking both of Eli's ports on the Hickman, Eli and I went to radiation oncology. I had to walk very fast to keep up with him because he was excited to show off the small EU basketball his mama had bought for him.

While Eli was having his treatment, I began to feel edgy about missing the hearing. But, there was nothing I could do about it anymore, so I pushed all thoughts of it to the back of my mind.

While Eli was sleeping, I picked up his birthday cake. My son wanted one even though we both knew it would just be for posterity, since he was not yet allowed to take food orally.

At 10:25 a.m., Ardy called and informed me that Henry won one night a week with Noah, which was to be on a Friday or Saturday night. I figured that the specific day during the week was going to mess with Henry's drinking habit with his friends, but I was also sure it would be my mother who would have my son that one night of the week.

There was nothing I could do about the decision. I just prayed my son would be safe around her. The rest of the hearing was continued until Eli was out of the hospital. I then called my lawyer Mr. Troy and we talked. He said that he was my sole representative, but that Ardy and Anna, along with others, were also there in the courtroom on my behalf.

Henry had with him the lawyer my mother paid for, my mother, and nine other people. A different judge presided over the hearing and he told Henry that he could have Noah for twenty-four-hour periods once a week, either on a Friday or Saturday night. Henry must let Ardy and I know what day each week he would have Noah, and this notification must be in writing. The notification had to be very specific, and the pickup and return times should also be stated.

The judge then decided the divorce would be handled when I got back to Durango with Eli. Atty. Troy told me he saw Henry, his lawyer, and my mother, talking earnestly after they left the court room.

I called Anna after speaking with Troy. She said maybe I should get a new lawyer to finish everything up because she thought a more prominent attorney would get things done to the boy's and my favor. Anna also said it might be helpful if I collected information on how my mother made money out of the insurance policies of her dead husbands. I gave it a lot of thought.

After that, I called Ardy so I could speak with Noah, and he told me he did not want to spend overnights with his dad. My heart simply broke for my son. He must be scared to be around his father or my mother to say something like that.

Social Security called and approved temporary assistance of $30 per month to Eli for each full month Eli was in the hospital, and a little more when Eli was not hospitalized.

At 2:00 p.m., Eli had his second radiation. Though Henry was awarded twenty-four-hour custody of Noah, I was still happy with the results because the court didn't allow my mother or Henry to take my son from Ardy. My mother must be raging mad about the decision.

I fell asleep in a sitting position in the chair bed next to Eli at around 4:00 p.m. and slept until 5:30 p.m. When I was about to get my dinner, Eli insisted on tagging along so I took him down to 1F with me. Eli played with some of the hospital employees and I ate a bite. While I was talking with one of the maintenance people at EU whom Eli liked, we found out that EU has twenty-seven miles of hallways, tunnels, and stairs. Astounding! Eli and I had a nice evening and when Emma called, she was able to speak with Eli and me.

The only thing that dampened the evening was when Henry called and told me that he would take Noah tomorrow at 2:00 p.m. until the same time the following day. As a last note, he said he had no refrigerator right now and he wasn't sure what he would do for Noah's food. Listening to Henry ramble on and on about it was very depressing as I knew it was just his way of hinting that my son would stay with my mother and eat her cooking. He was such a jerk!

At around 10:30 p.m., Matt called me and we talked for forty minutes. Eli slept through the entire conversation like he always did. When Matt and I hung up, I felt my spirit lift, and so I fired off another letter to my lawyer and also sent one to Noah. I sealed my letter to my son with a fervent prayer that my phone calls and letters were helping him while 230 miles separated us.

April 6, 1990 – Friday (Eli's 5th Birthday, 4th week of treatment)

Henry called at 7:30 a.m. to greet Eli on his birthday, but Eli was in the bathroom and he wasn't able to take the call. Henry got angry and started yelling again, so I did what I always did whenever he lost his temper—I hung up on him.

After telling my son "happy fifth birthday," I flushed and heparin locked both ports of Eli's Hickman, and we proceeded to radiation oncology.

Eli was in for a surprise. His nurse Vickie had a birthday present for him and the technicians had the radiation table decorated with balloons and toys. There was even a banner.

I took photos of Eli's delighted face with my camera and hoped that my shots would come out well. The staff also took a few Polaroid's.

After Eli and I got back to his room, Rita immediately hooked up Eli to his hydration fluids. As soon as she was done, a fellow nurse, Maci, together with Rita, asked us to leave the floor for fifteen minutes. I took Eli with me to 1F and waited there, all the while glancing at my watch. When fifteen minutes was up, I picked up Eli and carried him all the way to his room.

Upon arriving back to Eli's room, we were pleasantly surprised. I believe I heard my son yelp in glee.

There were decorations inside the room. Two birthday cards lay on the table. A remote-control cosmos car was beside the cards. As Eli and I walked to get to the center of the room, the nurses and the hospital staff started singing Happy Birthday.

That wasn't all. Dennis, the maintenance man who Eli liked, brought Eli an indoor basketball and hoop set. My son was so happy that day, and my heart felt so warm I was afraid it would burst in joy.

Afterward, Eli and I went down to 1G auditorium to see a circus bear. The bear was from the Moscow Circus, which came to visit the children at EU while they were in town. Eli loved the experience.

At 10:30 a.m., I held a party for Eli inside his room. All the nurses took turns coming in to greet Eli and the EU grade school teacher came to greet him as well.

Through the busy morning, Denise Simms, nurse for Dr. Benjamin, watched me as I did Eli's Hickman dressing change because my mother and Henry told her that I did not do them with sterile technique. Needless to say, Denise saw for herself that I did them correctly and in a sterile fashion, too. She stated she would document all this in Eli's chart.

I only wished my mother and Henry were there to hear Denise say that I did the change correctly.

Eli had an EKG done and the cardiology doctors checked in on him today.

I called Ardy and spoke with Noah. Ardy informed me that Roxie and Betty had verified to her that Henry did receive a DUI last Tuesday. She also said that Henry was waving around $400 in cash for a party at the bar. I also learned that my mother had just spent $10,000 on a trailer and was putting it out at Bow Mar for Henry to live in.

When Henry called, he said that he received a "ticket for speeding only because he was chasing Carter." That explained how he bonded out of jail so fast since Carter would have bonded him out.

At 2:00 p.m., I took Eli to his radiation treatment. The Heavens must be smiling down upon my son because the surprises still kept on coming. The receptionist gave Eli an Easter basket. It had turned out to be a great birthday, if only Noah were with us. I caught Eli's eye and I knew he was thinking about his brother, too.

While he was sitting on my lap, he whispered, "I miss my brother." I had to school myself to be brave so that I wouldn't shed tears. I loved my boys so much, and the way they had formed a bond between them made me love them even more.

Chemo started at 3:00 p.m. During this time, Ardy phoned and said that Henry had picked up Noah, and that per the court order, Henry should have my son back to Ardy by noon tomorrow. Then, Ardy spoke with Zoe Green of Child Protective Services and gave her updates, which consisted mostly of the DUI issued to Henry and the bond that was posted using Carter's money.

Henry was to go to court on May 20th regarding Noah's custody. Zoe Green said that my file had fifty-two pages in it, and they simply supported me in what has happened thus far. She said if Noah was not back at noon tomorrow, she should call the police.

At 7:00 p.m., Grace phoned and gushed about how nice Eli's cake was after I described the Ninja Turtles that decorated the cake. Of course, Henry had nothing to do with the cake—I doubt if he even knew that our boys fancied Donatello, Raphael, Michelangelo, and Leonardo. Eli's favorite was Donatello and Noah's was Raphael.

At 6:30 p.m., I called Anna and we spoke about the new information collected on Henry. My friend Calista verified that my mother did, indeed, buy a $10,000 trailer for Henry. She had the trailer put out at Bow Mar and had a rush job done to have it hooked up and ready by last Wednesday so that it would be completed before court. Ardy said she would drive through Bow Mar to see if a trailer was there.

Later, I dialed Ardy's number again, and she told me that there was a new, big trailer home with skirting around it placed down at the old Murphy place. The spot used to be owned by Ranae and her husband, but my mother owned it now. The trailer had some lights on.

This information confirmed the news about the trailer, and I wondered where Henry got the money. Regardless, somehow I knew that it was financed by my mother. The two of them worked hand in hand to take Noah from Ardy, and they supported each other in their scams.

Matt called me at around 8:00 p.m. and it was such a relief to hear his voice. I admit that when bad news kept on piling, my only salvation from all the drudgery was a conversation with him. Matt told me that there was to be NO traffic in or out of Silverthorne, which was thirty-five miles away from Durango, due to a Red Measles outbreak. This was very important due to Eli's compromised immune state while in treatment.

I fell asleep around midnight, tired but with a smile frozen on my lips. Eli had a great day, and a mother couldn't ask for more on her son's birthday.

April 7, 1990 – Saturday

I was up at 5:30 a.m. Eli had slept from 4:00 p.m. yesterday to 6:00 a.m. this morning, which was medication-induced since he was receiving the second round of chemo that started yesterday. This was Eli's thirty-fifth day in EU and it looked like it would be a two-month hospitalization this time. I took a break at 10:00 a.m. and what a morning it had already been. Even under sedation, Eli vomited. I changed his Hickman dressing twice with two groups of doctors and medical students wanting to see Eli's Hickman exit site. Eli became upset twice earlier in the morning and I blamed it on the chemo. He also had runny stools twice, and now Eli was angry about having to wear a diaper.

"Not for a five-year-old boy!" Eli shouted.

While Eli was getting change for one of his dollar bills, he threw a fit because the machine would not work. The medication was having the opposite effect on Eli, and I had to get help to get Eli back to his room. Eli was so stressed out from the medicine, that while in his wheelchair he almost hurt himself trying to get out of it. Eli could not stand up with this medicine on board. With assistance, I got Eli back to his room and into bed. The nurses put both side rails up on his bed. Then Eli started to dry heave and ended up vomiting. Eli's nurse gave him Ativan IV and Eli was asleep by 11:00 a.m.

It hurt to see Eli in such a rage from the medication, and now the medication had been listed as an allergy of Eli's. After grabbing a bite to eat at noon, I asked Eli's nurse for some Tylenol as I had a stress headache from worrying over my boys. I hardly touched my food.

At 12:30 p.m., I phoned Ardy and she said that Henry had Gavin with him when he returned Noah. Ardy informed Henry that due to the Red Measles outbreak in Silverthorne, she did not want to take any chances. She would take Noah to Durango for new tennis shoes.

Then, Henry asked Ardy if he could have Noah for a couple of afternoons a week. He also asked if he could take Noah to Denver and EU to see Eli, and then come back through Silverthorne to get Noah his tennis shoes. Ardy was steadfast and said no to Henry's request. It was careless of Henry to not heed the warnings about the measles outbreak, and what the germ could do to Eli.

The Shrine Circus in Silverthorne was called off because the outbreak was so bad. Noah said he saw his dad's new trailer and that Grandma came over to see him, and that she cried. Noah said that Grandpa was in the truck outside. Then, Noah went on to say that he went to Grandma's house, saw his and Eli's ponies, rode the donkey, saw the Billy Goat, and had cereal for breakfast with a sandwich for lunch. Then my son informed me that "Grandma had given him a big bunch of presents" because she loves me, he said.

Then out of the blue, Noah asked me if "Grandma was going to put him in jail." I told my son NO ONE is going to put you in jail and NO ONE had the right to even tell him that. I told my son it was another lie. Then I asked Noah if he wanted to live at Bow Mar.

Noah yelled over the phone, "No! I want you, Mama!"

I told my son I loved him many times and I reassured him that he was not to worry because Mama would fix everything.

At 1:00 p.m., Eli had another rough mood swing. Dr. Benjamin said the tumor in his brain was causing some of the changes in Eli's behavior.

After Eli calmed down, I took him to the Easter Party. There were clowns at the party and I could tell that the tricks and shows the clowns did made Eli feel better. The party was sponsored by Dream Factory, an organization that grants a dream wish to each child going through cancer or any serious long-term illness. They wanted to grant Eli a wish. I told them Eli would think on it.

Later, Ardy told me over the phone that she had spoken with lawyer Troy yesterday, and that Henry had received his Workman's Compensation settlement weeks ago. I certainly wished Henry would man up and help pay for Eli's medical bills.

Eli received a half dose of Ativan in the hopes he did not have as strong an adverse reaction this time. Eli woke up at 5:00 p.m. and we played.

At 6:00 p.m., Henry and Gavin showed up. I left and spoke with Eli's nurse about the "No Visitors" rule, and that meant Gavin. I also spoke with her about Eli's new Lacri-Lube for his right eye as this nurse has not worked with Eli for a while.

While down in 1F, I wondered how Eli's urine would test this time as it appeared to have blood in it earlier, and I wondered about the ketone level. I had to leave the room because it was not my time to be there. I was surprised that Henry and Gavin did not even stay with Eli. Instead, they came right down to 1F cafeteria and approached me.

It started so suddenly. Henry said that Noah was up from 3:30 a.m. onwards with a bad cough. Then Henry and Gavin started yelling at me, blaming me for Noah's cough. They made quite a scene in front of everyone in the cafeteria. Mortified, I left them and went back to Eli's room and upon arrival, I found signs that they had been drinking inside Eli's room. There were wet coasters that were still there.

I also noticed that there was a baseball cap, keychain, button, and a cup—at least today, Henry brought a few things to make Eli happy.

I looked at Eli and found him trying to drink water from the cup. I rushed to his side immediately and took the cup from him because he couldn't have anything oral yet due to his inability to swallow. Otherwise,

his lungs would be compromised, and he might end up suffering from pneumonia. I put the cup beyond Eli's reach to protect him.

Henry did not want to obey the "No Visitor" rule and Georgia, Eli's nurse, got involved. She had been told to call a social worker and that's what Georgia did. A few minutes later, one of the social workers came and made Henry and Gavin leave.

Later, Eli's urine test came back. The result showed high ketones, but the glucose level was okay.

April 8, 1990 – Sunday

It had been a fitful night for me and I woke up around 4:00 a.m. I managed to sleep again, and the next time I got up was at 6:30 a.m. Eli was still asleep.

I was afraid of what today would bring; the drama and asinine things Henry would do today.

At 8:00 a.m., I tended to all of Eli's needs and his favorite nurse, Rita, made copies of papers from my lawyer for Eli's chart. I then called Ardy and informed her to tell SRS of Noah's cough. Ardy said that she had been talking with Reese, and Reese said that Henry was in the bar the other night and told everyone that all I did here at EU at night was to party and leave Eli alone. I so hated that bastard for lying! I know the nursing staff charted everything as Rita said they did. She said they documented my presence here each night and all the cares I did for Eli and where I took him when he was not in isolation. The staff knew I had never gone out, partied, and left Eli alone.

Henry and Gavin showed up around 9:00 a.m. This was Henry's time to be with Eli. I left the room before Gavin went in and told the nurses where I was going so I could be reached if ever I was needed for anything.

At around 10:20 a.m., I spoke with Dr. Benjamin regarding some of Eli's medications that had been discontinued and the Ativan was down to ½ mg dose IV. Dr. Benjamin said the ketones in Eli's urine were caused by the mesna and ifosfamide chemo that Eli was receiving through his Hickman. Eli wanted me in his room at this time, but since it was still Henry's time, I went away, my feet barely touching the floor as I fled in a

rush and cried. My tears streaked my face as I passed the halls. I went to the chapel at EU and uttered some prayers.

The burden inside my heart had not yet lifted. I was worried about Eli. It wasn't right for a mother to leave her son in that condition, but what was I to do if the law did not allow it? I broke into another set of tears.

At 11:10 a.m., I phoned Ardy and spoke with Noah. My son's voice was like a knife that poked my heart when he asked me again "if grandma was going to put him in jail." The gash in my heart deepened as I felt sorry for my son.

"No! No one is going to put you in jail, honey. Mama will take care of everything. Don't worry," I said with utmost fervor. "Ardy will take care of you there while Mama is away," I repeated to him, and I wished for the millionth time that I could hold Noah in my arms as I whispered these words of comfort to him. Instead, I had to rely on Ardy's love and leave the care of my son to her. I prayed that Noah would no longer be tormented by my mother and Henry.

At noon, I came back to Eli's room. Evidently there were problems while I was gone. Henry and Gavin were yelling loudly. Then they used Eli's phone and talked loud enough to bother my son. Henry also demanded to see each nurse to know what I did or did not do. He just caused the nurses grief and he was harassing them so Rita called a social worker to straighten things out. She also called my lawyer Mr. Troy, and then she said I should call my attorney back in the morning. I now wanted a restraining order on Henry to keep him from harassing me mentally and emotionally.

Eli's chemo started at 2:00 p.m. and this time, Eli also had his TPN started; the TPN would now run 24 hours a day.

Henry showed up at 4:30 p.m.—half an hour late for his time with Eli. Eli was sleeping when I left. Due to the earlier incidents—Eli's plea for me to stay with him when I could not, and Noah's angelic voice asking me if Grandma would send him to jail—I knew I needed a breath of fresh air. I drove down Ward Parkway to Southwest Mall, then back to Ward Parkway, and then to McDonald's for a meal.

I arrived back to EU at 6:30 p.m. and went to 1F cafeteria to wait until 8:00 p.m. for my time with Eli. Henry and Gavin came down to 1F at 7:00 p.m. so I went back up to Eli's room as they were leaving. I posted an Easter card for Noah and wrote him a letter. It said:

04-08-1990

Noah, Mama thought she would write you a letter. Ardy told me that you liked the wrestling cards that I gave you. I'm sending you more. Eli is getting medicine right now to help him get better. He's sleeping right now. As soon as I can, I will come to see you, honey. Maybe in a week or so. I don't know when for sure. Be a good boy and help Ardy and Max. Always remember that I love you dearly.

Love ya lots, babe.

Love,
Mama

It was a difficult day for me, with everything that had transpired. I wanted to be in two places at once. If I could split my body, the right side would stay with Eli, and the other would go running down to Durango to be with Noah. Both my boys needed me now, but there was only so much I could do. I raised my hardships to God, and prayed Noah would understand that I was doing the best I could at the moment. For Christ's sake, my son was only six—but I prayed that his great love for his brother Eli would make him understand that Mama had to stay where she was needed the most.

At 7:30 p.m., I decided to call Matt. As soon as he said hello, I started crying. I felt so helpless. A lot of things were running inside my head. Eli's condition, Noah's emotional state, this whole big mess; I was having trouble trying to keep up with everything. And this time, I had to try to fight money—my mother. I knew she would try to use her money to make things harder for me.

At around 8:00 p.m., the chemo triggered in Eli an episode of tachycardia for a while, but the immediate attendance of the medical staff, coupled with prayers, made him well again.

April 9, 1990 – Monday

I was up early as usual this morning to take care of Eli's needs. Eli started his day vomiting and dry heaving, which made me curse yet again the effects of chemo to my darling boy. I was only able to give him Tagamet for his stomach in the hopes it would help him feel better.

At 8:00 a.m., I took Eli for his radiation treatment. His white blood cell count was dropping, and I was afraid that it would go so low he would be placed into isolation again. I prayed his immune system wouldn't be compromised.

Eli's red blood cell count was 7.4 so he would receive a blood transfusion again.

At 10:30 a.m., Henry finally showed up and I left Eli with him.

At 11:00 a.m., I spoke with the social worker, Lucy Stone, about going to Durango, and at 11:45 a.m. Lucy Stone made Henry sign papers stating that he would stay with Eli overnight. Eli went down to radiation oncology so that he could be platted for the second field that would require radiation. Afterward, Eli had his radiation treatment and a CT scan of his head.

On my way to the cafeteria I saw Lucy Stone. She told me to leave for Durango now or I would never get away from Henry, and so I left.

I needed to see my lawyer and most especially Noah. At 5:00 p.m. I called EU and Eli's nurse told me that he was in his room, sleeping.

At 5:30 p.m., I picked up Noah and treated him to a fine meal of chicken for supper. It was my special moment with Noah, and I sat in front of him, hanging on to his every word, as he talked about school. Talking to him over the phone was certainly different as compared to having him with me. I memorized the soft contour of his lips as he smiled, and I paid close attention to how his face pinched when he talked about his fears of Grandma and jail.

At 7:40 p.m., I called EU and I learned from Eli's nurse that he was still sleeping. She said that Henry was in the room with my son and that there was no word yet on the CT scan of Eli's head.

At 9:10 p.m., I called EU and again I was informed that Eli was still sleeping. I told his nurse Emily how I did Eli's treatments.

As I was putting Noah to bed, the bed broke and though I tried to fix it, the bed just wasn't stable enough. I took four padded blankets, folded them up and placed them on top of a sleeping bag and the small mattress, and then told my son he could sleep on the sofa or this makeshift bed for the night. He could choose. My son chose the makeshift bed I made for him. Noah had his ninja turtle toys beside him, and he played like he was camping out. I beamed seeing my son happily playing with his toys.

After that, I cleaned and dusted our apartment; and then Gavin showed his face at the door around 9:30 p.m. asking about Noah. I told him to leave, that my son was asleep, so he left.

At 11:00 p.m., I called EU back and Eli's nurse told me Eli was okay, sleeping, and there were no results yet on the CT scan. Henry was still in the room with Eli.

Tonight, although I missed hearing Eli's voice over the phone, I felt happy to be sleeping beside my other angel, Noah. I watched as my boy closed his eyes and fell into a comfortable sleep. I kissed him on the forehead before I retired to bed, too.

April 10, 1990 – Tuesday

At 5:15 a.m., I called EU to check on Eli. Penny was his nurse during the night and she told me that Eli had slept all night. The Ativan ½ mg IV worked for Eli beautifully during chemo as it kept him asleep. Penny said further that there were no problems, and that Henry was still there and that he, too, was sound asleep. I must change my pillow case and blanket when I get back to EU, that's for sure.

I stood up and went to the kitchen to prepare breakfast for Noah. I worried about both my babies so much. I wished that I could have them both with me all the time so that I could minister to their needs. Sadly though, it was impossible at this time.

Around 6:00 a.m., my mother and my younger sister Ella barged in, almost tearing their way through the front door. My mother said they had been parked at the Dairy Queen a block or so away. A cop then showed up at the door. Ella made the comment that her children, Ava and Emily, were in the van crying – she said this to my mother. Mother accused me of having Matt over the whole night and my mother said that she was in the parking lot and never saw Matt leave from my apartment.

My eyes widened in disbelief at the lie that she was telling. Matt had not been in my apartment last night, and certainly, my door is not visible from the Dairy Queen parking lot. My mother was again weaving another set of lies so she could thrive on drama. I hated to be used this way.

Then my mother barged right into Noah's room and woke him up. My son cried upon seeing his grandma and that was when the police officer made my mother leave the apartment.

After calming Noah down, I decided to take him out for breakfast instead of cooking for him. The morning had started so badly for my son, and I wanted to treat him to a good breakfast so I could take his mind off the horrible drama his grandma brought into the apartment.

Noah chose bacon, hash browns, toast, and chocolate milk.

I was at the sheriff's office by 7:15 a.m. and filled out a complaint on my mother for what she did. Noah said he wanted to write out a complaint also, but he was scared my mother would put him in jail and so the officer, Officer Gordon, told my son that no child could be put in jail and that my mother was just lying to him about it.

My son looked comforted and now that he was reassured he wouldn't be sent to jail, he narrated in his own words my mother's antics. The officer wrote out my son's complaint against his grandmother.

At 8:10 a.m., I took Noah to the grade school and spoke with his teacher about what happened early this morning so that they could attend to my son's needs should he become tearful. My heart ached knowing that I would have to leave Noah again.

Then I went to the post office and after that, to Ardy's place.

At 8:45, I called EU and Eli's nurse said that he was doing okay. I was proud to hear that Eli was currently doing his own mouth care and suctioning.

I was in my lawyer's office at 9:15 a.m., giving him copies of many papers. I also informed Atty. Troy of what happened early this morning.

Then I went to the bank and gave them a couple of Eli's medical bills. My son had funds from donation, and it was the bank that would directly settle the medical bills.

Upon leaving the bank, I met my friend Lucy outside. Lucy told me that her co-worker Betty got the information from my youngest sister Lily that I was on drugs. What a gossip my youngest sister was for saying that I was using drugs down at Prospector's Bar.

Lucy reassured me that both she and Betty didn't believe the lie.

My next stop was the SRS and I told them what my mother did early this morning, too. To my astonishment, SRS told me that Mother had phoned in already and that they were informed I was on drugs this morning. SRS told me that they knew it was all a lie. I was still shaking from anger. How dare she?

I only had two days in Durango to spend with Noah and to meet with my lawyer, and my mother decided to ruin this time for me by spreading lies so she could take Noah from me.

Mother would make me upset and then record our conversation when I was already upset. She was just horrible. Maybe horrible was too mild of a word to describe Mother!

I pushed all thoughts of my mother aside and called EU. Rita told me that Eli was playing and that he would have two radiation treatments today as well as his chemo. Aside from these, Eli would have a visit to the eye clinic, too.

I called Anna and we went to eat lunch today at Prospector's—not on the bar side. At 2:00 p.m., I headed back to Denver and EU. I arrived at 4:50 p.m. and went straight to 5D to immediately see how Eli was doing. Upon learning that my son was fine, I decided to heed my lawyer and the SRS to undergo a drug screening due to my mother's and youngest sister's accusations.

I went to the nurse's desk and told them I wanted my urine screened for drugs and alcohol. One of the nurses on 5D obtained a urine sample from me. All through this process, the nurse was with me so that there would be no question as to the validity of the sample I gave.

After that, I mailed letters to Noah and to Mr. Troy. Then. I went to 1F cafeteria to grab a bite and stayed there for a while since it was not yet 8:00 p.m.

Henry caught me in 1F at 7:30 p.m. and told me, and to everyone present in the room, that all I wanted to do was "breed." Henry seemed to want everyone to think that I was a whore and a druggie, and that my life was worthless. Though embarrassed, I was somehow getting used to all his oral lashings.

I walked away with my head held high. It didn't matter what he said anymore.

I went to Eli's room instead, and I was happy to find him awake. We talked for a while, and then Eli yawned and I had to put him to sleep.

I phoned Anna and told her about Henry's actions to which Anna simply advised me to be strong. An hour later, I spoke with Matt and told him about the incident, too.

Matt said, "Everything will work out and everyone here is pulling for Eli and you." It was a simple statement and yet, it managed to bring me calmness and hope.

At 10:00 p.m., I was glad to receive a phone call from Ardy. She simply wanted to know how Eli was doing. Her concern brought a weak smile upon my lips. God bless her kind soul.

April 11, 1990 – Wednesday

I was up at 5:30 a.m. this morning and gave sweet Eli his usual morning cares. I couldn't believe how being away from him for even a short time made me miss him so much. I just wished that I could show my love to my son in ways other than taking him to radiation, or cleaning after his vomit. What I would give to show him my affection by teaching him how to play basketball, or taking him to the movies, or chasing him in the park. But as I tended to Eli's needs, I realized that the best time a mother could show love for her son, was when loving him took so much of her that it hurt to love anymore. Yet, she didn't give up on that love, and instead drew more from her heart to shower and cloak her son with the affection blooming inside her very core.

I brushed a tear that almost streaked down my cheek. Then I took Eli down for radiation and back to his room. Eli said he was happy I was back with him. With my son's words, all weariness left me, and I felt rejuvenated like an athlete after a full night's rest.

Henry came in at 9:00 a.m. "wanting to do business" so I spoke with the social worker, Lucy Stone. She informed me that my mother had called all over the state of Colorado yesterday to relate how I was on drugs and not a fit mother. I shook my head in disbelief. Would Mother never stop? She'd been doing this because she wanted to take Noah from Ardy. If she had proven to be a good mother to me, or a good grandparent to my sons, maybe I would have considered leaving Noah's care to her. But sadly, she was neither.

Later, I took Eli to the EU gift shop to purchase a couple of things with his birthday money he had received in some cards. Eli was delighted to shop and his face was glowing as he looked at me as though he was so happy to have me back.

I went up to the 5D nurse's desk and checked on my urine screening, but there was no result yet. I was informed that the tests were currently being run.

Henry was in with Eli so I had to wait somewhere else. When noon came, I went to Eli's room. Then, I took him down to radiation so that the medical staff could check on the boost volume on Eli's new platted field. The blocking was wrong and so they did not radiate. They were to re-do the blocking tomorrow morning and then radiate.

I took Eli back to his room and at 1:00 p.m. The treatments to his radiation-burned skin areas were completed. This brought much pain to Eli so Rita called the hospital pharmacy for morphine suppositories.

Casey Hunter, a friend from Durango, was working in the pharmacy and she was also attending pharmacology school at EU. We spoke briefly as Eli received his morphine. It was always nice to talk to her as I didn't feel so alone in the city.

At around 1:45 p.m., Rita took Eli to an Easter egg hunt while I went down to Family Practice. While there, the medical staff drew two tubes of blood serum. They did not do a urine sample. The one urine test done with the nurse present would back up the blood tests.

I was back in Eli's room by 3:00 p.m. and we played. Henry arrived at 4:10 p.m. for his time with Eli so I went down to 1F and updated my journals. That man knew I wrote in journals and he never acted like he was interested to see what I've written, but since I did not trust him, I took the journals with me anywhere I went.

I was at the nurse's desk by 5:30 p.m. for an update on Eli and I was relieved that he was doing okay.

After dinner I sent off another letter to Noah. I would call him later so as not to miss my daily habit—a habit which I love doing—because Noah missed me so badly. I knew this because I missed him just as badly.

At 8:00 p.m., I was back in Eli's room for my allotted time with him. We talked for a while, and then I phoned Ardy.

Ardy told me that Henry called to say he would pick up Noah tomorrow afternoon to which Ardy responded prudently, telling Henry that it wouldn't happen because tomorrow was only Thursday.

Ardy read to me a letter that Atty. Troy had sent to her; and then she checked with SRS and the Health Department, and she was assured that Henry would not be able to take Noah from her on Thursday. I silently applauded Ardy for her courage. She proved to me yet again that she was taking care of my boy just fine.

I asked to speak with Noah and as soon as he was on the receiver, he told me he was scared of Grandma whenever he was at Grandmas. I calmed Noah down while tears streaked my cheeks. I understood my son's fears for I was once there, too. I experienced my mother's abusiveness, and it was not a memory worth keeping. I praised God in all his glory, but at the time, I couldn't help but wonder why He allowed my mother to have my son from time to time.

My conversation with my son ended with my promise to him that Mama would take care of everything and that I loved him very, very much.

Much later in the evening, as Eli was sleeping, I phoned Anna and updated her about today's events. It was such a comfort to have her in my life. After our talk, I went to sleep.

April 12, 1990 – Thursday

Eli woke me up at 1:00 a.m. this morning, wanting me in bed with him so I climbed into the bed and gave my son comfort. I hugged him tightly and told him I loved him dearly.

At 4:30 a.m., I changed Eli's bedding and cleansed my son. I could not go back to sleep so I remained awake until dawn. Eli vomited and dry heaved a lot, and each time his body curled in helpless fashion, my insides tore. I had to see the horrid effects of the treatment that was supposed to save my son's life.

5D did not have any Reglan on the unit so the nurse gave Eli some Thorazine. When the Reglan arrived, she gave him that as well.

At 7:00 a.m., I gave Eli his Tagamet. As usual, Eli and I strode to radiation oncology at 7:30 a.m., where Eli's blocking was re-done, and he received his first radiation treatment on his new field.

Henry showed up at 9:00 a.m.; and he took to the phone without even a hello or good morning to Eli.

I sighed knowing that I had to leave Eli's room again. The schedule was just driving me insane. To make myself useful though, I decided to check on my old car as it had been using a lot of oil. After checking the oil, I checked the water in the radiator, too. The oil was one quart low and so I added a full quart.

After that, I went to Medical Records in the hospital and signed releases for my lawyer. The administrative staff told me that they would call Mr. Troy first before sending the medical records.

At around 10:00 a.m., Henry came down to 1F looking for me, and as soon as he did, he started yelling. I couldn't take any more of his ranting so I left and went over to the Boone Entrance of the hospital and fell asleep in a chair in the lobby after mailing out four letters. I was exhausted after being up most of the night with Eli, but I would gladly do it again for my son in a heartbeat.

When I woke up, I grabbed a bite and then walked into Eli's room at noon. Dr. Benjamin stopped by and said that Eli's hemoglobin was 6.6. It meant that another blood transfusion was required and the plan to infuse 180 ml. of packed red cells would be done.

The CT scan of Eli's head finally came and it showed the main tumor mass unchanged. I was heartbroken. The main mass was not bigger, but it was not better either. We would know more after radiation was completed.

Later, Dr. Benjamin came back and said that the radiation would have an additive effect. Although the radiation, of course, would not stay in his head and neck, the effect would be cumulative. In essence, we wouldn't know the real effect on my son until all the radiation was completed.

On the positive side, the radiation had done a lot of good; it stopped the cancer cells from dividing, which, in turn caused them to die, which, in turn diminished them.

Eli received 180 ml. of packed red cells at 4:00 p.m. and the remainder would be transfused tomorrow. He also received ½ mg. Ativan IV before the transfusion, and every six hours after that. TPN was running in. Eli had two radiation treatments today and he had twelve radiation treatments left to complete. It was still a lot of vis-its, but at least Eli had a lot of fun placing stickers on the calendar I made out of construction paper. This calendar tracked the days where Eli had radiation, and a sticker would mark each day that he went to treatment successfully. It was one of my efforts to make the stay at EU bearable for my little Eli.

Eli was assisted into the bathroom and upon coming back out, he sat down on his bed. All of a sudden blood was backing up in his tubing and I immediately clamped his Hickman. Then, I pushed his intercom button and yelled that I needed a nurse in the room now.

Most of the blood was flushed back into Eli, and his tubing was also changed. After the arrival of his cross matched packed red cells, Eli received a transfusion right away. Then, he started to choke and I had to suction him several times, only God knows how many times. My senses were alert so I could be of assistance to my son immediately. I feared that he would have died if I had not been there.

Eli's doctor came in to assess him.

At 5:30 p.m., Henry called to say he lost track of the time. He arrived at 5:45 p.m., and I had to leave.

I grabbed a bite and started writing in my journals. I even called the Durango Reporter as many people in Durango wanted to know about how Eli was doing.

At 8:00 p.m., I walked into Eli's room. He was still vomiting with blood in his emeses. I was able to advocate for Eli in speaking with a resident and obtaining orders for Eli's previous medications. The cumulative effect of chemo lasted for five more days so all in all, there was a total of ten days.

Eli said that he spoke with Grandma on the phone while his father was in the room. He told me she asked him many questions, and that she told him she was taping his answers on cassette. Eli said grandma told him about his pony and his father's new trailer. Eli also said she asked him if he "wanted to live at Bow Mar." He said he told her NO! Damn that wicked witch of a woman! I would have to be stronger for Eli all the more now — the strongest I could ever be for him.

At 8:20 p.m., I called Ardy and filled her in on Eli's condition. Then I related the hardest thing I ever had to tell Ardy, that tonight I wouldn't be able to speak to Noah because Eli was so very sick. Instead, I asked her to give him my love, tell him I called and that I love him very, very much.

Between 8:00 p.m. and 11:30 p.m., I had to change Eli's beddings twice. I was too tired already and found myself asleep soon enough.

April 13, 1990 – Friday the 13th

I awoke at 5:30 a.m. but felt so very tired whereas Eli slept through the entire night. The Thorazine/Ativan helped with his emesis and helped him get some sleep. Eli has twenty-three radiation sessions left after this morning's session.

I went down to breakfast at 8:45 a.m. and chatted with Dee Hardy, RN, and Social Services at the hospital. I told them of all the recent happenings and left nothing out. Then I thought maybe I should ask for an evaluation to determine my sanity (so to speak.) I prayed they would have me tested for my children's sake. Henry had left to go to Bow Mar, and before I went to breakfast, I completed Eli's cares and Hickman dressing.

After mailing off another letter to Noah, Eli and I played. Then we went to the school room on the unit and he saw the egg named after him, Eli. The egg was getting ready to hatch and Eli thought this was so cool! I had gone down to 1F for lunch and Eli's nurse, Emily, came down and fetched me because Eli was crying hard. Eli said he was scared of what Grandma had said to him and asked of him on the phone just now, and that Eli knew I was here in the hospital eating (I would not eat in front of him), but he was scared of the things she told him on the phone after I had gone for some lunch. After comforting Eli, I phoned Ardy, spoke with Noah and then spoke with my lawyer, Mr. Troy. I hated my mother for tormenting my children. That was the kind of mother I grew up with. I took Eli to the eye clinic for another suture evaluation and then Gavin showed up. I made Gavin leave. Eli had his second radiation treatment and back in his room pentobarbital was given to Eli.

At 3:30 p.m. I was finally able to sign the surgery form for Eli's right eye stitch. I also signed a release form for a more permanent surgery on his right eye next Tuesday, which would be administered under an oral anesthesia with medicine for preventing a bronchospasm. The surgery on Tuesday might cause blindness in Eli's right eye eventually, but the eye must be protected, and there was no other way to make this so. It struck me as odd as I realized for the first time that Henry had NEVER signed any medical papers or any release on Eli. That was fine with me. I had better control of Eli's care as I knew all that was going on with Eli, and his father did not—nor did he care or ask.

Dr. Benjamin enlightened me somewhat this afternoon. He said that although the CT scan of Eli's head and neck showed the tumor was still the same size, it didn't show how much of it was dead. Only a Magnetic Resonance Imaging (MRI) could do that. Eli was still pretty out of it with the pentobarbital, and by 5:00 p.m., his eye surgery was over and he was doing well.

At 7:30 p.m., Henry phoned Eli's room and said he "did not have Noah," but he asked about Eli so I told him all I could before he cut me off.

Eli went to bed at 8:30 p.m., too tired to speak with Ardy or Noah. Ardy told me the biggest lie that Mother had fabricated, and Henry was the one who delivered this gossip to Ardy. According to him, my mother had my apartment staked out all night, that Matt arrived at 1:00 a.m., that Matt left at 6:00 a.m. squealing his tires, that mother knocked lightly on my door, that I opened the door with no clothes on, that Noah was huddled down in a corner with only a blanket and in a fetal position, that I was speaking softly...Mother also supposedly said that she did not want my kids—she was only concerned. Then Henry lied further by telling Ardy that as soon as my allotted time frames with Eli were over, I'd walk out the door of EU, and a boyfriend would be waiting for me. This was all bull shit! This was so NOT true! I hated my mother and I hated Henry.

At 11:00 p.m., Eli's doctor called me to see how my son was doing. I was still awake at midnight pondering everything. I called Anna and we talked.

At 2:00 a.m., Matt called and there was so much to say to him. He was doing a family type of outing for his one-and-a-half-year-old daughter Reba, an Easter Eve supper at Prospector's. That should give my mother something to talk about. Among other things, Matt told me that my mother had called Matt's ex-in-laws, Lucy and Bobby, and asked many questions about Matt. He had found out from their daughter.

April 14, 1990 – Saturday

I was up and going by 6:00 a.m. and had actually slept in a half hour later than usual. I found Eli crying when I came back from breakfast. This just tore me up. Emily had been there and started talking with Eli. This was the second day that he had been scared, thanks to his grandma. I finally got it out of him that he was afraid Grandma would make him move and live at Bow Mar. This was part of what had frightened him yesterday and caused him to be so scared, since he was forced to listen to his grandma on the phone late Thursday night, and she recorded the conversation like usual. I did all of Eli's morning care and then took him to the eye clinic for the dressing on his right eye to be changed. Then, we went back to his room.

At 9:45 a.m., my doctor, Dr. Alex Hughes from Family Practice, was on the floor and informed me that only caffeine and nicotine showed up in my drug screening; I knew this was what would show up anyway. Regardless, this would make my mother so angry! No, Mother, I was not on drugs or anything and my blood and urine proved it!

Gavin showed up at 10:15 a.m. and Dr. Benjamin came into Eli's room not long afterwards. Eli's ANC was now 600 and he had a temperature of 102 degrees. Dr. Benjamin explained to Gavin about hand washing and wearing a mask and isolation gowns around Eli. I could tell that Gavin totally ignored Eli's doctor. Eli would most likely be on five days of antibiotics yet again, and isolation would be initiated. Eli had a fairly good time the rest of the morning playing with me.

Around 2:00 p.m., I took Eli down to radiology for a chest X-ray of his lungs in order to check and see if he had pneumonia. Blood cultures were also drawn. It was nice outside and so I placed a mask on Eli. Then, we went outside so he could ride his red Big Wheels. Eli knew he had to wear a mask so he would not breathe in any germs from anyone else walking around the hospital, and he was okay about that.

Around 5:00 p.m. a medical student came in to draw blood. He hurt Eli badly and he totally just "fished" for a vein. Blood cultures were drawn from Eli's Hickman and they had to be drawn peripherally as well to make sure Eli's Hickman was not infected. Eli needed really good people to get his blood since his veins were so poor. I finally told the medical student, "Take the needle out now." I had to repeat that several times and threaten to take the damn needle out myself before he finally took it out. Then, I asked Eli's nurse for the resident in charge, Dr. Mark, to come to Eli's room. I informed Dr. Mark that there would be no more medical students practicing on Eli for blood, as his veins were too small and hard to obtain blood from. Dr. Mark then drew the blood himself. He used a twenty-five-gauge butterfly needle instead of the twenty-three gauge needle the medical student was using. Dr. Mark said my request was valid because Eli's veins were poor due to the chemo, radiation, and anemia, brought on by his treatment protocol. I already knew that, of course, and thought that the medical students could just practice hitting a vein on each other. That was what we did in nursing school!

At 7:00 p.m., Dr. Mark told me that halfway down one of Eli's lungs was a questionable spot. He said it could be pneumonia and that we would know more tomorrow. Eli was wide awake at 8:00 p.m. so I placed a mask on him as he wanted to leave his room. Eli also asked me fill up his 60 ml. syringe, minus a needle, so he could go and shoot staff in the hall. Eli had a water fight with the staff for almost an hour off and on, and he had a grand time as the nursing staff got involved and played with him.

Before 9:00 p.m., I could see Eli was getting tired, so I helped him change and get ready for bed. Eli started vomiting and having dry heaves around 10:00 p.m. and he was given Ativan. At 2:00 a.m., Eli did a repeat act and he received more Ativan in small doses.

When the clock struck 3:00 a.m., I found Eli pulling on his Hickman, and trying to get out of bed. The nurses thought the Ativan in small amounts would be okay, but the doses were given too close to each other, and they had adverse side effects on him. Eli reacted with increased excitability. He was awake and he was agitated. The opposite effect expected from the Ativan.

April 15, 1990 – Sunday

Today marked day forty-three that Eli and I spent at EU. I was up as usual by 6:00 a.m. By 7:00 a.m., the resident came in to see Eli after his morning labs were run. Eli's red blood cell count was 6.7 so that meant more packed red blood cell transfusions. To my chagrin, Eli's ANC hit an all-time low at 270, and this would render him room bound for now.

At 10:45 a.m., I phoned Ardy and spoke with her and Noah. Ardy said Henry came by with Easter candy for Noah and that they talked for about two hours. Ardy overheard Noah ask his father if Grandma was going to put him in jail. To my relief, Henry actually told Noah that Grandma was not going to do that. Apparently, Henry also took my advice and called Stella about Noah's fears.

Henry told Ardy that he had received a Workers' Compensation Settlement last fall for $6,000. That money must be all gone by now; most likely spent on liquor. Then, Henry started telling Ardy that at night, I left EU and went to Durango with my boyfriend, and then I would come back to EU, and that this happened many times already. What a load of crap. Should the need arise, the nursing staff documents would prove that I spend all my nights with Eli except for those times I went to Durango to visit Noah, my lawyer, and the SRS. The lies Henry spreads were interesting. He told them frequently enough that I wondered if he actually believed with conviction the erroneous stories he fabricated with my mother.

By 1:00 p.m., I flushed and heparin locked the red port of his Hickman. By this time, too, Eli was ready for a blood transfusion. The highest his HGB ever got from his last transfusion was 7.8 so his doctor said the blood must have been nearing its expiration date. By 2:00 p.m. Eli was receiving Rh Negative Type O blood.

Around 4:30 p.m., Henry arrived from out of the blue and I had to leave then. I just took off walking and exploring the hospital, but consciously evading all Intensive Care Units, the Burn Unit, and the unit for Tuberculosis (not that I would go to these units). After spending more than a month at EU, I had grown familiar with the hospital's layout so this time, I decided to look at all the medical students who graduated from EU and walk their hall of fame which was full of photos. I am still amazed at the hospital's size.

At 7:50 p.m., Henry found me at the nurse's station on 5D asking Eli's nurse how he was doing. He had a snarl on his face.

"You will pay for not allowing me to have Noah over the Easter weekend."

I looked at him, aghast. By this time too, I had become familiar with Henry's unwanted presence. He lurked around and when he felt like it, he would just burst out of nowhere to threaten me, or to say mean things. Still, there were moments that he caught me off-guard.

"I could have just taken Noah, you know. But I want my lawyer to see that I didn't," he added.

The nurses were gathered all around us, stiff. Whatever they were doing seemed to have been forgotten due to Henry's sudden attack on me.

"You can only have Noah for a twenty-four-hour period on a Friday or a Saturday as per the judge. You can just take it up with the judge if you want your time with him reconsidered." I was composed when I said these words, but of course it didn't mean I was strong. It only meant that I would fight for my child.

Henry knew he couldn't do anything aside from jab me with his constant attacks. With a sour face, he turned around and left me.

Eli's nurse applauded me for telling him that. She knew about the judge's order because a copy of it was on Eli's chart.

At around 8:00 p.m., I phoned Ardy. Again, I spoke with Noah and told him I loved him very much and that I would be back to see him as soon as I could.

By 9:00 p.m., I spoke with Matt. He always seemed to know the right things to say. He was sensitive enough to pick out the words that would offer me comfort, even with the distance that separated us. After our conversation, I fell asleep next to Eli in the chair bed.

April 16, 1990 – Monday

Eli woke up at 2:00 a.m. and he wanted his mama to hold him. I was still tired and sleepy, but my son's call was like a plea. So, with all my love, I did just that. I held Eli in the chair bed and he finally fell asleep. The next time he opened his eyes was at 5:30 a.m. I smiled at my little boy.

Eli received his usual morning cares from me. I changed his Hickman dressing, his eye dressing, and heparin locked his white port so that the rest of the packed red blood cells could be transfused into Eli.

Henry showed up about 10:00 a.m. so I had to leave. I spent time walking the halls and reading down in 1F. Noon found me at Eli's door and Dr. Benjamin showed up. He said Eli had an infiltrate of pneumonia, and that we would treat it with broad spectrum antibiotics.

I played with Eli, held him, and when he fell asleep, I laid him gently in his bed. Later, I phoned Ardy and spoke with Noah. I was happy to hear Noah's voice. He was in high spirits this morning and he had voiced no concerns this time. I was able to joke with him and he retaliated with quite a funny joke, too.

At around 4:20 p.m., Henry arrived. I went for a walk again, and this time I decided to stop in the chapel and offer prayers for both my boys.

Even with everything that was going on here and at home, I still believed that the Lord worked in ways we did not understand. The Lord lent you a child just like he lent you your life. This was how Eli must be getting his inner strength even at age five.

At 6:15 p.m., Henry sought me in 1F and told me he had to leave because he had business to take care of. After going back up to 5D, Eli, Rita and I had a water gun fight. All of us were laughing so hard. Eli was very happy and I had to blink back tears several times upon realizing that Eli's happiness was like the sun's ray during a storm—it very seldom appeared.

I sent Noah another letter:

Hello, Noah!

How are you? Eli wants to know if you are okay and he also wants to know how school is. Eli wants you to have these stickers. He said, "Brother will like them." We both love you very much, Noah, and we both miss you very much. Eli still has a temperature and has started a new medicine. We also want to know how your field trip to the zoo went. Was your lunch okay? Did you feed a lot of the animals? If we had not been here, we would have gone with you.

Take care, Noah—we love you lots!!!
Mom & Eli

At 7:45 p.m., something had gone awfully wrong. Eli's little body was red due to hives and the medication he took, but overall, his temperature was okay. I wondered what Eli was allergic to this time? Rita gave him IV Benadryl and the rash started to vanish.

By 9:00 p.m., Eli was back in bed, and I read one of the books Dr. Cameron and Lucy Owens had sent to me. I silently thanked Lucy, a classy lady, for the book that now kept me company; I knew it was actually her who took the time to send me this book.

I talked with Anna before I finally fell asleep.

April 17, 1990 – Tuesday

I woke up at 4:30 as Nanci, Eli's nurse, made such a racket in his room. I had to remind her about saving all medication labels for me. I always wanted to see what Eli received while I was sleeping. I wanted the best care for Eli.

Eli was still sleeping at 7:00 a.m. so I went down for breakfast after telling his nurse where I was going. I was back by 8:00 a.m. and did all of Eli's cares, his oral care, and his Hickman dressing change. Eli had been having daily Hickman dressing changes due to the fact that he was allergic to the adhesive on the Tegaderm clear plastic dressings. This allergy required a sterile change using sterile 4 x 4 gauze; and to do away with the adhesive, I fashioned an elasticized tank top shirt of sorts for Eli out of elastic netting to hold his Hickman dressing in place. It was better for Eli's skin this way and the nurses liked the way this was being done.

Henry arrived around 9:45 a.m. and he asked me to pick up an EU employment application for him. This man was nuts and maybe I was, too, because I did pick up an employment application form. I then left and went down to Volunteer Services. I spoke with the director, Dina Clark. Dina told me that if ever I wanted to talk or wanted a place to go for a couple of hours or even for overnight, that her home was open to me. She was a nice, kind lady and we talked for a good forty-five minutes. At noon I went back to Eli's room and gave Henry his employment application.

Eli wanted to have another water fight so I placed a mask on him and he let loose on the nurses and doctors. Everyone laughed.

Dr. Benjamin came in about 2:30 p.m. and told me that Eli's ANC was 240, his HGB was 10—-and a shock that was, as it had been a long time since it reached 10—-and that Eli's platelet count was 35 – no wonder Eli had been bruising so easily.

At 3:15 p.m. I went down to the radiation oncology department to speak with Dr. Goodman. She said to use Aquaphor on Eli's radiation burns on his skin, three times a day.

Henry came at 4:15 p.m. for his time with Eli. I informed Henry that I was leaving for Durango this evening and I had a social worker, Lucy Stone, with me when I informed him. At 5:45 p.m. I phoned Ardy and spoke with Noah. I told them both that I was having car trouble on the turnpike near Lawrence and would get going again as soon as I could. I finally got to Durango about 10:00 p.m. and called Ardy to check on Noah. He was sound asleep. I decided to go and see Anna, but my car wouldn't start. I thought the starter had gone out and my car had to be towed to a shop. Now what would I do?

April 18, 1990 - Wednesday

I woke up at 9:00 a.m. and called EU and I was on hold for at least fifteen minutes after which they hung up. I think the unit was just really busy. At 10:00 a.m. I called EU again and spoke with Eli's nurse, Jackie, who told me that Eli was okay but that he had a temperature and they were going to do blood cultures and get a chest x-ray. That was standard procedure. Then, I called my old boss, Bob, at Bobby's Auto and he said he had a starter for my car. I called Ardy and told her of my car trouble and that Bob had a starter for me. Then, I phoned SRS and spoke with Nora about how things were with Eli and my car troubles. I walked down to the office of my lawyer, Mr. Troy, and we discussed how Eli was and what Henry had been up to. Then, I walked over to Bobby's Auto and spoke with my old boss, Bob, after which I walked to Prospector's and met up with Anna for lunch.

Using Anna's car, I ran all over town trying to get my car ready for the road. My car required one starter, one battery cable end, one battery cable (positive), brake fluid, power steering fluid, a quart of transmission fluid, one PVC valve, one fuel filter and one alternator. After Brody, Matt's cousin, fixed my car, I went and picked up Noah from Ardy. From there we went to the grocery store and then we headed home. It felt so good to have Noah with me and I gave him lots of hugs and kisses to make up for the ones I had missed giving him in the past days.

I phoned EU around 5:00 p.m. and was told that Eli was sleeping and that he was to receive one unit of platelets. I called Eli's nurse back at around 7:00 p.m. and spoke with another nurse, Olive. She said she would have to call me back so I called into Eli's room and Henry answered the phone. He started ripping into me. All I wanted was to find out how Eli was and to inform Henry that I was bringing Noah back with me tomorrow to see Eli and that this was worked out between EU social worker, Lucy Stone, Dr. Benjamin, the SRS and Zoe Green in Durango. If I had told Henry before I left EU of my intentions all hell would have broken loose so I had to do it this way and the hospital agreed with me.

At 9:30 p.m. I called Olive back, and she said Eli's platelet count was 16 so he was receiving another unit of platelets. His WBC was 0.2, his HGB 3.64 (low), Segs were 30, Bands – she did not know, so I was not able to compute Eli's current ANC. Eli had a 102-degree temperature, so he was given an ice blanket to make him more comfortable. Eli could be better. Eli could be much better.

Matt stopped by my apartment for about an hour and we talked a lot. He talked to Noah as well, and Noah smiled for Matt more than once and I was glad about this. After an hour, Matt left for home. "Mommy Dearest," my mother, should like that Matt came over for an hour and spoke not only to me, but to Noah as well.

After a long day, I tucked Noah into his bunk bed and went to sleep, too.

April 19, 1990 – Thursday

I woke up at 5:00 a.m. as if I was at EU. Noah and I most definitely felt Eli's absence.

At 7:30 a.m. I phoned EU. The nurses were in a meeting and Nanci, Eli's night nurse, had already left. After breakfast I took Noah to school. He had half day school as a kindergartner. I spoke with his teacher, the school office, and Stella in order to give updates. Then I went to the SRS and spoke with Zoe Green about Noah not being in school tomorrow as I wanted to take him to see Eli in Denver. Zoe Green asked to see my apartment so I took her to my apartment and then back to the SRS office. My mother must have wanted my place checked out and I know Zoe Green saw fresh milk, healthy food, frozen foods in the freezer, all laundry washed, dried, and put away. There was no trash or dust to be found. My mother was not going to like what Zoe had to write in her report at all!

While Zoe Green was in my apartment looking around, I phoned 5D at EU to check on Eli. I spoke with Jackie and she told me Eli had received some Tylenol. He had blood cultures and urine cultures done, and Henry actually went with Eli for his chest x-ray. Come to find out, all he wanted was time to read Eli's medical chart and he told me about it. Of all the times I took Eli to see a doctor, have x-rays, CT scans, MRI's, or radiation treatments I never once read Eli's chart! I never felt the need to do so and the nurses always answered my questions. I gave Zoe Green some information for Nicole, another SRS employee, and Zoe Green agreed with me that I should take Noah out of school for one day so he could see his sick little brother. I went to the store for gas, soap, shampoo, film and a flip flash for my 110 camera.

By 10:30 a.m., I phoned the county attorney's office, Mr. Ethan Reynolds, and he was to call me back in forty-five minutes or so. I then went to Mr. Troy's office and updated him. I also updated Ardy on Eli, and then my lawyer called me back and said to hold off on slander for now against my mother after my double drug screen returned negative. Then, Mr. Reynolds called me back and said he was fully aware of what was going on as Mr. Troy had informed him of everything. I was to check back at 1:00 p.m. Then, Ethan Reynolds said to me, "I said you would need me as a county attorney for you and I was right to suggest you see Mr. Troy for your divorce." I had forgotten he had told me that when I filed for divorce.

I spoke with Anna and then picked up Noah, and after we ate lunch we left for EU at 2:00 p.m. Ardy called me to say that Henry had phoned and that he would leave Denver for Durango after I got back to Eli's room. The arrangement made prior was for Henry to go back to Durango after the boys got to see each other for two days. Henry knew he was set to have Friday night with Noah at the Ronald McDonald House so I think he was just spouting off.

We were in Eli's room at 6:00 p.m. and Eli was sound asleep. I called the Ronald McDonald House and they informed me that Henry had checked out early in the afternoon even though he knew I was bringing Noah to see Eli. Henry just pulled a very dirty trick on all three of us, Noah, Eli, and me. That bastard knew that the arrangements were made with social services at EU so Noah would have a place to stay, the Ronald McDonald House, as siblings could not stay the night on the hospital units. Henry did this on purpose – out of malice – damn him! Henry just abandoned Noah out of malice! He cared not one damn bit about either Eli or Noah.

My lawyer, Mr. Troy, and Zoe Green from SRS would find this behavior atrocious as would social services at EU! So here were Noah and I both wearing masks, in Eli's room, with Eli asleep; I explained and showed Noah that Eli did not have any hair and tried to make him understand the treatment was the cause and that Eli's golden blond hair would grow back. I told Noah to not be afraid of the bandage on Eli's eye as it was for protection, and that the redness on his neck from radiation burns did not hurt, even though I knew they did and Eli never complained.

Noah began playing quietly with some of Eli's toys, and I knew he had heard that his father abandoned him in Denver. Henry was such an asshole, but it would come back to bite him I knew. Now I must make arrangements for Noah to get back to Ardy's and I would. Sadly, the boys would not have two days together as planned. Damn that man! Eli was sleeping on his right side and he woke up around 6:30 p.m. and in his left eye he saw Noah sitting on the floor playing.

Immediately Eli yelled out, "Brother, Brother!"

Eli bounded out of bed and grabbed Noah in a big bear hug. I was deeply touched by this display of affection between my boys and knew right then that even after all the trouble we went through, Noah not having a place to stay for the night, it was all worth it. It was so awesome that I know I must have been smiling big time as I watched my boys play.

Dr. Benjamin walked in to see Eli and to tell me that he did have a small touch of pneumonia, but that it should clear up fast. Of course, visitors should still wear masks around Eli and the usual precautions like hand washing were still to be adhered to. I had explained this part to Noah before Eli woke up.

At 7:30 p.m., I left a message with Anna's husband Spencer and requested for Anna to call me back. There was no way I was splitting up the boys' reunion, and no rooms were available at the Ronald McDonald House, plus I did not want to stay the night there with Noah anyway as I wanted to be with Eli. The staff said that as per policy, Noah, could not stay the night. I was waiting for Anna to call me back.

Henry would always be an ass. He did not care to see if I actually made it back to Denver and EU, and he left Eli! In a sense, he also left Noah since Henry chose not to wait and see his son. I think Henry wanted to tell his lawyer that I denied him his Friday or Saturday twenty-four-hour visitation. But I am sure, by the time social services at EU and SRS in Durango presented letters to the court stating Henry had agreed to the arrangement, the judge would not look too kindly on this.

I spoke with Ardy at 8:15 p.m. and told her about Henry's latest stunt. Ardy informed me that after I had spoken with her earlier in the day, Henry called her to say that he would be bringing Noah back tonight, and that he would get in around 2:00 a.m., and drop Noah off at Ardy's at that time. I shook my head in disgust.

At 8:30 p.m. I signed the release for another spinal tap on Eli. We then went into a different room for the procedure and chemo was placed into Eli's spinal fluid area. I was forced to leave Noah alone in Eli's room, and so I told him to be very quiet and to keep the door closed and that we would be back as soon as possible.

Afterward, back in Eli's room, the boys played and talked up a storm while I phoned my lawyer and told him the scoop. Eli had grown tired and fallen asleep by 10:00 p.m. and Noah curled up next to me in the chair bed and fell asleep around 10:30 p.m.

Around 1:00 a.m. Anna called me back and said she would come and rescue Noah. I was keeping Noah really quiet so I would not get in trouble with the nursing staff. They knew I had no place to take Noah to, nor could I afford a hotel. I kept telling them people were coming to pick up Noah, and they gave up asking about what time they would get here. Eli's nurse knew I would not leave Eli, and she did not say much except that it was a really bad, rotten thing Henry had done to both boys.

Before the day came to an end, I was shedding tears for my boys.

April 20, 1990 – Friday

(*No School Day in Durango*) I was awake by 6:00 a.m. and slept about two hours the whole night with so many worries running through my head. Noah awoke and started to play with toys while Eli was asleep. I gave Noah grape juice and cereal from the kitchen on the nursing unit. I had to sneak in and get it since the food was meant only for the patients. They allowed parents to get things for their sick children, and they kept coffee in the unit's kitchen for the parents.

Eli woke up about 6:30 a.m. and saw Noah. Eli jumped out of bed, ran to his brother and hugged him. At 7:45 a.m. Anna, Matt, and Ginny (a friend) arrived at Eli's room. I think they made good time by not leaving the club until after 3:30 a.m., since Anna couldn't close the club until then. They had early morning traffic congestion problems. We all talked and visited; everyone wore a mask.

At 9:00 a.m. I flushed and heparin locked Eli's Hickman and Eli had a slight temperature, so I gave him a Tylenol suppository. Eli informed everyone that Grandma had talked to him over the phone again this morning while I was in the shower, and she asked him if he would like to move to Bow Mar. Eli also told the four of us that his daddy had told him yesterday that I was NOT coming back to care for him, and that I would be staying in Durango. That non-human of a man was so cruel! Who told children these kinds of things? I asked Eli in front of the four of us if he believed me when I had told him I was coming back, and Eli said yes. Eli told us he "just did not let his dad know that." At just turning five years old, Eli was more grown up than his father would ever be.

Around 10:30 a.m., Noah left with Anna, Matt, and Ginny to go back to Ardy's home. Noah asked me why his dad was not here to take him back like planned? I told him that Daddy forgot that Noah was going to Denver with me. What else could I say? I thanked the Lord for my boys and their time together, and for my friends who came to my son's rescue and took him back home. This did not bode well for Henry at all, yet I was not happy about that, as my boys would be subjected to more mind games that were mean and just not necessary! Yes, it made court and child custody better for me, but the cost to my boys was too much. I knew one thing for sure—my boys only trusted me.

Ardy phoned around 11:30 a.m. and I told her to expect Noah this afternoon. Then, I updated her about how Eli was doing. Ardy told me that Henry called her around 11:00 p.m. last night and woke her up. Henry told Ardy that Noah was spending the whole weekend in Denver, and that I was preventing Henry from his allotted Friday or Saturday twenty-four-hour visit. Obviously, that would not fly since Noah would be back this afternoon. But Henry did not know that.

In talking with Anna and Matt in the evening, we had come to the conclusion that Henry would manipulate the facts. That was why they decided to leave for Denver very early this morning, so that Noah would be back in time for his visitation. Henry's plan was not working and he messed up the perfect opportunity for a good "family" thing this week-end. Then, I fell asleep cuddling Eli in my chair bed as he was drifting off to sleep, too.

I woke up at 1:30 p.m. and Eli was still sleeping next to me. Infectious Disease doctors came in to see Eli around 2:00 p.m. They saw no reason why Eli had a temperature. Eli's WBC's were zero, his ANC zero, and HGB of 3.1 – not good at all! More packed red blood cells were coming and everyone wore masks and did great hand washing today to avoid contaminating Eli. Platelets were 47,000.

At almost 4:00 p.m. I phoned Ardy and she told me that Noah, poor baby, had arrived at her house at 3:30 p.m. Thank the Lord for my friends and support system. I told Ardy to let Henry know that Noah was back, and that he can have his Friday or Saturday twenty-four-hour visitation this weekend. I phoned Henry myself twice to tell him he can also visit, but he did not answer the phone. Both Ardy and I left voice messages for Henry saying he could arrange a visit, but he ignored those voice mails. So Ardy took Noah out shopping and then for some bowling. The rest of the afternoon and evening was peaceful.

Around 10:00 p.m., I called Ardy and told her they might have to put Eli on another antibiotic – a very toxic one – due to Eli's up and down temperatures.

April 21, 1990 – Saturday

Eli still had up and down temperatures during the night but I was able to still wake at 6:00 a.m. and did all of Eli's cares after my shower. Ardy phoned me at 9:30 to say that Henry had phoned her. Henry told Ardy that he had called me last night but I wouldn't talk with him. He was lying yet again. LIAR! He never called, never answered my calls, and most likely was drinking. He also had the nerve to tell Ardy that he "met me at the toll booth" on the turn pike. It never happened! Henry also said to Ardy that his lawyer told him to leave Denver, and that there would be a court hearing on Monday. He asked Ardy who brought Noah back from Denver and she told him. He told Ardy that I was in big trouble for having my friends rescue Noah and take him back safe and sound to her home.

I spoke with Noah on the phone for fifteen minutes and told him I loved him and would see him again as soon as I could.

I played with Eli then, and we also started new treatments for the radiation burns on his neck. This was just for the visual burns, but Eli had burns on the inside, too. Eli was tough as he never complained of pain. I was only too thankful for the few brief hours Eli and his brother managed to have quality time with each other.

Eli saw Dr. Mark from his door and cornered him from his doorway shooting his water gun at him. We just laughed and I closed the inner door again. Eli had a WBC of 0.3, ANC of 900, HGB (hemoglobin) of 8.8; platelets were 63,000, Segs of 30 and no Bands. From these numbers, it was easy to figure out his ANC except I came up with 90. Eli's temperature was 101 degrees and I gave him two Tylenol suppositories. Maybe they wouldn't need to use the nasty amphotericin B on Eli. I was hoping to avoid it since Eli could react to it negatively and die. Amphotericin B was like calling out the big dog in the world of antibiotics.

I called Anna around 3:30 p.m. and she told me that Ginny drove the car back all the way, that Matt chatted up Noah then fell asleep in the car, and that she stayed up the whole time Noah was chattering away and they had many conversations. I knew my son was a talker, especially around people he knew. She said they had lots of bathroom stops for Noah.

Later in the evening, I phoned Ardy and spoke with Noah for a while. He told me he had a good trip back and that Matt and Anna made it a fun trip. This confirmed what Anna told me.

After getting off the phone, I did, in a sterile fashion, debridement on Eli's neck. The procedure was done correctly, but the Tylenol was not enough for the pain.

Even a little morphine did not help the pain Eli was in. There was just so much pain. Too much for a child, even an adult, to go through. Throughout the debridement of the dead skin, I just cried. Eli could not see my tears as I had my mask on, and Eli was crying so hard himself.

I cried myself to sleep after Eli nodded off.

April 22, 1990 – Sunday – (Day 50)

I was awake at 5:30 a.m., but exhausted. Eli had been up twice during the night. After my shower, I came out and Eli's IV pump was beeping. I followed the line on his most important IV antibiotic and found his white port unconnected and his antibiotic all over his bed. This was the second time that Eli's nurse had not taped the needle and port correctly, and I was ticked off to say the least. After speaking with Eli's nurse, I knew we could not give Eli another dose and risk renal failure.

Eli still had a temperature this morning, but it was 99.9 degrees and we sent a stool culture down to the lab. This was improvement in his temperature. After Eli's usual morning routine, I was reminding Eli of how we were going to make him feel better so that I could take him home soon and we could be with his brother.

Eli started to cry hard. He said, "Daddy told me I wasn't going home. I have to stay here all the time."

I asked Eli's nurse, Rita, if she knew of this when she came in with medicine for Eli. Rita said yes, she had heard Henry say that to Eli and she had tried to comfort Eli after Henry left last Thursday, but she had not been back to work until today to tell me. I cried hard as I held Eli in my arms in the chair bed. That man was the very epitome of cruelty.

At around 11:00 a.m., Eli became restless so I placed a mask on him and then took him outside to get some sunshine. Eli rode around on his red 3-wheeler, on the outdoor patio area that was adjacent to the EU bookstore. Eli was reacting well for a child with his condition. I took a lot of photos; some of Eli watering the flower plants in the garden pots with his water squirt gun. When Eli started to get tired, I took him back inside to his room for a nap.

While Eli slept I went to the bookstore and got him a new headband to help keep the dressing on his right eye covered. When checking his temperature, I was glad that it was normal. Eli woke up asking for apple juice. Eli's nurse and I talked about it and we got Eli some. Then, we both told Eli to sip just a tiny bit and he did. Eli did not choke or take it down his wind pipe. We were both smiling. Eli only ended up drinking about 15 ml. of apple juice, but it was great to see him able to do this and not choke. Both Eli's nurse and I considered this a miracle.

Labs today were HGB 8.7, platelets 72,000, WBC 3 and that made his ANC 300 per Dr. Mark, but my calculations made it 30. Eli wasn't on his way back up yet.

By 5:30 p.m., Ardy called in to Eli's room. She said that Henry had stopped by about 4:00 p.m. for about fifteen minutes. She said he spoke with her and her husband, Max, and that he did not talk with Noah. Henry told them to just let him keep on playing outside in the yard. I wondered why he didn't want to talk with his son. So, I spoke with Noah after updating Ardy. Eli's nurse left a note in Eli's chart for his doctor, regarding the apple juice he drank. I decided to ask the doctor in the morning for another esophageal X-ray, to check if there were improvements on his ability to swallow. Maybe Eli could start drinking other liquids and receive more nourishment.

Eli went to sleep at around 9:00 p.m. and I fell asleep soon afterwards.

April 23, 1990 – Monday

Eli and I were both awake a lot during the night. I had a few choice words for Dr. Mark for telling me that Eli's ANC was 900 on Saturday. But when I figured it out, I came up with 90. On Sunday it was 30 – not 300. I told him that senior third year residents should be able to calculate an ANC. Dr. Mark was in his last semester as a resident and he could have done much better. Thank the Lord I could calculate what Eli's ANC's really were. Eli had on a mask when he went outside, and we all wore masks in his room. This kind of thing makes me wonder about other children whose parents were never here – the children were pretty much dumped and that was usually on a Friday. I spoke with Dr. Benjamin regarding his chief resident's mistakes.

Eli had more energy so I placed a mask on him and he rode around 5D on his red Big Wheels. Then, Eli fell asleep around 4:00 p.m., but he had a great, interactive day. While Eli was asleep, I took the opportunity to speak with Lucy Stone, Ardy, and Anna.

Henry stopped by Ardy's and took Noah for the afternoon. On the other hand, Eli and I had a quiet evening, and after speaking with Anna and Matt, we fell asleep almost simultaneously.

April 24, 1990 – Tuesday (Day 52)

Our day started at 6:00 a.m. like usual. I just didn't know if I was ready for this day to start or not. So much had happened and it would be nice to have a drama free day for both Eli and me.

Eli was scheduled to receive another MRI of his head and neck today. When Eli had his MRI's or CT scans and chest x-rays, I helped him get through them. For the MRI's, I removed any metal I had and locked it up. Then I sat at the head of the MRI machine talking Eli through it and keeping him still. I told him stories and how much I loved him. For the CT scans and x-rays, I had to wear a lead apron and we did the same thing. Eli's doctor knew that he reacted adversely to some medications, so we did it this way to prevent any adverse reaction.

Ardy phoned at 8:45 a.m. and informed me that Noah had told her he was at Grandma's house with his dad yesterday, and that Grandpa, who's bound to a wheelchair due to a stroke, had come out on the porch.

An hour later, I was on the phone with my lawyer and informed him of what Noah told Ardy, and that I wanted him to check on the status of my divorce from Henry.

Eli went to the school room on the unit this morning. He liked the teacher, Kristy Davis, and Eli painted a picture which I taped on the wall of his room. His wall was decorated with lots of birthday cards, and the calendar he placed stickers on when he had treatments. Stuffed bears, turtles, and fish were neatly arranged in his room, too.

I looked at Eli's printout of his labs and he had 70 Segs, no Bands, an HGB of 7.4, WBC 0.5 and 76,000 platelets. This meant Eli's ANC was 350 per my computation.

Eli eventually had the MRI and he did well this time. Then, my little boy sucked the juice out of one orange, slice by slice. Eli so loved food and flavors. I was both happy he could do this and sad that he was not able to eat properly.

In the afternoon, I was able to teach Eli some American Sign Language. I thought it might help him communicate when he had trouble talking. I made it into a game. I spoke with Noah in the afternoon and he told me he was so scared about grandma. I assured Noah that none of what she said was true, and that he shouldn't believe any of it. But I understood that at age six years, that was very hard to do.

Ardy called me back around 9:30 p.m. after Noah had gone to sleep. Noah told Ardy that "Grandma chases him," "Dad was working somewhere," and that he was NOT to tell Ardy anything! That meant Henry was passed out, and my son was in my mother's clutches. My lawyer would hear about this tomorrow.

April 25, 1990 – Wednesday

I woke up at 5:00 a.m. from a horrible nightmare. After doing Eli's morning cares, I called the SRS in Durango as well as the grade school counselor, Stella, and apprised them of what had happened the day before while Noah was out at Bow Mar. My lawyer, Mr. Troy, called me around 10:30 a.m. and said that Henry could end up in jail if the judge was to see it that way.

Eli was somewhat tired most of the day, so I decided to take him around inside EU, stopping in the gift shop for a new toy on our way back to his room.

In the afternoon, I received the MRI results from Eli's doctor. He stated that the main tumor was down $1/8^{th}$ or $1/6^{th}$ cm. from the MRI done at Frisco and that there was no tumor extension now. This was great news. That thing trying to kill my son was being killed instead. Overall, the main mass went down 1 cm. That is, after growing two more weeks before Eli's actual treatments began.

Eli had HGB 7.7, WBC 1.4, platelets 66,000, Segs 67 and Bands 13. That made Eli's ANC 1,120. Eli could now receive radiation treatments again. The eye doctor came in and examined Eli. He told me the radiation treatments damaged Eli's right optic nerve and that Eli was blind in his right eye. I cried over this, but not in front of Eli. I kept telling myself that the tumor was being killed and Eli could still see with his left eye. I have seen little kids with amputated legs, but Eli still had both his legs. These thoughts did not comfort me as my heart still clenched tightly at the thought of my son having lost his right eye vision. New TPN solution started this evening.

April 26, 1990 – Thursday

Both Eli and I were up way too early because his nurse, Nanci, couldn't be quiet when she was taking care of Eli.

I called down to radiation to let them know of Eli's ANC. The radiation staff told me that Ardy, Henry, and both lawyers, were discussing visitation rights. Upon learning that, I had them add Zoe Green from SRS in the discussions, as she could assist in this matter. I had no doubts about Ardy. I knew she would do what was best for Noah.

Radiation staff came out to tell me that that Eli's 6 MV, a multi-million-dollar machine, broke down while Eli was in it. Thus, his radiation was not completed.

I also informed Ophthalmology about Eli's blood counts, and since it was a good number, we went down for Eli's eye surgery. We were in the holding area at 12:30 p.m., and thirty minutes after that, Eli was in surgery.

At 2:30 p.m., while Eli was in recovery, Dr. LaGreca came to see me in the waiting room. She told me two things. First, Eli had optical nerve atrophy from the radiation; and second, he would need another surgery, a one-and-a-half-hour process to be done on another day.

After two and a half hours, Eli was out of recovery. The good thing was that there was no need to place an airway down Eli's trachea this time.

At 6:00 p.m., Dr. Cole came into Eli's room. He was the third Pediatric Hematologist Oncologist in the group and he took over with his team at noon today. They took every third month between the three of them (Dr. Landon, Dr. Benjamin, and Dr. Cole).

Later in the evening, Eli answered the phone when I asked him to. To my delight, Eli engaged in a conversation with Ardy and Noah. This was the first time this happened since Eli was admitted at EU. I strained my ears to listen to my son's words, hope blooming in my chest as he talked.

From Eli's side of the conversation I gathered that Oriana, a child Ardy babysits, was doing some scooting and crawling. Eli received a big kick out of hearing that and he giggled. That night I went to sleep with a smile on my face, running through my head the great conversation Eli had with Ardy and Noah. I fell asleep uttering a prayer of thanks to the Lord for this wonderful blessing.

April 27, 1990 – Friday

I was up earlier at 5:00 a.m. this morning. Dr. Cole came in and according to the new MRI, the improvements were tremendous. In my conversation with the doctors, the words amazing and astounding cropped up repeatedly.

I was not sure what to make of this, but if this were true then the hard-hitting protocol Eli was on must be working. Oncologists always treated children the hardest with chemo, and they always told me it was because kids had a better chance of having a great rebound from treatment and a long life ahead of them if they survive! I prayed that this was the case for Eli.

Eli's HGB was 6.6 so there would be another blood transfusion. Eli was in bed most of the morning watching *Superman* on the VCR as he received the packed red cells.

Eli had a CT scan of his lungs today.

By 1:00 p.m., I spoke with both Ardy and Noah; and Eli did, too! Things were looking up even more.

Henry called at 1:30 p.m., and he could not believe that Eli could now talk on the phone. Henry had no words to say nor did he ask how Eli or his surgery was. Instead, he ended up telling me that he was going to go pick up Noah from Ardy and then he hung up.

Chemo started at 2:00 p.m. At 5:00 p.m., Dr. Cole came in. He said cancer cells were found in Eli's spinal fluid. He also stated that a network of doctors from many places such as Cambridge, Mayo, UCLA, and St Jude, were discussing a new protocol to start on Eli come Monday.

Eli liked Dr. Cole and the way his name sounded, so he kept repeating it to the kind doctor. In moments like this, when Eli was so playful, I could certainly say he was cut out to make everyone laugh. His natural jovial mood was back, and so was the sparkle in his left eye.

Matt called me and we chatted for some time after Eli fell asleep. Our relationship was changing in a scary yet good way. I had decided to step gingerly. I did not want to get involved with Matt and be hurt yet again.

April 28, 1990 – Saturday

After Eli's morning cares, I stopped his TPN since it was already complete. Then, I thoroughly flushed both ports and obtained a CBC to send down to the lab. Henry called and I spoke with Noah. Then, Dr. Cole came in and he said the CT of Eli's lungs showed no change. He also said that Eli could try some applesauce. Eli's eye lit up upon hearing that. He listened to the doctors when he heard something interesting and he ignored them when they were discussing Eli within their group, the blue team.

Eli sorely wanted to tear down the hall on his red Big Wheels, but he must be hooked up to his normal saline hydration fluids for a few hours.

By 1:00 p.m., Eli was receiving another blood transfusion. The blood transfusions gave Eli more energy. Labs were Segs 30, 10 Bands, WBC 1.4, 63,000 platelets, HGB 3 and low ANC of 560.

Henry phoned at 1:30 p.m. asking if he could keep Noah longer and I said no!

Eli started chemo at 2:00 p.m. and Noah was returned by Henry to Ardy at 3:00 p.m. After Eli had fallen asleep, I called Ardy. I was itching all morning to give her a call, but refrained because I didn't know what had transpired while Noah was with Henry and my mother. I feared I might react upon hearing whatever antics they pulled, and end up upsetting Eli.

I learned that Henry told Ardy more good lies; that Matt spanked Noah and only refrained from doing the same to Eli because he was sick. This was an outright lie. Ardy also said that Floyd Fleming, Henry's ex-employer, said Henry had told him that I had gone back to Durango with two men and $1600 cash money, and that when I got back to EU I did not have any money left. It was impossible to do as it would mean that I traveled 460 miles in one night to party in Eagle, go back to Durango, party, and then head back to Denver. If he would concoct up some more lies, the least he could do was make it sound feasible. The lies he told only discredited him further. All this information would, of course, be relayed to my lawyer come Monday.

April 29, 1990 – Sunday – (Day 57)

Eli had slept all night, and in the morning, I performed his usual cares. Dr. Cole came in to see Eli.

At 10:45 Henry called and started yelling at me so I just hung up on him. Labs were 70 Segs, 6 Bands, WBC 1.4, and ANC of 1,064. It was a lot better than his ANC yesterday so radiation would resume tomorrow. Platelets were 78,000 and HGB was 10.3.

Eli and I talked with Ardy and Noah around 2:00 p.m. We had a nice conversation. I especially enjoyed hearing Eli talk with his brother and Ardy.

Chemo was finally started later than the usual schedule, at 4:00 p.m., and I wasn't sure why this was so. I didn't think two hours would make any difference anyway.

Eli and I watched *Ghostbusters* and *Batman* movies while he was confined to his bed due to the blood transfusion and chemo.

At 7:30 p.m., Henry popped in with no warning and abruptly left. I really did not need him in our lives right now.

After Eli had fallen asleep, Matt called and asked how Eli was and if I needed anything. We had a long talk and Matt ended up telling me that his anxiety was gone now – ALL gone - and that he loved me. I didn't know that I was waiting for those words to come out of his mouth, and that hearing these words from him would make me cry so hard. Needless to say, I loved this man so much! I kept crying, engulfed with a different kind of emotion, which was raw, unfamiliar, and overwhelming in a very good way. I had never ever felt this way about any man before. What started as a good friendship had blossomed into love. Tonight, even with everything that I was going through, I fell asleep with a smile on my face.

April 30, 1990 – Monday

Today, I woke up feeling like I had a good night's sleep. I handled Eli's morning cares, and I was smiling all throughout the procedure. I blushed, I think, for feeling like a high school girl with a crush who had just been told that the object of her thoughts felt the same.

Eli received radiation at 8:00 a.m. and Henry popped in at 9:30 a.m. so I had to leave.

I wandered in the hospital and picked up our mail. I checked on Eli's labs right before noon and his ANC was 990, 105 for platelets, and HGB of 10.3. Then I walked into Eli's room.

Dr. Cole came in and said Eli's treatment protocol was to remain the same and that one more medication would be added. First dose would be tomorrow for his new IT Protocol.

Eli had his second radiation at 2:30 p.m. and now he had twenty planned radiation sessions left to complete. Chemo was started at 3:00

p.m., and Henry showed at 4:00 p.m. I left for a walk to give him his time with Eli.

I was back in Eli's room at 7:45 p.m. and Henry was already gone. The nurses never saw him leave so I had no idea what time he left my little boy alone. It was scary thinking that maybe he followed me around the hospital without my knowledge. How unnerving it was to think of that possibility. Eli was awake when I came in, so we played until he became tired. Afterward, I tucked him in bed for the night and slept soundly too.

One month into treatment

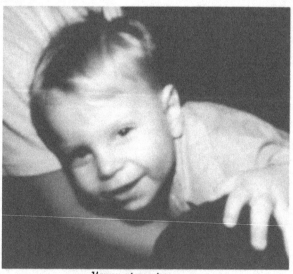

Happy at age two

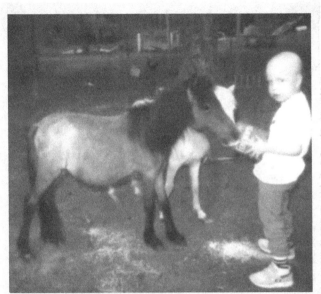

Feeding Ginger

Half way through treatment

Happy and well at age three

Outside hospital

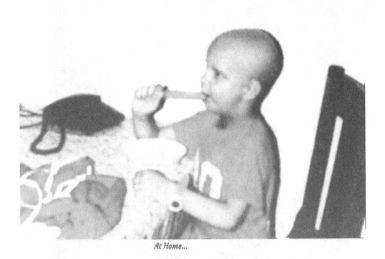

At Home...

December 1988

Age four

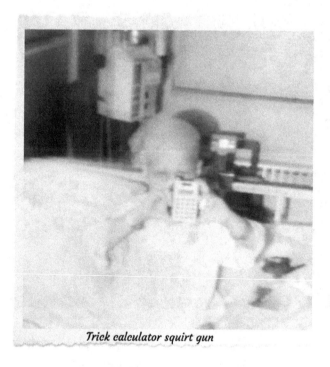

Trick calculator squirt gun

Chapter Fifteen

May 1990

May 1, 1990 – Tuesday

It was Day 59 since Eli and I went to EU. Eli had his early morning radiation treatment. At 9:50 a.m., my mother called Eli's hospital room, threatened and bitched at me for calling SRS on her. Her husband, my third step-father Bob, yelled at me as well. SRS knew what my mother was up to. Up until now, my mother was still livid because my son stayed with a sitter 24/7 and was paid for by the State of Colorado to watch him and keep him safe for me while I was in Denver with Eli.

Today, my mother taped the entire phone call as she wanted to upset me on the phone so she could try and use it in court. She told me she taped the whole conversation after the fact. She threatened me with court so I hung up on her.

Henry popped in at noon and Eli received his new IT Protocol today. I had to help Eli's nurse, and then after Eli fell asleep I made my escape when Henry went to eat lunch; otherwise I never would have been able to leave for Durango as he would have chased me down in the city.

At 6:30 p.m., I called up to 5D and spoke with Rita. She handed the phone to Eli, and from the other line, Eli told me that he and Rita were headed to the gift shop. Afterward, Rita said that Henry left the unit about half an hour earlier and never asked where I was – he did not know I had left to see my lawyer.

At around 7:00 p.m. I called over to Ardy's and spoke with her and Noah. I told him I was in town and coming over to pick him up. Ardy said Noah had already eaten supper and had his bath. When I picked up my son, I thanked Ardy for her great care and for putting up with Henry and my mother. I so wish life was not a soap opera, but life had always been that way ever since my first memories as a child. Noah and I talked a lot, and then he went to sleep in his bunk bed and I fell asleep to music on the radio.

May 2, 1990 – Wednesday

After waking up, I called EU and Eli was fine and headed down for his morning radiation. I told Eli's nurse I would call back later. After breakfast, I dropped off Noah at school and went back home after picking up groceries. I then called back Eli's nurse, Marci, and she told me that Henry was with Eli. Afterward, I went out to the Stoneybrook nursing home to visit Great Grandma Brown.

Evidently, my mother caught up with Spencer (friend) and she hounded him, wanting to know where I was. I found that comical because I was at the nursing home visiting my boy's great-grandmother and the nursing home was a mile or so from town. My mother was clueless. After lunch, I called EU again and Marci said Eli was doing okay and that Henry was there. She also observed that Henry did no morning cares for Eli. I told her he had never done so. Marci did Eli's cares and took care of his radiation burns on his neck, too. I was glad she did. Henry would have hurt Eli badly if he tried.

The County Attorney, Ethan Reynolds, was still not back from court at 1:15 p.m. I had Noah with me, so we went to the park and played instead. We ate supper at the Dairy Queen and Noah wanted a chicken nugget meal so that was what he had for supper followed by ice cream.

At 8:00 p.m. I called EU and Eli's nurse, Maci, was busy so I called Eli's room and Eli answered the phone! Noah talked with Eli first for a long time and then I talked with Eli. It was great to be able to have this conversation as Henry had already left! We talked for over forty-five minutes. At 9:30 I phoned Ardy and she said she had just gotten off the phone with Henry and that he was back in Eli's room. At 11:00 p.m. I called EU and Eli's nurse told me Eli was fast asleep. She also told me the eye doctor was going to do another tarsorrhaphy, a surgical procedure in which the eyelid was partially sewn together to narrow the opening so as to protect the cornea, on Eli's right eye at 11:00 a.m. tomorrow. Eli was to have radiation treatments at 7 a.m. and 1 p.m. if up and out of recovery.

I fell asleep while listening to some soft country music on the radio.

May 3, 1990 – Thursday

I was up at 6:00 a.m. and it was a GREAT morning with Noah. At 8:00 a.m., I took my son to school and spoke with his teacher and the school principal with updates regarding custody and Eli. Afterward I phoned EU and spoke with Eli's nurse, Emily. I reminded her that they would need to use a bronchodilator on Eli during his tarsorrhaphy. Emily told me the radiation machine was down so Eli did not receive his a.m. radiation treatment.

By 9:30 a.m. I was back at the school to see the kindergarten program dress rehearsal with Noah in it – I took a lot of photos and I felt great inside because although I would miss the program, I was in attendance for the dress rehearsal and my son knew it! Noah needed to know that I was still here for him, no matter what, even when I'm in Denver with Eli.

After the dress rehearsal I saw my lawyer, Mr. Troy, and I gave him more papers to use in the custody and divorce as well as another journal book. After that I went to the Health Department to check on whether or not Noah should have a Measles, Mumps, Rubella (MMR) vaccine, if one was due. Noah was given an MMR booster shot.

At noon I picked up Noah from school and we had lunch. Then I called EU and spoke with Emily who told me that Eli was still in surgery.

Ardy called to say that Henry had called her wanting to "know what I was up to."

Then we went to the City of Silverthorne Ambulance Department to take care of the big ambulance bill when Eli was first taken to EU.

When I phoned EU at 4:30 p.m., Mitch, Eli's new nurse, said that my son was doing fine in his room. Mitch was a great nurse and I trusted him. Conversely, Henry hated Mitch because of his different lifestyle. He was gay. This didn't bother me at all. Mitch proved to be a good, capable, and caring nurse for my son, or any patient, for that matter.

Then I phoned my lawyer to update him on Eli's status. Troy informed me that my mother bought Henry's house in Kiowa. Oh well! I knew her angle there, she wanted to tell my boys that the house would be theirs to live in with their father, and that they would inherit the home someday even though I KNEW she was lying purposely.

After 7:00 p.m., I phoned EU and spoke with Mitch. He told me that Eli was fine and that his favorite nurse, Rita, had played with him. Mitch told me that Eli had a grand time as he drenched Mitch with a water gun. Mitch transferred my call into Eli's room and Noah talked with both Eli and his father who was in the room at the time. When I took the phone to talk with Eli, Henry refused and he let me have it full force, verbally deriding me for not being a "good mother" and for "abandoning Eli today." None of that was true, but he refused to let me talk with Eli and I had to finally hang up on him due to his abuse.

At 7:35 p.m., my sister Ella was knocking on my door. She stated that "Mother and entourage (Ava and Emily—Ella's kids)" were outside in the parking lot. Ella stated that she wanted to see how I was holding up. I told her I was fine, and I asked her where Henry was going to live—Bow Mar or Kiowa. Ella said Kiowa would be too convenient due to the three bars in one town of 700 people so Henry would have to live at Bow Mar where he would not have easy access to alcohol.

Noah fell asleep around 8:30 p.m., I spoke with Ardy by phone to update her on Eli and then I went to bed as well.

May 4, 1990 – Friday

I was up at 6 a.m. like usual and Noah and I had another great morning at breakfast. He was a little chatterbox. After I took him to school I phoned EU and talked with Rita and she informed me that Eli's ANC was 920 yesterday. I thanked her for the information and I told her that I was happy she took the time to play with Eli. Rita really liked Eli, but I knew that she could not always be his nurse when she worked as she had grown too fond of Eli and Eli was now like a son to her. The closeness was a double-edged sword—Rita would have emotional times when Eli went home.

Then I spoke with Zoe Green at SRS and discussed my return to Durango with her, what had transpired, what Noah and I did, and everything Ella and my lawyer had said.

I liked keeping SRS aware of what was going on even though it drove my mother and Henry nuts. I had nothing to hide and they needed to be aware of things. On the other hand, I think both my mother and Henry had much to hide! I was in the office of Ethan Reynolds, the county attorney, by 10 a.m. and picked up the warrant on my mother – for a Protection from Abuse order and her harassment of me at my apartment.

Ethan told me that Judge Sterling was in Genoa Bend today, and since I could not wait until next week to see the judge, I had to drive to Genoa Bend and have him witness my signature, upon which he must then sign it and then it must be notarized.

I went to Ardy's with Noah's things and told her of my need to go to Genoa Bend. Henry phoned Ardy while I was there. He just had to make sure his visitation with Noah was not denied. Ardy informed Henry that he could have Noah Saturday night and all day Sunday. Then I went to the grade school and spoke tearful goodbyes to Noah in case I didn't see him later. I didn't know how Genoa Bend would go and I was feeling nervous. I called EU and found out that Eli was doing okay so then I went to Genoa Bend.

Judge Sterling and I talked and then we signed the warrant. I brought the papers back to the Clerk of the District Court, and Penny Troy filed them after giving me a copy of the warrant. My mother's Conditions of Bonds meant that she must come up with 10 percent of $1,000 for her bail. Nobody should have to have their own mother arrested, but for all the harassment mine did to Noah, Eli, and me, it was the right thing to do. Her cruelty was just too much.

I spoke with Ardy and called EU, and I was informed that Eli was down in radiation having his treatment.

Noah had been picked up by Ardy at noon when kindergarten got out, and I told Ardy I was going to try and set up my sister, Lily, by going into Prospector's for supper. I wanted her to tell people I was on drugs and very drunk, but she did not take the bait. I wanted to have a reason to do another drug screening at EU to prove her wrong! After dinner I went to the club and spoke with two of my friends, Denny and Piper Brosnan. We talked about the current status of everything, and mostly about Eli.

My sister Riley came in and started to talk with me, when I noticed my brother, Gavin, pull up outside. Riley and Gavin had just been to the police station with my mother following her arrest and subsequent bonding out of jail. Gavin started to harass me about being friends with Anna and Matt. Then, Matt pulled up at the club. Things were going to get interesting really fast! I left by the back door and went down to the police station and filed complaints on Gavin and Riley.

I had not intended for this to happen at the club, but I was not going to let this go by without being addressed.

Then, I went home and called Ardy. Noah was already in bed by then as it was past 9:30 p.m. Ardy told me that Henry already knew my mother had been arrested. Word traveled fast to him somehow. Finally, I crashed and went to sleep listening to country music on the radio.

May 5, 1990 – Saturday

I was up by 5 a.m. as I wanted to get an early start and I left Ardy's by 6 a.m. with Noah to go to Denver. I repeatedly told Henry that he had to be there in Denver when we arrived so he could take Noah back home after he saw his brother.

By 10:45 a.m., Noah and I walked into Eli's room. My Eli looked great! And the two boys instantly took to playing together and talking non-stop.

Eli's ANC was 282 so that meant hand washing and wearing of masks was again needed. The boys did not mind abiding by these strict rules as long as they got to be together. As a mother, I was proud to see them both so loving toward each other.

At noon, after placing a mask on Eli, I took both boys down to the main cafeteria as I knew Noah was hungry and I also knew that I could not separate them long enough for him to eat lunch – it just would not be fair. At 2 p.m. both Henry and Noah went over to the Ronald McDonald House after he told me, in front of both boys, that I had "sexual problems." He just never stopped with his BS. Several hours later they both came back and we all four actually went down to supper together, which was rather amazing. It went okay as Noah and Eli kept chattering away and Henry did not get a chance to say much. Eli was pretty tired after supper and playing with his brother, so I did Eli's cares and tucked him into bed by 7:15 p.m.

At 8 p.m. both Henry and Noah went over to the Ronald McDonald House together. After they had left, I phoned Ardy to let her know that Henry had indeed waited for Noah, and that they were together for the night. Matt called me later around 9 p.m. and we talked for a long time. Matt was good to my boys and me. He was my rock.

May 6, 1990 – Sunday (Day 64 – 15 radiation sessions left)

Eli woke up at 4 a.m., but I waited until 6 to do his morning cares. Eli chose to go down to the cafeteria with me and he tried to eat some hash browns with ketchup.

At 9:30 a.m. I took Eli outside in his wheelchair as the day was nice and he wanted to go out so much. All that was required was for Eli to wear a mask. Eli begged to go over to see his brother at the Ronald McDonald House as it was across the street from the Boone portion of EU.

Eli said, "Daddy took me over to the Ronald McDonald House the other day in the morning." I finally relented.

Noah and Eli played so well with each other and it was really nice. On the way back to EU half an hour later, Henry argued the whole way. The man refused to shut up so that I could assist Noah in pushing Eli's wheelchair. On the sidewalk outside the hospital main entrance, Henry asked me to step aside from Eli and Noah so that other people could go by. I stepped aside and then Henry yelled loudly at Noah and this startled and scared him. Noah let go of the wheelchair and Eli fell out scraping his right knee. Then, Henry left to go back to the Ronald McDonald House leaving both boys with me (not a problem usually), but Eli started to cry for his brother because Noah was so scared. At last, we were back in Eli's room. Another family staying at the Ronald McDonald House saw how Henry was behaving.

I took care of Eli's needs first when we got back into his room, and then I held Noah. Noah told me that "Daddy had hurt his feelings."

Then, Henry started arguing yet again! It was all BS nonsense and what he was really doing was taking away some good time for the boys to be together. I left the room so that the arguments would stop and the boys could continue playing together, but Henry followed me out the door of Eli's room and he went up to the assistant head nurse, Marci. Henry told Marci that he "did not want me doing some of Eli's cares at the hospital." I told him to "stop making it hell for everyone" and

I left the floor.

At least this way, the boys would not witness more arguing. Up until now, I still couldn't understand why this man had to make things a living hell for the children and myself. Why? It seemed as though he didn't realize that one of us must be capable of doing Eli's cares when he went home!

At noon, I phoned up to 5D to see if Henry was still there. He had just left with Noah, by way of the elevator.

Around 1 p.m., I spoke with Dr. Cole's nurse about maybe taking Eli home for one or two days since he could not have radiation due to the very low ANC. Eli was pretty tired all afternoon and he barely watched *Ghostbusters*. I spoke with Ardy to let her know that Henry had just called, and that he still had Noah, and he would be returning him around 7:30 a.m. tomorrow.

Eli played with me for much of the evening and by 8 p.m., he was already sound asleep. Henry phoned me at almost 11 p.m. to say he would drop off Noah at Ardy's in the morning.

May 7, 1990 – Monday

I was up after about five hours of sleep. Eli was awake two hours later and his skin felt a little warm to me and I knew Eli's nurse would be in soon to check on him and to see if he had a temperature. I had Eli flushed off both IV lines by 8:30 a.m. and was waiting on his doctor to come in and see him. I figured Eli's ANC to be 90 this morning and he had a HGB of 7.3.

I wondered when all this would end. It seemed like another blood transfusion would be needed. This was becoming cyclical after each chemo series.

Eli and I played and read part of the day, but he was pretty tired mostly due to the effects brought on by his treatment. I took Eli to the eye clinic twice today (he wore a mask) and Dr. Cole stopped by. He informed me that Eli's results from his spinal tap slide was lost! Dr. Cole and I had a really good talk; I refused to let the doctor leave Eli's room until I was good and ready. I was so upset that the slide that would show if cancer cells were present was lost, and this impacted Eli big time – it impacted his chemo, nothing could be adjusted until we knew the results. Another spinal tap might have to be done. The list was endless.

Then I showed Dr. Cole an area on Eli that looked like a spider or insect bite and he ordered a cream for this spot. Eli had three Hickman dressing changes today because of him developing an allergy to the adhesive dressing. Eli spiked a temperature of 101.5 and so he was started on vancomycin IV again. This time Eli had an adverse allergic reaction to the IV vancomycin and he developed really bad hives. I was glad I was there when it happened. Eli had hives on his head, neck, back and stomach and he received some Benadryl IV that helped him, as well as helped him to sleep the rest of the day. I phoned Ardy around 9 p.m. and I spoke with both her and Noah. Noah told me that "Daddy told him that I was going to have him put in jail!" This man must stop this crap. It was enough that my mother used this sadistic way to hurt Noah and now his father was telling him that "I" would have him put in jail?

I was informed by SRS today that I didn't have protection at my apartment from Henry, and from my mother so I couldn't take Eli home with me. Sigh.

Out of this endless stress, there was one laugh for the day though – I caught Eli trying to give his goldfish 7-up to drink.

May 8, 1990 - Tuesday (Day 66)

I knew the day would be a long one from the start. I slept hard and woke up around 5:30 a.m. Eli had a different IV antibiotic attached. As always, I wanted to know what he had received while I slept. In looking at the label, I noticed that the antibiotic was semi-synthetic penicillin. Eli was allergic to penicillin and he could have an anaphylactic reaction! While waiting for his nurse to come in, I watched Eli closely as I knew my son was prone to delayed reactions. By 7 a.m. the medication was discontinued, thankfully without any adverse effects.

Today's labs were HGB 6.9 and Eli was to receive one unit of packed red blood cells. His WBC was 0.6 with 20 Segs and 0 Bands making his ANC 120. This time his platelet count was 11,000 and Eli was to receive three and a half units of platelets. I was worried about overloading Eli with IV fluids and decided to watch him closely for overload. Nothing was settled yet in Durango, as per the county attorney, Ethan Reynolds, and Mr. Troy was not in the office.

Eli started the red blood cells around 2 p.m. and at 3:30 Ardy phoned Eli's room. At first Noah did NOT want to talk with me again. I was hurt and I was scared that Henry or my mother said something horrid to him again. Finally, Noah did speak to me and then he said that "Grandma and Daddy told him to never talk to me on the phone again."

"*DAMN THEM!*" went through my head at this. Why were they still doing this kind of thing to my boys? I prayed something would happen soon for their sakes. I asked Ardy to visit with Stella (grade school counselor) at the school music program this evening so that maybe she could help Noah. Dr. Cole popped in around 4 p.m. and said that Eli's last spinal tap was clean of cancer cells. After much study, the doctors had come to the conclusion that the spinal tap done the week of April 20 was clean as well. The cells that were different were damaged during the spinal tap process, and all other spinal taps showed no cancer cells. I would feel better if they found the actual slide to know this for sure, but I was happy to hear the news. Dr. Cole also stated that Eli could try some real food!

After the packed red cells were infused, Eli broke out in hives so he received Benadryl IV before starting platelets. Around 9 p.m., I was able to speak with both Ardy and Noah. My son asked me if I was "going to put him and Eli in jail." Noah told me that his dad had said I was going to put everyone in jail. I fell asleep crying for my boys tonight. I must let SRS know what had happened.

May 9, 1990 – Wednesday

After usual morning cares I found some blood in Eli's stool. The stool did check out as heme (blood) positive. I informed both SRS and Mr. Troy about Henry's call, which he made at around 11 a.m. Henry said he wanted to work out a deal when school was out. He wanted Noah at Bow Mar for the summer while I was tied up with Eli.

He really had the gall to ask me this? We started arguing about his request and it was going in circles, so I decided it was for the best that I hung up on him.

Mr. Troy had to help me ensure this would not happen.

At 3:00 p.m., Henry phoned back and asked if someone else could pick up Noah for his visitation until he could get back tomorrow. My answer was a resounding "NO."

Labs today gave me the following results: WBC 0.3, Segs 20, and no Bands so ANC was 60. HGB 8.3 and platelets were 65,000.

Eli actually ate well at supper. He enjoyed the applesauce, mashed potatoes and some watermelon. It was only soft food that was served to Eli to avoid aggravating the radiation burns in his throat.

Eli was in bed by 7 p.m. as he was tired and he had been up all day long. At 8:00 p.m. I noted that the white port on his Hickman had a small tear just below the clamp. I asked the nurse why she did not say anything or tell the doctor about it. Eli's nurse today was a fresh graduate and she made the mistake of trying to flush without undoing the clamp. The only saving graces were the fact that the port could be mended and that all of Eli's medications were compatible with his TPN.

May 10, 1990 – Thursday

I woke up to the sound of Eli vomiting around 4 a.m. I hated seeing Eli so sick. I hurt for him and I wished the cancer could be mine and Eli could be a happy little boy again.

I was angry at God this morning for allowing Eli to be so hurt and so sick. Life wasn't fair. "Take me Lord! I have known love with a significant other, a first kiss, eighth grade promotion, high school graduation, driving a car for the first time, getting a driver's license… The list is endless already for me. Please let Eli experience these things and more for the first time and just take me instead." But of course, it didn't work that way. All I could do was wish and pray that Eli could get better.

Eli's ANC was zero this morning. Well, he couldn't really go any lower than that. Dr. Parmalee stopped by and she wanted Eli to have a radiation treatment.

Dr. Parmalee and I discussed this a bit. I knew that with an ANC of zero, Eli was in no condition to have one. I prevailed for my child. Just after 1 p.m. Eli's Hickman was repaired and it could be used after twenty-four hours had passed, and a good seal on the Hickman repair was obtained.

Eli was wearing a mask and in his wheelchair when I took him to his eye clinic appointment that afternoon. Then, he told me he had a stomach ache. I touched his frail body and tried everything, but not even my softest caresses and whispers of reassurances could make the pain go away.

The nausea medications were not helping my child. Around 6:30 p.m. Eli wanted to eat so I gave him his meal. Eli ate a single hash brown shredded into bits and that was it. Night was kind as we both crashed in bed after we spoke to Ardy and Noah.

May 11, 1990 – Friday

We were up at 3:30 in the morning when Eli started a new antibiotic. Thirty minutes later, Eli was actively throwing up. When Eli felt a little better later in the morning, I gave him his bath. My son looked probably as exhausted as I did.

At almost 11 a.m., Dr. Cole and the blue team came in to see Eli. I informed them that I should be consulted prior to Eli receiving any antibiotic. Dr. Cole agreed that it was a valid request, given the circumstances. The cancer treatment that was supposed to save Eli in many ways was actually doing the opposite. But I would be damned if an antibiotic would endanger him due to anaphylaxis!

Eli napped at around 11 a.m. Later, Eli was filmed for the "Children's Miracle Network Telethon," which would be used in promoting children who are receiving critical medical care. Eli's video would air June 2nd and 3rd. I signed releases for both internal and external EU use.

Morning labs were HGB 7.7, platelets 53,000, 0.2 WBC's, 10 Segs, and no Bands so Eli's ANC was 20. This was so much better than the zero of yesterday.

By 3:30 p.m., I spoke on the phone with Ardy and Noah and learned that this was the second day now that Henry and my mother picked up Noah from Ardy's. I was livid about that.

At around 6:00 p.m., Eli was sick again and Dr. Landon came in to see him. He said that Eli would have sinus x-rays tomorrow.

After Dr. Landon left, I watched Eli fall asleep. My poor boy was suffering so much. It hurt me that there was nothing more that I could do about it.

I called Matt and told him about the day's events and my worries about Eli. We had a long conversation and before I fell asleep, close to midnight, I thanked God that there was Matt to somehow ease away some of the pain inside.

May 12, 1990 – Saturday (Day 70)

I was up at 5:30 a.m. and Eli was up half an hour later vomiting. He was so sick and this time he had a fever.

The good guys (chemo and radiation) were supposed to get the bad guys (cancer cells), but in the process they took the fighter cells Eli needed.

Eli's room was special and had been from the start—seventy days ago. His room allowed for the air outside the hospital to circulate inside and blocked off the air coming from within the hospital. It was a special positive pressure room, which was what most hospitals provide to patients with compromised immune systems. Filtered air would flow out of the room instead of in, so that any airborne germs that may infect the patient were kept away.

This damn fever really made me upset. I did all I could to make things as germ-free as possible like hand washing and wearing a mask. Eli always wore a mask to the clinics and back; and yet the fever still came. Nothing had ever been cultured as to germs. It was so frustrating. I wished Eli's father would wear a mask and wash his hands.

Not an hour went by and Eli was vomiting again. It hurt to see Eli so very ill. Morning labs were WBC 0.3, Segs 4, and Bands 4 makes Eli's ANC 240. HGB was 7.9 and platelets of 59,000.

About 3:00 p.m., Henry, Noah, and Gavin walked into Eli's room. I did not know they were coming to Denver. Thirty minutes later Noah was upset and crying so I took him out for a walk.

Noah told me that he wanted me home with him and Eli. Then he said to me that he did not want Daddy or Grandma.

My heart just ached for my son and I gave him much love and held him tightly telling him that Ardy and I would keep him safe until I was able to come back home. I almost cried because I knew that with Eli's cancer, it wasn't only him that was hurting—my other son did, too.

Reassuringly, I told Noah not to worry and not to believe the things he heard from his father or grandma. His eyes were still liquid and sad, but somehow, behind his clouded eyes, I knew he understood. I had to bite my lip to not cry in front of him.

Later I took Noah back up to Eli's room. Eli had sinus x-rays at around 5:00 p.m. and afterwards he was tired and fell asleep. Finally, Henry Gavin and Noah went over to the Ronald McDonald House and I was able to get some of my much-needed rest.

May 13, 1990 – Sunday (Mother's Day)

I heard Eli vomiting at midnight. I cleaned everything up and he fell back to sleep. Matt phoned at around 1:00 a.m. and we talked for an hour. Then he greeted me with words I wasn't expecting to hear from him "Happy Mother's Day." All of a sudden, I missed him. I clutched the cradle of the phone tightly as I listened to Matt's soothing voice.

At 3:00 a.m., Eli was up and vomiting yet again. I cleaned my little boy up and then at 3:45 a.m. Eli was asking for a doctor! That had never happened before and I knew Eli had to be feeling really, really horrible to ask for a doctor. Even in the middle of the night, somehow this recently-turned-five–year-old child knew he could ask for one.

The doctor was called, but he did not come to see Eli. I really wished the nausea medicine would work. Eli fell back to sleep at 5:30 a.m. and thirty minutes later he was vomiting again. It was so much and very forceful. My son hurt and he had not had good rest. I was tearing up inside.

At 7:00 a.m., Eli opened his eyes and he wasn't sick to his stomach. My prayers were answered! Thank you, Lord.

Eli simply played lightly with his stuffed animal, Precious, and Dr. Cole came to see Eli. I told Dr. Cole how I felt about Eli having so much emeses without relief and asked him if we could just try some other anti-nausea medicines please. Dr. Cole was hesitant due to Eli reacting adversely to other medicines.

Eli started napping mid-morning and Henry, Noah and Gavin walked in the door. I left so Henry could have his time with Eli. Henry came down to 1F cafeteria and verbally harassed me. I walked away from him and went back up and then to the nurse's desk area. The staff told him to leave me alone or they would call EU police. He did leave me alone, and then the three of them headed back to Durango at 3:30 p.m. I gave Noah extra hugs and told him to remember that he was not to believe anything Henry or Grandma said to him.

Eli fell asleep at 7:00 p.m. and new TPN was hung at 8:00 p.m. so then I decided to try and get some sleep. I was terribly exhausted, but I knew Eli must be even more exhausted.

May 14, 1990 – Monday

I was up like clockwork at 6:00 a.m. and so was Eli. Eli was tired, but he just really needed me all night long so we went back and forth between his bed and my chair bed. I did what I could to comfort Eli.

Morning labs were 32 Segs, no Bands, and WBC 0.9 to make ANC 288. Eli just did not feel like playing today so we watched the *Superman* movie three times in a row. I wrote Matt a long letter voicing how I felt our relationship had grown and how I thought of him. At the end I wrote, "I love you." Then I dropped "The Letter" off in the mailbox at the nurses' station. My mother had not scared Matt off and for that I was thankful. Matt had been my rock. Most men would have been run off by now yet Matt was stronger than my mother.

Tonight, I did not remember falling asleep and yet my head floated lightly in a really good way.

May 15, 1990 – Tuesday

I was awake at midnight again and both Eli and I spent a restless night going between his bed and my chair bed. We had a big, bad, thunderstorm with lightning bolts splitting the night sky. I could not watch the weather on the television as the service was knocked out. Come to find out Hesston was hit with a F5 tornado late yesterday, which then spawned one in the town of Goessel. I had no idea that the storm last night came directly from the same weather system we experienced.

Morning labs were 56 Segs, no Bands, and WBC 1.2 for an ANC of 672. HGB was 7.2 and platelets were 94,000. I called down to radiation oncology with Eli's ANC and I was informed that their whole area had been flooded from last night's storm. All the radiation machines were standing in a foot or more of water, as this area of the hospital was in the sub-basement. The medical crew was not able to do treatments for anyone today. To make matters worse, the clouds outside still looked fierce and ominous this morning.

After the cable television was restored, I watched the Hesston tornado on the news. I took Eli down to Cardiology for an echo of his heart.

No mitral valve prolapse was seen today. I did not know why, and I made a note to ask Dr. Mattioli as soon as I could. This was Eli's second echo. The first was done in Silverthorne, Colorado, through Dr. Mattioli and EU, before Eli was ill last year. Dr. Mattioli cared for children with heart issues. He was also my little brother Gabriel's doctor.

At 4:00 p.m. we were at the Eye Clinic and they told me that Eli's eye showed signs of improvement. It was good that he was healing so well after the surgery. Between the sutures and the care I gave, his eye did not hurt now. I was thankful.

Eli ate a few bites for supper, and he kept the food down. If Eli could eat more, then we could cut back on the TPN some. Real food was better by far than nutrition via parenteral (intravenous) infusion.

Kristy Patterson, a nurse on Dr. Landon's team, stopped by Eli's room. She was the third of three pediatric hematology oncology nurses. They rotated just like the three pediatric hematology oncology doctors. Of all times to do an EKG (electrocardiogram) on Eli, they chose to do one at 8:00 p.m. Afterwards, we both talked with Ardy and Noah before finally falling asleep.

May 16, 1990 – Wednesday (Day 74)

I woke at 2:30 a.m. for no reason. Eli was fast asleep. I could not fall back to sleep so I continued writing in my journals.

Morning labs were 28 Segs, 21 Bands, WBC 1.9 made ANC 971. HGB was 7.7, platelets 126,000 and blood glucose was 291.

After the usual morning cares, I took Eli down to radiation oncology for his treatment. The flooding was still present, but not as much as it was yesterday. We saw one of the doctors sitting on a stool, in a foot of water, writing orders. Eli thought he looked funny with all the water and I had to giggle myself.

The medical staff told us Eli's treatments would resume tomorrow.

At 10:00 a.m., Eli started a packed red blood cell infusion. I knew that was coming as his HGB was 7.7. I spoke with my lawyer, Mr. Troy, near lunchtime and he told me that he had not received any word yet from Henry's lawyer regarding Noah spending the summer at Bow Mar.

For two hours, I read every report and looked at every X-ray, CT scan or MRI done here at EU and at Frisco in Silverthorne, Colorado, as I had requested them for my lawyer. I decided to read them and see how Silverthorne, Colorado, missed the main tumor mass the size of my fist in one of Eli's tests.

Eli's full bone scan showed no cancer, but did show Spina Bifida Occulta of Eli's S1. The mildest form of Spina Bifida, Bifida Occulta, describes a group of neural tube birth defects that can affect the spinal column. This was composed of bones, or vertebrae, that support the nerve center of the spinal cord, which was responsible for carrying all nerve signals in between the body and the brain. Most people were unaware that they had Spina Bifida Occulta, although an estimated 10 to 20 percent of the population carried this type of condition. There may be no outward sign of any defects in the spinal column until an X-ray is carried out for some other reason, because in this type of Spina Bifida there aren't any problems with the nervous system.

As far as outside films from Frisco in Silverthorne, EU's findings on the CT scan of Eli's head done on February 19, 1990 showed a nasopharyngeal soft tissue mass extending into the region of the pterygoid fossa.

Nasopharyngeal cancer is a rare type of head and neck cancer. It starts in the upper part of your throat, behind the nose. This area is called the nasopharynx. The nasopharynx is precariously placed at the base of your skull, above the roof of your mouth. Your nostrils open into the nasopharynx. When you breathe, air flows through your nose into your throat and nasopharynx, and eventually into your lungs. Scientists are not sure what exactly causes nasopharyngeal cancer. However, the cancer has been strongly linked to the Epstein-Barr virus (EBV). Eli had been diagnosed with EBV in the fall of 1989.

Although EBV infection is common, not everyone who has EBV will get nasopharyngeal cancer. In the U.S., most people who have had an EBV infection never have long-term problems. That's because the body's immune system destroys the virus. But sometimes, genetic material (DNA) from the virus mixes with the DNA in the cells of the nasopharynx. The change in DNA causes cells to grow and divide abnormally, causing cancer. This is rare. The chance that EBV will fuel cancer growth goes up if you eat a diet rich in salt-cured fish and meat. That type of diet is common in Asia, particularly China. Scientists believe that chemicals in such foods further damage the DNA in cells.

Only about seven in one million people in North America get this type of cancer, according to the American Cancer Society. Sadly though, Eli was one of the seven people.

In the U.S., nasopharyngeal cancer has also been seen in African-Americans, Hispanics, and white people. One is more likely to get this type of cancer if the following conditions are present/ true: male, younger than 55, eat a diet rich in salt-cured fish and meats, have a family history of nasopharyngeal cancer, have certain genes linked to cancer development, and have come in contact with EBV.

Some of the symptoms of nasopharyngeal cancer may include: blurry or double vision, difficulty speaking, including hoarseness, ear infections that keep coming back, face pain or numbness, headache, hearing loss, ringing in the ears, or a feeling of fullness in the ear, lump in neck or nose, nosebleeds, stuffy nose, and sore throat.

Keep in mind such symptoms are more likely to occur with many other diseases and health conditions that are less serious than nasopharyngeal cancer. Eli also ground his teeth together.

Knowing what it meant to have a loved one with this type of cancer makes me want to spare any other parent from what I'm going through. So, as soon as any of these symptoms persist, the best course of action is to consult a doctor immediately.

I feel like I'd be doing someone a favor if I also post how this type of cancer is diagnosed, so here goes:

The doctor or nurse will examine you. This includes a detailed look at your ears, nose, and throat. He or she may send you to a doctor that specializes in these areas, called an otolaryngologist. The doctor or nurse will feel your neck. Most patients with nasopharyngeal cancer will have a lump in the neck. This is a sign that the cancer is spreading to the lymph nodes. Small mirrors and lights or a flexible, lighted tube may be placed through your mouth or nose to help the doctor better view the nasopharynx. This is called a nasopharyngoscopy. It helps the doctor check the area for abnormal growths, bleeding, or other problems. If the exam is abnormal, your doctor may recommend a biopsy. A biopsy is the removal of a small amount of tissue for examination under a microscope. A biopsy may be taken during the nasopharyngoscopy if it is done using the flexible tube, called a scope. Other times, the biopsy is done by placing a very thin, hollow needle into a lump in or near your neck.

Imaging tests can help spot nasopharyngeal cancer or determine if it has spread. Imaging tests may include chest X-ray, CT scan, MRI, and ultrasound of the neck.

Further, the following tests may also be done to confirm or rule out cancer: complete blood count and other blood tests, urine tests, genetic testing, and EBV testing.

If someone is diagnosed with nasopharyngeal cancer, other tests will be done to determine if and where the cancer has spread. This is called staging. There are four stages of nasopharyngeal cancer. The lower the number, the less the cancer has spread to other parts of the body. (Eli was stage 4).

Stage 1 is called *early stage nasopharyngeal cancer.*

Stage 2 is called *intermediate-stage nasopharyngeal cancer.*

Stages 3 and 4 are called *advanced or late-stage nasopharyngeal cancer.*

If nasopharyngeal cancer returns, it is called *recurrent cancer.*

The treatment procedures for this type of cancer will include the regular follow-ups with the medical team before, during, and after treatment; and the treatment plan will depend on many things, including: location of the tumor, stage of the tumor, and the patient's overall health.

The treatment plan may include:

Radiation therapy uses X-rays to kill cancer cells and stop them from growing. It is the standard treatment for early stage nasopharyngeal cancer.

One type called IMRT delivers high-dose radiation directly to the tumor, while minimizing damage to nearby healthy tissue. It may cause fewer side effects or complications than conventional radiation treatment to the nasopharynx, which can lead to: dry mouth, inflammation of the lining of your mouth and throat, blindness, brain stem injury, and death of healthy tissue.

Surgery can cure nasopharyngeal cancer if all the tumor and cancer cells are removed. But the surgery can be difficult because of the tumor's location near the skull. It may cause permanent damage to the eye and other nearby structures. Not all people with nasopharyngeal cancer can have surgery. Your doctor will consider the location and stage of your tumor when discussing your treatment options.

Biologic drugs affect how your body's immune system fights disease. They are also called monoclonal antibodies. A biologic drug called bevacizumab blocks production of a substance called vascular endothelial growth factor (VEGF). Studies show that patients with nasopharyngeal cancer who have lower levels of VEGF are more likely to remain disease-free after treatment.

Bevacizumab is currently being evaluated to see if it will help improve your overall survival when combined with other treatments, such as chemotherapy. Chemotherapy uses drugs to kill cancer cells. By itself, it is not usually helpful for treating nasopharyngeal cancer. But it may help you live longer when combined with radiotherapy or biological drugs. At this time, there is no cure for head and neck cancer that has spread, or metastasized. The goal of treatment is to control your symptoms and make you as comfortable as possible. This is called palliative therapy. If treatment does not work, consider joining a clinical trial. Researchers are always testing new ways to treat cancer, and they need your help. Ask your doctor or nurse if there are any clinical trials for nasopharyngeal cancer in your area.

Now, the question that I want answered is can nasopharyngeal cancer be prevented?

Taking these steps may lower the risk of nasopharyngeal cancer: eat a diet rich in fruits and vegetables. Avoid salt-cured fish and meats, smoking, and drinking a lot of alcohol.

The pterygoid fossa is a term used for a V-shaped depression that is located at the back of each of the two pterygoid processes that the sphenoid bone bears. Shaped like the wings of a butterfly, the sphenoid bone is one of the bones of the human skull, responsible for helping to form the back of the sockets where the eyes are situated. The pterygoid fossa is created from the two plates that converge from each pterygoid process of the sphenoid bone. The adjective "pterygoid" is applied to the depression because of its location at the sphenoid bone. (This is where the mandible and maxilla meet).

Now, how was all this missed by so many medical professionals in more than one city over a period of months?

Frisco in Silverthorne, Colorado, only picked up sinusitis!

After reading EU's findings on this scan, I just sat in my chair bed and bawled. I cried for Eli, I cried for Noah. Then I cried some more. I looked at the scans and even I could see the main tumor mass! The tears just ran down my face in a total uncontrollable way and I was thankful Eli was asleep.

The MRI done at Frisco in Silverthorne, Colorado, on 03-06-1990, showed a 5.5 cm AP dimension by 4.5 cm transversely by 7.0 cm vertical soft tissue mass; in the right parapharyngeal space, involving the pterygoid muscles, the right mandible, and the parotid over to the lateral (side of head) right orbital wall.

The esophageal x-ray, done at EU on 03-30-1990, showed Intermittent Failure of the epiglottis.

CT scan of Eli's head, done on 04-09-1990, both with and without contrast, showed NOTHING intracranial at that time! (Nothing in Eli's brain).

A lung CT scan, done on 04-09-1990, showed a 7 mm nodule in the posterior right lower lobe and in his left lower lobe only one pulmonary nodule remained. The other one previously seen is now gone!

An MRI of Eli's head, done on 04-24-1990, showed no tumor extension into Eli's head!

I had many things to now give to my lawyer, Mr. Troy. While Eli slept, I slipped down to the EU post office and picked up our mail and then I went back to Eli's room.

Eli's phone rang at 5 p.m. and it was Matt. I was nervous when I picked up the phone. I heard his voice and KNEW he had just read the letter I sent declaring my love for him. Matt told me he LOVED me, too! We spoke for over an hour as Eli slept. We spoke about us, Noah, and of all I had read on Eli today. Matt was strong and comforting.

Eli's nurse came in around 6:30 p.m. needing me so I got off the phone. Eli was still sleeping. His nurse told me that a biopsy of Eli's lung may have to be done. We talked about the pros and cons and I knew that Eli must have open lung surgery. My heart just broke. I fervently prayed for Eli, as I knew what he must have to suffer through in order for this biopsy to be accomplished.

Ardy phoned Eli's room at 8:15 p.m. She informed me that both Henry, and my mother, had brought Noah back to her house about an hour earlier. Noah had not had his supper yet and Henry had said he would feed him. I hated my son being hungry, but I also knew this would look bad on Henry and mother in court, and they brought this on themselves.

Ardy waited until Noah had his supper before calling Eli's room. I spoke with Noah. He told me his father had said he mowed the lawn all evening and had not had time to cook supper. Then my son said his father was in a big hurry to take him back to Ardy's house early.

I phoned my sister, Riley, after I was done talking with my son and Ardy. I explained all this to her and asked her to call Henry and have him explain himself. I know he wouldn't do this but I knew that I must try to find out what happened for my boy's safety and eventual custody determination.

After the phone conversation, Eli was still sleeping and I fell asleep exhausted.

May 17, 1990 – Thursday

Eli woke up around midnight for about two hours. We watched *Superman* on the VCR again until we fell asleep to the black screen of the TV.

Eli was up at 6 a.m. and I was so glad he actually had some restful sleep yesterday and last night. These little things were some of what I overlooked in the past, but I found myself thankful for them now.

Eli received his morning radiation therapy and while down there I spoke with Dr. Branson about another radiation schedule this Saturday. Eli missed several treatments due to the effects on his body and he had to make up for them.

Dr. Branson said they would let me know. Henry phoned around 9:30 a.m. not to ask about how Eli was, but rather, about what I told my sister, Riley. Then the usual bitching followed, making me hang up on him again. It got really old; the way things had been pirouetting between us; all the jealousies, lies, anger, and not one ounce of respect for the boys or myself.

The only undeniable good that came out of my relationship with him were my boys. I wanted Noah and Eli to have a father to look up to, but a father who didn't behave in the manner Henry did. The abuse must stop, but how would I put an end to it?

I wish it were as easy as closing a door on an irksome stranger. Sadly though, it wasn't an irksome stranger at my door, but rather the irksome father of my sons. I could not prevent him from coming to EU, nor go against the court ordered visitation rights.

In the afternoon, Eli had his radiation treatment, too. Afterwards, I took him to the eye clinic and he saw ALL cards today with his "bad" eye. Eli's vision was back! Once more, there was another good thing to thank God for. I read it once before, that the key to happiness really was gratitude. As I bent my head in prayer and whispered a prayer, I realized how true it was.

The evening would not be complete without Henry phoning in and doing another round of bitching, which he did at 10:30 p.m. He was half drunk, and he started yelling. And as the day came to a close, I hung up on him.

May 18, 1990 – Friday (10th Week of Treatment)

Eli woke up around midnight last night, but he did go to bed early so it was just as well. He wanted to see *Ghostbusters* again so I started up the VCR. Then, just like our usual nights at EU, he fell asleep with the list of credits scrolling on the TV.

I woke up at 4:30 a.m. and Eli was wide awake again. He went back to sleep, but it wasn't for long. My son woke up one hour later sick to his stomach and vomiting like crazy. His night nurse came in and gave him medicines to help his stomach.

Morning labs came back early and Eli's ANC was 1169. It was a good figure as it meant that Eli's immune system was rising back up!

After Eli had his morning radiation treatment, I took him back to his room. When he was asleep, I just sat there and bawled for a long time. It was an everyday battle. To care for your son, whom you love so much, and see him in all his sufferings, and then to put on a smile for him so he wouldn't worry about me when he woke up. The physical stress was easier to cope with. It was the constant dread of the unknown that almost-always drained the energy out of my body.

Early in the afternoon, Henry and Ella picked up Noah from Ardy. Ardy phoned to tell me about it and to chat with me. We had come to the conclusion that Henry's driver's license was taken away due to the DUI and not because his car had broken down. That was truly the only explanation for all these people taking Henry over to her when he picked up Noah.

I phoned Anna after Eli's afternoon radiation treatment and asked her to deposit money into Eli's medical fund account from the donation jar as I was running short and had more bills to pay. I was sending the bills to Citizens State Bank and they would disperse the funds accordingly.

Around 3 p.m. Eli was given sleepy medicine as well as anti-nausea medication so that his chemo – doxorubicin given IV slow push, followed by a hanging bag of IV ifosfamide, could be given. Eli slept and I was nervous. I just knew Eli would start throwing up again and that this round of chemo would drop his counts, his immune system, his platelets and red blood cells. We must try. God does hear us. I sat staring at my son's fatigued body that lay before my eyes, unblinking. My eyes had dried up. No tears would come out. And it was only the gritty feeling like having sand in my eyes that kept on reminding me that all of this was my reality.

May 19, 1990 – Saturday

Eli and I were both up at 6 a.m. If Matt phoned during the night I had no recollection of the phone ringing.

When we got back to Eli's room after his morning radiation (yes – Dr. Branson agreed that Eli could catch up on his missed treatments), Eli ate many bites of soft food, hash browns, applesauce, and some chocolate milk.

Labs came back and HGB 10.2, 46 Segs, 16 Bands, WBC of 3.0 made his ANC 1960. Eli was still on the rise, but I braced myself knowing that the vicious cycle of low counts and the need for blood transfusions would happen again.

Eli ate pretty well at lunch, too; mashed potatoes and other soft foods such as watermelon, and he sure loved his apple juice. I thought, today will be a good day! In the early afternoon, Henry, Noah, and Gavin showed up. I had not been expecting them so I just played things cool until I could find out what was going on. Henry did not want to go with Eli down to his afternoon radiation treatment, so I took him.

Around 3 p.m., Eli's temperature was checked and it was 101.3. Eli received sleepy medicine and chemo was hung. Afterwards, I went for a walk with Noah, leaving Eli with Henry.

I took Noah down to the chapel in Murphy building and we prayed for Eli. I wanted my boys baptized, but Henry never would allow me to take the boys to church as he was an atheist. Noah and I talked about God; and I showed my son many things in the chapel and what each one signified.

After going back up at 6 p.m. Henry took off with Noah and Gavin for the Ronald McDonald House. They all popped back into Eli's room around 9 p.m. as Eli was just about to fall asleep. Henry agitated Eli, and I pushed the red button to call the nurse and when she came in, she saw what Henry had done. She made them leave so I could calm Eli down. When I did, it was already 11 p.m. and two hours of sleep had been lost.

May 20, 1990 – Sunday (9 Radiation Sessions Left)

After morning cares, I flushed off Eli's IV. He then promptly got on his red three-wheeler and peddled up and down the hall just like any other little boy would do at his age. By 9:00 a.m. Eli was hooked back up, this time for his hydration fluids.

Henry, Noah and Gavin came to Eli's room at 11:30 a.m. I asked Henry if he drove to Denver because he technically couldn't. He replied that not being allowed to drive would not stop him from driving. He admitted that his driver's license had been revoked. I just sighed. I had seen this man get more than twenty DUI's since we were together. Some things never changed.

I told Noah how much I loved him and how I couldn't wait until Eli and I were home so that all three of us would be together again. Noah whispered in my ear that Uncle Gavin spanked him really hard lots of times. I looked up and locked eyes with Gavin, and I told him to never lay a hand on Noah again. I told Gavin that he had better learn what "time out was and how to use it."

Henry and Gavin started to make a loud scene over this matter. I did not want Eli to get upset, so I took Noah for a walk. We stopped by the pretty water fountain just outside the EU bookstore and we made some wishes. The fountain was full of flowers.

I took Noah back up at 1 p.m. so he and Eli could be together for a while. By this time, Eli had already simmered down.

After ten minutes, Henry said they were going back to Durango and goodbyes were exchanged between my boys.

Chemo was started by Eli's nurse. I looked to see how much Eli ate for lunch, and was satisfied upon seeing that he finished half his mashed potatoes. This was definitely an improvement. I was glad Eli could keep taking in some nutrition. I delayed removing the tray from his room in case he wanted more.

Casey stopped by Eli's door when she brought up medications from the pharmacy. Casey grew up in Durango and she knew Eli as I had taken my boys to the swimming pool quite a bit when she worked summers there. She was in Pharmacy School here at the medical center. Her presence yet again brought me comfort.

Eli's morning labs were pretty good–70 Segs, 8 Bands, WBC's 3.4 meant his ANC was now 2652. HGB was 9.7 and platelets were 152,000.

By 7:00 p.m., Eli was already asleep. I phoned Ardy at 9:00 p.m. to update her on Eli, Noah, and their father. I also mentioned the story Noah told me about Gavin hitting him and Ardy said she would keep an eye out for that. I hung up, thanking God for the wonderful blessing that was Ardy.

May 21, 1990 – Monday – (Day 79)

Eli woke up bright and early at 4 a.m. He demanded food to eat! Eli wanted watermelon and there wasn't any in the patient refrigerator. The nursing supervisor went and looked in the medical center kitchen and she could not find any. I told Eli I had to go out and find some at a store that was open all night, and so I did just that. I brought watermelon into Eli's room and he ate quite a bit of it, and he also stayed awake and never went back to sleep. Eli was wearing watermelon juice with a grin on his face – the best grin he could do, using the left half of his face, since his right side was paralyzed due to the cancer. The travel just to get the watermelon was all worth it.

After I cleaned up Eli, I took him down for his morning radiation and then we went to the eye clinic. Eli was still able to read all the cards with his right eye! Between eating and being able to see again, I just knew Eli would be coming home soon! Eli was a pure ray of sunshine from God. A miracle was happening before my eyes.

On the way back to Eli's room, we stopped off at the EU gift shop so he could spend a few dollars of his birthday money. Eli always looked closely at what his choices were and invariably picked out something he really wanted.

Eli kept his dollars in a Batman child's wallet and he shared them with Noah when the latter came to visit.

Eli's morning labs were 82 Segs, 6 Bands, WBC 2.0 making his ANC 1760. Eli's ANC was dropping; the chemo and radiation was doing this to him again. His HGB was 9.4 and platelets were 221,000. After Eli's 1 p.m. radiation treatment, Dr. Goodman checked on Eli's protocol with the network of hospitals that were with EU. Because of radiation treatments missed and due to having a really low ANC, Eli was required to add four radiation treatments to his regimen. This meant eleven sessions were left. Dr. Goodman said they couldn't stop anymore due to low ANC's. I prayed Eli was able to do this, to get through all that was demanded of him.

Dr. Goodman said one thing and Dr. Landon said another though, and this confused me. I wished they would just be on the same page for once.

Eli's chemo was started in the middle of the afternoon and an hour later both Eli and I spoke with Ardy and Noah. It was a wonderfully nice call.

Eli and I spent a quiet evening watching his favorite movies and his chemo went okay in the evening. I did tell Eli that he needed four more radiation treatments and Eli wanted to use my fingers to count them all. Then Eli wanted to know if he had enough stickers to place on his construction paper calendar for each one. We looked and counted. Eli was happy we had enough stickers. With all that Eli had been through, he took the news of four additional treatments without complaint. Such a brave little boy.

May 22, 1990 – Tuesday – (11 Radiation Sessions Left)

Eli woke up at 6 a.m. just like me this morning and he was hungry again! That was just great and he had leftover watermelon so he ate that and some applesauce.

Then my silly little boy opened a packet of mayonnaise and ate that too – just for the flavor! Eli loved the sheer taste of food since he was born and proof of it was in that mayonnaise he ate. I just smiled. I loved seeing Eli really enjoying himself.

Eli had his morning radiation and after arriving back in his room, Dr. Cole came in to see him. He said Eli may need antibiotics again since his numbers were going down. I had already figured that one out. Dr. Cole said he had phoned Dr. Roan, pediatrician in Silverthorne who worked with Dr. Brown, about Eli's current medical status and update. Then he added that Dr. Landon would be on tonight, Dr. Benjamin tomorrow, and then Dr. Landon for the rest of the month. I felt like Eli had three great doctors with these men. In this sense, my son was a lucky patient, no matter how grossly ironic this statement sounds.

Eli's weight check this morning showed he weighed in at a little over 39 and one half pounds. This meant he had gained over two whole pounds! It isn't much, but for a five-year-old boy with cancer, it was reason enough to celebrate. Things were looking up. Eli smiled as best he could when his nurse, Rita, smiled at his weight gain.

Eli's labs came back at 86 Segs plus 5 Bands times WBC 1.9 equaled ANC of 1729 with HGB 8.8 and platelets of 147,000.

Eli ate a pretty good lunch for him, most of his mashed potatoes and some corn. He followed that up with the contents of two mayonnaise packets.

Rita hooked up Eli to his ifosfamide (chemo) after Eli came back to his unit, all fresh from his 1:00 p.m. radiation treatment.

We watched movies and played with toys and had a quiet afternoon which was nice for a change. Around 8 p.m. I phoned Ardy. This gave us the chance to talk to each other and bridge the distance.

We spoke of Noah, and how good a day Eli had. By 9 p.m., Eli was sound asleep.

May 23, 1990 – Wednesday

Eli was awake at 5:30 this morning. He woke more than once during the night, but he was not sick to his stomach. I was thankful for that.

After he had a little breakfast, I took Eli down for his morning radiation treatment. When we got back to his room, Henry phoned. I gave

Eli the phone so he could speak with his father. I chose not to speak with Henry as I did not want to start an argument. I told Eli that when he was done speaking with his father to just hang up the phone. Eli said, "Okay, Mom."

Morning labs were 94 Segs plus no Bands times WBC of 1.9 equaled ANC of 1786. HGB was 8.0 and platelets were 145,000. I know it was a matter of time before Eli dropped much more as the cycle was repeating itself. After Eli's early afternoon radiation treatment, I took him over to have X-rays of his head and chest areas done. Finally, Eli would stay positioned for them so I didn't need to hold him in place wearing a lead apron.

Afterwards Eli had another echo done on his heart and then we went back to his room.

Henry's cousin, Kinsey, stopped by to visit Eli. I wasn't aware she was in town and do not know her well enough to expect a visit from her. She was cordial and I was glad for that. After she left Eli ate a pretty good supper and no emesis yet. Again, I was thankful. Today had been peaceful for Eli.

In the evening, Eli and I talked with Noah and Ardy. I was happy that my boys could tell each other good night.

Afterwards, Matt phoned and we had an interesting conversation. The sort that's both familiar and comfortable. We were becoming so close to each other. It was a good feeling but scary at the same time. How would our relationship turn out? When I started to nod off while on the phone Matt told me, "I love you and good night." I said the same back of course as I fell asleep in my chair-bed at Eli's side.

May 24, 1990 – Thursday

Today, only seven radiation sessions remained.

Eli and I were up by 6 a.m. and I took him down to have his morning radiation treatment. Then, we went to the eye clinic. Eli's eye doctor placed dissolvable plugs in his tear ducts to help keep his eyes moist. Per multiple internet references, "Punctal plugs are tiny, biocompatible devices inserted into tear ducts to block drainage. This increases the eye's tear film and surface moisture to relieve dry eyes." Eventually the body absorbs the collagen and the plugs dissolve. It was such a heart break to find out that Eli could NOT see with his right eye today. Atrophy of Eli's right eye remained. I was just so heartbroken inside for my baby. Eli's seventh facial nerve was bad. It seemed each time something good happened, something bad happened.

After arriving back to Eli's room, his hydration fluids were stopped so we could see if Eli would be able to drink enough when awake. He still received the TPN at night though, unless we could be sure that Eli was drinking enough to no longer need the hydration fluids.

Eli's Tagamet was discontinued as well, and I was not so sure that was a good thing. But we would see how Eli's stomach did without Tagamet.

Morning labs consisted of 92 Segs plus 4 Bands times WBC of 1.4 equaled ANC of 1344. Eli's immune system was taking a hit again. I knew this scenario too damn well by now. All I could do was pray for my son. I know God heard me; He had allowed many beautiful moments with Eli, but I just wished it could be me undergoing all the treatments Eli had done and had yet to do. Eli's HGB was 8.1 and his platelets were 142,000.

It was 2 p.m. by the time Eli received his second radiation treatment, and during this time, I spoke with Dr. Goodman. She said we may not be able to radiate Eli if the machine gave more trouble like it did today. Eli had to wait an extra hour down in radiation oncology this afternoon because the machine was not working correctly. Dr. Goodman said Eli may not receive radiation treatments at all this coming weekend.

Dr. Benjamin popped in around 4:30 p.m. to tell Eli hello and to see how he was doing. Dr. Benjamin said that Eli had a sinus infection, but that his lungs were clear. I took Eli outside on this beautiful day in May and I just wheeled him around and around letting him see the sights, the busy people, and the cars. When Eli tired I wheeled him back to his room, and after settling him in bed, I phoned Ardy. Both Eli and I spoke with Ardy and Noah.

After Eli fell asleep I did the same and I have no recollection of even getting into my chair bed. I woke up at 8 p.m. and realized the phone was ringing. It was Henry and Gavin calling to say that tornadoes were hitting Durango. After hanging up I watched the weather on the news.

At around 11:30 p.m. Matt phoned to tell me that one of the tornadoes had hit Lucy and Bob's home out in the country, and that he and Spencer had gone out there to help them collect things from what had been their home. The area and home were completely leveled. I could not be there to help so I prayed for all of them. Gavin said he had just missed the tornado on Highway 14 near Gainville, Colorado. Tornadoes are something I really hate. The tornado funnel was large and had a rope tornado with it. After destroying the trees and Bob and Lucy's home, it crossed in front of Gavin's car and kept on moving northeast.

As if the tornadoes weren't enough, the day worsened when Eli started having dry heaves, and then vomiting around midnight. His nurse gave him some Benadryl IV.

May 25, 1990 – Friday (5 Radiation Sessions Left Plus 1 For Eli's Proton Field)

Eli woke up around 2 a.m. with dry heaves and vomiting. It was too soon for more Benadryl and the doctor did not want to try anything else at this time considering Eli's sensitivity to medication. Eli next awoke at 6 a.m. again with dry heaves and emesis. This time he received Benadryl IV. Two hours later, he was vomiting again.

Eli's voice was hoarse and he said his throat hurt. The Tagamet was restarted and when Eli was feeling better I wheeled him down to radiation oncology, where he received his morning radiation treatment. My son felt better after radiation and wanted to go outside. I took him up to his 5D nursing unit and we dropped off his patient chart and I told his nurse that we would be back soon, that Eli wanted fresh outdoor air.

I wheeled Eli all over the EU complex where he absorbed everything around him. I was glad for this speck of time that let Eli experience the regular days of an ordinary little boy again. But time flew by, and not long after that, we were once again back in Eli's room.

A hospital representative caught up with Eli and me and she asked us if Eli would like to appear in more videos later today with Cynthia and Brandon of Denver Channel Four News.

Right before noon Eli was ill again. I asked his nurse for more IV Benadryl. Lucy Stone, a social worker for EU, stopped by for the first time this week. Lucy can't walk and uses a mechanical wheelchair to get around in. I spoke with Lucy regarding my plans for Eli when he was well enough to go home and she agreed with me.

After she had left, Eli required suctioning as he produced more oral secretions than he had all week. This was disappointing as Eli had been off suction and was swallowing his saliva all week long.

After assisting Eli with his suction, I went out to see his morning labs. Eli had 84 Segs plus 10 Bands times WBC of 0.9 equaled an ANC of 846. Sure enough Eli was headed back down (immune-wise) fast again. Eli's HGB was 8.3 and his platelets were 36,000.

Right before Eli went down for his second radiation treatment a video was made of Eli with Brandon of Channel Four News. This video would be part of the presentation of the Children's Miracle Network Telethon. Eli and Brandon played Monopoly in the segment filmed and afterwards Eli received a small pin to wear that represented the telethon. Eli started dry heaving and then throwing up almost as soon as we got back from his afternoon radiation treatment. I did not have enough time to drop off Eli's chart at the nurse's desk and he was throwing up right there in front of them.

Due to Eli's sore throat from radiation and his inability to drink and keep down enough liquids, Eli would restart six hours of normal saline hydration therapy. That was a good thing.

Eli would not receive radiation this weekend due to the machine malfunctioning, as well as his sore mouth and throat.

Dr. Landon stopped by right before dinner to see Eli, and was positive that Eli would get through his treatment protocol since he had shown so much progress. The doctor made no changes in Eli's orders.

After dinner, a man called from "Dream Factory." He wanted to know what Eli's wish was so they could get it going. This group provided one wish to ill children. Eli was trying to decide if he wanted to have a pedal push "Batman Car" or if he wanted to go to Disney World in Florida and see his favorite Disney character, Donald Duck. I told Eli he had plenty of time to think about what he wanted. Eli went to sleep right after we both spoke with Noah on the phone.

May 26, 1990 – Saturday – (Day 84)

Both Eli and I were up by 6 a.m. A medical student came in with Dr. Landon. Labs this morning consisted of 60 Segs plus 20 Bands times WBC of 0.5 equaling ANC of 400. Eli was dropping fast. We would start wearing masks again. Eli's HGB was 7.8 and platelets were 101,000. Dr. Landon said Eli would have a full IT, a combination of several medications used in children to prevent cancer from getting to the brain. The medications included: methotrexate, cytarabine, and hydrocortisone. This would be Eli's fourth full IT regimen. It had been found that combinations of medications are often more effective against cancer than a single medication used alone. We are keeping our fingers crossed that Eli would react positively to the meds.

Dr. Landon added that Eli would have a full medical evaluation on Friday to ascertain his progress at this point. Henry, Noah, and Gavin stopped in at 2 p.m. I did not know they were coming. I wished they would come when Eli's counts were higher, but I know the boys needed to see and talk with each other. I left twenty minutes later. I had wanted to swipe Noah and take him with me for a visit with Mom, but he and Eli were playing together so well, and having so much fun that I just couldn't separate them. I missed Noah so much, but I knew it would be better for Eli to see and play with his brother than for me to take his brother away for half an hour. That would be totally cruel to both boys in my eyes.

While out walking the halls, I decided maybe now was my chance to go to Durango and take care of a few things. So, without telling Henry, I left for Durango. Had I told him prior to leaving, he would have prevented me from doing so. After arriving in Durango, I phoned Anna to let her know I was in town and then I went out for supper with Anna as I had nothing thawed from my freezer at home. We talked a long time and then I went up to the club with her and we talked some more. I spoke with more friends than I had in a long time and the adult conversation was nice.

Later that evening, I phoned EU and I was told Eli was asleep and that his father, Noah, and Gavin, had gone back to the Ronald McDonald House.

May 27, 1990 – Sunday

I was awake by 8 a.m. so I decided to call EU. Eli's nurse, Mitch, spoke with me and we discussed Eli's plan of care. Mitch was great, but I knew Henry wouldn't want Mitch anywhere near Eli. It wasn't my problem if Henry was homophobic.

Mitch was the kind of affectionate nurse that patients warmed up to easily. He said Eli would receive packed red blood cells today. He also said Henry was not happy I had gone to Durango, but nothing ever made that man happy except for liquor and women.

I had packed summer clothing from home, which Eli and I would need in Denver, as well as a few other things that were essential. I also put together a large packet to give my lawyer in the morning. Then, I went out to the cemetery near Bow Mar for the memorial services they were having. After placing flowers on my son Joshua's grave, I spoke with my Aunt Lucy for quite some time. Lucy was a splendid and educated lady.

I went back to Durango so I could call EU and see how Eli was doing. The nurse told me that Eli was okay and shared with me his care plan for the day. I asked to be transferred into Eli's room in the hope that Eli or Noah would pick up the phone. Unfortunately, it was Henry who did. He started yelling at me so I hung up.

At 4 p.m. I tried calling into Eli's room again hoping my son would pick up the phone, but it was Henry who answered. Henry said that he and Gavin would NOT bring Noah home to me like I asked him to. I tore at my hair in frustration. It was not fair! I wanted to see Noah so badly before I headed for Denver tomorrow. I had the sinking feeling that Henry was keeping my boy from me on purpose. He also refused to let me talk with Noah or Eli over the phone, and I had to finally hang up.

I phoned Ardy after that to tell her how Eli was doing and what Henry had to say and what he was up to. After supper, I just listened to country music and let the melodies wash over me; a quiet evening and bed came early. I fell asleep crying for my boys.

May 28, 1990 – Monday (Memorial Day)

I was up by 8 a.m. and called EU right away and spoke with another one of Eli's nurses, Jackie. She told me that Eli was having a good morning and eating a banana, which he had taken a liking to for the past three weeks. Jackie said she changed Eli's Hickman catheter dressing the way I had been doing it, so Eli wouldn't react to adhesive and I was happy. She had left Eli watching *Ghostbusters* on the VCR. Jackie then transferred my call into Eli's room, but my son did not answer.

By 10 a.m. I tried calling into Eli's room again. Henry answered and he let me talk with the boys. Eli wanted me to come back. I longed for that, too, but I wanted Noah all to myself for a bit. Maybe I was being selfish. After getting off the phone, I went over to Ardy's and picked up all of Noah's papers, which she had collected for me while he was in kindergarten. I glanced at them and my heart twisted as realization dawned on me that I had already missed out on almost three months of Noah's life.

Janet, my best friend from high school, was Ardy's daughter-in-law, and lived across the street from Ardy. She came over to see me before I left. Janet had seen me at my best, my worst, happiest, and saddest; she had seen and heard my mother yell at me more than once in person and so much more. After hugs and tears, Janet left. I then went back home with Noah's school papers and to finish packing for Denver.

Aunt Lucy stopped by while I was packing and we talked for more than an hour. Noah was supposed to be back by now so I could have some quality time with him, but he was not. After Aunt Lucy left I went over to Anna's house about 2 p.m. and we chatted for a while. It was good to let out some pent-up emotion. I was back home by 3:30 p.m. and Ardy phoned me for current updates on how Eli was and when Noah would be back home. I was able to give her the updates on Eli, but I had no idea when Noah would be back. This was not in the plan. Henry was to have him to me by now. I so hated that man! He knew that anything that would hurt my boys would hurt me more and he never gave a care how badly the boys got hurt. In Henry's sick and twisted mind, he rationalized that God wanted it to be this way. This was a sharp contradiction to his beliefs because he was an atheist. I wanted both boys baptized, but Henry did not allow that to happen.

I called Eli's room after I got off the phone with Ardy. Henry answered and told me I could not have Noah. Damn him to HELL! I got off the phone and bawled. My heart was simply breaking and I had no control over events with Noah right now. I tried calling my lawyer but nobody picked up. I called EU at 6 p.m. and found out that Henry was still there. I was not sure what that man was going to do, but I had to stay here and wait for Noah since Henry promised to drop off my son when he got back. I wouldn't leave for Denver until I had seen and spoken with Noah. I must know the lies he had been told. I needed to see how my son was truly doing. I phoned back Eli's room at 6:30 and Henry answered. He said they were just leaving the hospital and that if I wanted Noah, then I should go to his place at 10 p.m. I put out some codes (for help) to Anna, Ardy, and Matt, so that if I needed assistance, if I got into trouble at Bow Mar, they could get me some back-up. Later, when Noah and I were together, I realized that even though he may be six years old now, I still could cuddle with him. We also talked for a long time even though it was late. When I saw my son's eyes closing, I knew he needed to go to bed. I tucked him in and watched him the rest of the night. I missed him so much.

May 29, 1990 – Tuesday

I hardly slept last night as many things kept running through my head. I almost did not get away from the "Lion's Den" (Henry's) last night. One of the things Henry said was that I had to bring Noah back to him today, so he could have him the rest of the week. That was pure bull. He knew I didn't want Noah around my mother if I could prevent it from happening.

Today was going to be a busy day and it had barely started. I phoned Ardy with updates, and then I tried to reach Judge Sterling. He was not having his usual morning coffee yet. I phoned EU and spoke with Marci, Eli's nurse, and with Eli. Marci and Eli knew I would be back sometime today. Eli, albeit barely a boy, understood that I must protect Noah the best I could. Eli knew this was why I went to Durango – so that I could keep Noah out of my mother's clutches this summer. Eli understood that I was trying to ensure his brother stayed cared for at Ardy's. Eli also wanted me back with him, but he told me he also wanted, in his own words, "his brother safe." It broke my heart that Eli, at age five years, already knew so much about the bad things in life. Were my boys robbed of their childhood by Henry and my mother?

Judge Sterling was still not with the guys drinking coffee yet so I called his home and finally reached him and informed him of what was going on. Then I spoke with Lawyer Shlock, and with my lawyer, Mr. Troy, about Henry's recent demands. We were going to get legal papers drawn up, signed and delivered. I called Ardy so she would be aware and be home. I called SRS for Zoe Penson so that SRS would know what we were trying to legally do for Noah. Lawyer Shlock was going to dig up an order previously signed by a judge. Finally, I woke up Noah and fed him breakfast. Afterwards Noah and I went to Shlock's law office, and then we went to the courthouse with the court order Mr. Shlock found. The Clerk of the District Court for Durango County received one copy of the court order. Another copy went to the Durango Sheriff's office, one to the SRS in Durango, and one copy to Ardy. Then I called Henry at home and I informed him that he would have to adhere to the original court order. The man went ballistic so I hung up. My mission was accomplished – Noah would have Ardy for the summer, or as long as I was at EU with Eli.

Noah and I headed over to Ardy's house and my son told me that while his father was at the Ronald McDonald House, Noah and Uncle Gavin were left with Eli. Then my son told me that "something" happened yesterday and that Gavin grabbed both of Noah's wrists and threw him into a corner of Eli's room. I looked at my son's wrists and saw that

Gavin had left bruises. I was livid. What could a little child do to cause him to be thrown into a corner? We were almost to Ardy's house and Noah simply told me that Gavin said to say "that Matt spanked him" even though Matt never did. Only God knew how much I hated Gavin right now.

At Ardy's I looked over my son for further bruising and found none. I told Noah that Mama would make things right and then I headed for EU after informing the county attorney, Ethan Reynolds, of what had happened. Ethan said something would be done about this abuse and that I had to make out a complaint at EU since it happened at EU.

I arrived at EU around 2:30 p.m. and went straight to Eli's room. I gave Eli a big hug and kissed his head. Eli smiled and I just beamed back at him. Eli informed me that he had received two radiations today. I took Eli to the eye clinic and they said Eli's right eye was getting better again, that it looked almost healed. On the way back to his room Eli told me he had not had a bath yet, so when we got back, I gave him one. I then took care of his right eye medication and the radiation burn areas on his head, neck, and chest. Eli liked having Mama back. Later in the evening Ardy phoned and she told me to check with SRS and Zoe Penson about "mental abuse" as she felt Noah was being mentally abused by his father and Gavin. Ardy hoped that something could be done in this area, too, for Noah's sake. I looked at Eli's labs. Eli had 20 Segs plus zero Bands times WBC of 0.3 equaled ANC of 60. Good thing my mask was on. I wondered if Henry and Gavin ever wore a mask. I doubted it. Eli's HGB was 9.1 and platelets were 20,000 yesterday and so Eli received a platelet transfusion today. On re-check Eli's platelet count was 46,000.

Ardy phoned at 7:30 p.m. and told me that Henry was demanding to take Noah from 9 a.m. to 9 p.m. Wednesday through Saturday. The man was nuts if he thought I would allow that to happen. I called Henry and told him his demands would not be met and hung up. I phoned Matt and told him what Noah had told me. Matt was angry and he wanted to talk with Gavin so I gave him the phone number, but Gavin was not there.

Matt spoke with Riley instead and then he called me back. Matt wanted to know how to protect everyone including himself and I told him to go and talk with the county attorney and see what he had to say. I slept restlessly.

May 30, 1990 – Wednesday

At 4:30 a.m. I was awake for the day. I caught one medication error on Eli and I let his nurse know about it. It was a simple oral liquid medication, but she had brought in one prepared for another child and it did not have Eli's name on the oral syringe. I spoke on the phone with Matt before he went to work and we discussed the "power of positive thinking" and our continued growing love for each other. Today was a busy day and Eli received both his radiation treatments so now Eli was ALL DONE with radiation!

Morning labs were 40 Segs plus zero Bands, times WBC of 0.5 equaled an ANC of 200. Eli's HGB was 8.8 and platelets were 52,000.

After Eli's early afternoon radiation treatment, we went back to his room and the Durango county attorney, Ethan Reynolds, phoned into Eli's room. Ethan asked me what I thought of a diversion on my mother for a year. I told him the diversion was fine with me if he thought it would work. Then, he told me that I must go through the proper channels here at EU and file a complaint on Gavin for what he did to Noah. I asked Eli's nurse to please have a hospital social worker and an officer from the EU police come up to Eli's room. At 4:30, I gave the EU police a full report on what Gavin did to Noah in this room with Eli watching and crying.

The officers wrote up a report and I signed it. I also gave them a report that I had written up myself and signed it as well. Afterwards, I cuddled Eli. We both want Noah safe.

Around 8 p.m. Ardy called and both Eli and I spoke with Noah. I needed to know he was safe and I could sense that even Eli needed to know his brother was okay. Children can be intuitive. I went to sleep after Eli fell asleep.

May 31, 1990 – Thursday

Eli and I were awake by 4:30 in the morning. We just seemed to have crazily erratic sleeping hours. No radiation today so we were able to go down to the eye clinic earlier. The eye doctor found Eli's tear ducts were plugged again. I felt frustrated, but I placed a bandage over Eli's GOOD eye and asked him to walk to things, he balked at doing so. Then Eli's nurse, Rita, tried to get Eli to walk to his stuffed animal, Precious, but Eli refused. So much for trying to ascertain how much Eli could see out of his bad right eye. Dr. Landon came in and said that Eli would go on IV vancomycin for his fever that had just spiked over 101. Dr. Landon wanted to stop the germs as fast as he could.

Today's labs showed 10 Segs plus zero Bands times WBC of 0.7 making for ANC of 70. *Oh, Eli honey, we are doing this again.* I knew it was a matter of time for Eli's counts to drop. Eli's HGB was 8.2 and his platelets were 53,000 and holding for now. I was glad that Eli's body was making platelets.

Zoe Penson of Durango SRS phoned to see how Eli was. Afterwards, Kristy Patterson, nurse practitioner for the pediatric hematology/oncology doctors, did a lumbar puncture (spinal tap) on Eli and placed his chemo in at the same time. The entire procedure took less than fifteen minutes with Kristy.

Eli's vancomycin was started 4 p.m. and at a slow IV rate so he would not react to the antibiotic. Eli still had a bad reaction though, this time he broke out in hives that felt hot to the touch.

My son was given additional IV Benadryl through new IV tubing as the one with the vancomycin was removed so that Eli did not receive more of it. It was then decided to start a new antibiotic in the morning for Eli's staph infection.

Henry called at 9 p.m. and I let him know that Eli was now allergic to vancomycin. I doubt he even understood what I said. I then told him I was going to sleep and hung up on him. Ardy phoned thirty minutes later to tell me that "Noah was sick with a cold, and that he said he had played all day long with his cousin Ava and that he only went to Daddy's house to take a shower and clean up." Then Noah got on the phone and he told me that "Daddy wanted him back home." I told my son not to worry about things and that it would all work out okay. In my effort to reassure him, I told my son over and over how much I loved him.

But as I put the phone back to its cradle, I knew that saying I love you wasn't the same as being there to protect him, and I fell asleep crying softly to myself, wishing that my two boys and I could be together again—loved, painless, and free.

Chapter Sixteen

June 1990

June 1, 1990 – Friday

I woke up just a little after midnight and Eli was asleep. At about 12:30 a.m. Matt phoned and we talked for about two hours. I was mostly worried about my mother causing further grief to the children. The future was bleak in that area, and only time would tell what Mother, Eli, and I would do back in Durango.

Afterwards, I listened to soft music on the television on low volume and read a romance novel I had picked up weeks ago, so I had something to occupy my time when Eli was asleep.

By 2:30 a.m., Eli woke up and asked for something to eat. I gave him watermelon and apple juice. Then he fell back to sleep. I watched him as he slept, his chest rising and falling slowly. He didn't stir and when I was certain he was fast asleep, I took a shower and applied my makeup.

When I was finished, I walked over to my son and grazed a hand over his forehead and that was the moment I panicked. His skin felt hot to the touch. I kept pressing the nurse call button, and she came rushing in to check Eli's temperature, which was 39.7C or 103.4 F.

I gave Eli some liquid oral Tylenol – this was the second time Eli had taken the Tylenol this way. I guess he was tired of all the Tylenol suppositories, and I was just so scared for Eli for he had never had a temperature this high before.

Kristy Patterson, nurse of Dr. Landon, who gave Eli's last IT chemo, came in later, too. She informed me that Eli's spinal fluid was clean of cancer cells.

Frances, another nurse with a home health agency, called from Durango to assist me in the preparation for Eli's return home. We discussed home care, the essentials on how to care for Eli when outside the hospital premises. Basically, I would still do all the things I already do for my son including adding multiple vitamins and a couple more medications to each bag of TPN before giving it to Eli. I had done this several times so the nurses could chart my efficiency and competency. Eli would require lab work to be done and I already drew his labs from his Hickman so there was no change there. We just needed a home health agency in place so that I would not be falsely accused of not caring for Eli correctly.

I took Eli down for another MRI of his head and neck. Before, I had to sit near his head during the MRI talking to him, keeping him from moving so that good films could be obtained. This was preferable to giving Eli medication to make him sleepy and then the possibility of Eli having an adverse reaction. Eli's ANC was only 48 today and his HGB was 7.7 so I was sure packed red blood cells would be given soon. Regardless, Eli was still making platelets at this point.

I took him down for a CT scan of his chest at 2 p.m. and when we got back to his room I gave him leucovorin calcium, which was a derivative of folic acid. Eli received it since he was given methotrexate (MTX TIT) chemo during his spinal tap.

For Eli, leucovorin calcium meant rescuing the gastrointestinal lining and bone marrow cells from MTX toxicity. Most of the complications and side effects of methotrexate could be either prevented or treated by using leucovorin calcium, which is usually given twenty-four hours after methotrexate. Leucovorin calcium was well tolerated and had almost no side effects of its own, but this medication must be given under the supervision of a medical oncologist.

At around 3:30 p.m., I called Cate, with the Children's Telethon, and she gave me the times that Eli would be on TV. Eli's time slots were 11:40 to midnight tonight, 12:40 to 1:00 a.m. Saturday night, and then on

Sunday Eli had two: 10:40 a.m. to 11:00 a.m. and 3:30 p.m. to 4:00 p.m. Hopefully, Eli helped to make an impact on the plight of children suffering from horrible diseases.

Henry called after I got off the phone with Cate. I hung up on him as soon as he started with his mind games, blaming me for Eli's cancer, God is getting back at you for leaving me, etcetera. That man didn't even believe there was a God, and here he was throwing his accusations to my face.

Two more antibiotics were started this afternoon so that now Eli was on three different antibiotics for the presumed staph infection in his sinuses. My son would now receive tobramycin for the second time, and clindamycin phosphate had been added.

Ardy called at around 9:30 p.m. and she told me that Henry brought Noah back to her this evening. Henry has had him every day this week. He brought Noah back with sopping wet feet, and Henry informed Ardy that Noah had a temperature of "101.6" and that Noah had taken a nap." Henry never took him to the doctor so I told Ardy that Noah was to see the doctor tomorrow no matter what Henry said. Noah had a cough, sore throat, headache, earache and fever. Henry had never taken either child to the doctor – not even once their whole lives thus far. Henry could just shove it. Looking back, I remember Noah had a cough Tuesday morning this week, although he did wear a mask to protect Eli.

Matt phoned me around midnight and we talked for over an hour. It was a good call and we talked of dreams we both had regarding life in the future and how it would impact us. We discussed what we wanted for the children and what we wanted out of life in general.

June 2, 1990 – Saturday

Eli was up for three hours during the night last night. Eli ate little of his breakfast, but I knew that would happen given his fever from yesterday and how he was feeling. Eli's ANC today was only 80 and his HGB was 7.4. Platelets were okay still. I know they would transfuse packed red blood cells to Eli soon.

At noon and without warning, Gavin showed up to Eli's room. I asked Gavin if he had been around Noah and he did not say anything. Then I asked Gavin if he was going to answer me and he shook his head. I informed Gavin that I did not want Noah's germs brought to Eli because Eli had no means of fighting the infection.

Eli was so neutropenic right now. Gavin left and went to the nurse's desk and he must have asked them about Eli being susceptible to germs as he came in next wearing a mask. It was the first time for Gavin to wear a mask. Maybe he was starting to see that I had been telling the truth to everyone, that this must be done to protect Eli.

I phoned Ardy about thirty minutes later and found out that Dr. Owens put Noah on an antibiotic, Ceclor, as well as a generic form of Benylin cough syrup and expectorant for children. Ardy said she had asked Henry if he would take Noah to the doctor, and he had told her he would see if he could. Then he called Ardy back to say he could not, and so Ardy took Noah to see the doctor.

I had no more expectations from my boy's father, but time and again, he kept on reminding me how irresponsible he was; how badly he was wired to be a father.

Early in the afternoon, I put a patch on Eli's good eye, his left eye, just like on Thursday and asked Eli to look for different people and objects and then walk to each item when he saw them. Eli was able to see and do this EIGHT times from his bad right eye. His optic nerve must be better. Afterwards I rewarded Eli with a new toy.

Gavin popped back in around 6 p.m. and he put on a mask before entering Eli's room. Gavin did not say one word to Eli or me. Eli's phone rang with Henry on the line. It seemed like it took him forever to get off the phone and put SICK Noah to bed. He really didn't have his priorities in the right place. Gavin finally left an hour and a half later, still not saying one word.

Ardy called me later in the evening and said she had seen Henry's trailer for the first time today. Ardy said it was clean all decked out with new furniture, toys, pictures everywhere and religious statues here and there – for a man who was an atheist! Matt called later in the evening and I updated him on the day's events, Eli, and then we were able to talk about the two of us. I was drawing incredible strength from Matt. This left me wondering what I would do without the support of Ardy, Matt, my friends and some of my family.

June 3, 1990 – Sunday

This morning, I noticed Eli's right ear had bled some during the night while we were sleeping, and I informed Eli's nurse, Lisa, of my findings. Lisa told me I talked during my sleep last night. She added that she didn't really know what I said as the words were mumbled. Maybe that was a good thing.

After I did Eli's regular routine this morning, I took him to the exam room on 5D where procedures were done to have his ears examined. Each spinal tap had been done in this room so Eli was not fond of going into this area. Marci, RN, assistant head nurse, and the residents did check Eli's ear. While they were inspecting his right ear, they told me that the report was back on Eli's chest CT scan, still showing two spots. We were looking at a biopsy this week, I think. Right before lunch, I took Eli back to have his right ear irrigated. A "lot" of wax came out, and in a piece of that wax was the tube, which had been put in his ear back in Silverthorne months ago. Apparently, the tube never stayed in his ear during that surgery and the wax just built up around the tube. Eli's eardrum appeared intact and no bleeding was noted. No signs of infection or perforation were noted either, and his left ear still had the tube intact and in place. No differential was done on Eli's complete blood count this morning, so I wasn't able to figure his ANC, but with WBC of 1.0, I knew it was low. HGB was 7.8 so a blood transfusion will happen soon. Eli's platelets were hanging at 87,000 so no transfusion there as yet.

Right before noon, Eli's name was announced on television on the Children's Telethon with a $5 pledge, and Eli had part of the segment devoted to him. Eli was just tickled and loved seeing himself on television. He couldn't stop grinning and neither could I to see him that happy to see himself on TV. We watched *Spider Man* using the VCR this afternoon, and I had thought things were rather quiet for once. In the evening, Henry phoned twice but not to speak with Eli. He just wanted to yell at me and to try and find out what I had planned down the road. I hung up on him twice. I was not sure if he wanted to know what I had told my lawyer lately, or if I had reported him to the SRS for not taking Noah to the doctor. I decided since I wasn't sure what his problem was, I would just let him stew instead. After Eli had gone to sleep, Matt called me and we spoke for an hour or so. A more than perfect way to up the day even just a bit.

June 4, 1990 – Monday

I awoke as usual around 6 a.m. and by 8 a.m. I had all of Eli's cares completed. After taking Eli off his TPN we just watched TV and waited for the doctors to get to Eli's room. I wanted to hear Dr. Landon's thoughts on the CT scan of Eli's chest and also the most recent MRI. Dr. Landon changed Eli's TPN mixture to incorporate more lipids for healthier growth.

By mid-morning I took Eli to feed the frogs for the last time. They were in the schoolroom and the teacher, Kristy Davis, would take them home with her for the summer. While there Eli painted a picture and I would be framing it later for my wall. Right before lunch time, Dr. Landon and the Blue Team came to Eli's room. Eli now had both an ENT and Dental consults. There might be more consults before the day ends. Kristy Patterson came by to do discharge planning. Eli only took bites and sips for lunch, but I was happy to see him eating anything and to be able to savor the food in his mouth as I knew how much my son enjoyed the sheer taste of food.

At 8 p.m. Eli had his ENT consult. We would not replace the tube in Eli's right ear at this time. Eli's hearing would be checked tomorrow and he was started on new ear drops to his right ear four times daily. Eli and I both talked with Ardy and Noah, and Eli also talked with other children in Ardy's care that he knew. This was a first for Eli. It was like he was getting back to a more normal life, and I was so happy to see this.

After Eli fell asleep Matt phoned and we had another long talk. I updated Matt on today's events and Matt and I prayed together for Eli. I loved this man more and more each day and he loved me back. Our love kept blossoming. It occurred to me, as I lay huddled in the chair bed that I looked forward to each phone call I would share with Matt. It was like my own dose of medicine, something to rejuvenate me for the long day I had to face tomorrow.

June 5, 1990 – Tuesday

Eli woke up ill and sick to his stomach. After he was cleaned up he vomited again an hour later. I had no recourse but to clean up once more. It was probably the antibiotic Bactrim that was doing this to him. Neither Eli nor I ever got along well with sulfonamide antibiotics. Eli took after me in this regard. I informed Dr. Landon about it, he immediately changed it, and things became better.

By midmorning I took Eli to the eye clinic and found out that Eli's right eye was not getting any worse.

Ardy phoned around 11 a.m. to tell me that Henry picked up Noah and that he took him over to the SRS to speak with Zoe Penson. I think this man made a mistake, but I wouldn't wait to hear from Zoe. I wasn't the least bit concerned about what Henry told Zoe, as I knew that the social workers I worked with would vouch for my character.

Dr. Landon stopped by about noon and said Eli's MRI showed no changes. He also said that Eli had received all the radiation he could have.

In the afternoon, I took Eli to the dentist who thought he could save the one bothersome tooth. Eli received diligent dental care from me, but he had been limited in using a toothbrush due to his tender mouth, which was riddled with sores from chemo and radiation. No amount of soft tipped tooth sponges and toothpaste could protect the enamel of my boy's teeth from the effects of chemo, radiation, and all the throwing up. The best that could be done now was to have Eli's tooth fixed with sealant just like what I had always done for both boys each year.

After lunch I spoke with Anna on the phone and she told me that she had no idea what Henry was up to now. I called Ardy and she had not heard anything back from the SRS. Later on, Ardy called and it had been decided, per my request and the request of Zoe Penson, that Noah needed counseling. So many people had been lying to my son and treating him badly and I prayed he would open up during counseling.

Afterwards I was able to speak with Noah. He told me that he was happy to be staying with Ardy again, but sad that Eli was asleep and could not talk to him. Then Noah giggled and told me about the babies Ardy cared for. He thought it was funny to watch them crawling and scooting around.

At around 10 p.m., Matt called me and we talked for at least an hour. He agreed that it was best for Noah to receive counseling. Matt was so caring. I was blessed to have him in my life.

June 6, 1990 – Wednesday

I woke up for no reason at 4 a.m. Eli was okay. I don't know why I woke up, but I didn't go back to sleep until 6 a.m. After doing Eli's usual morning cares, I found out Eli would receive packed red cells today as his HGB was 7.2.

Eli's labs showed an ANC of 3999. Platelets were hanging at 65,000. By midmorning I spoke with Mr. Troy, who informed me that we could not get the divorce going unless I wanted to give up my boys and I sure didn't want to do that! Henry's lawyer wanted a deposition on Friday the twenty-second. Troy and I decided that would not be a problem as we were going to ask for the same with Henry. I could answer any question thrown my way just fine, in the same manner that I knew Henry would hang himself on many questions.

Troy said I was also required to obtain something from Horizons Mental Health this coming Monday, stating that Henry had not contacted them nor made an appointment for an evaluation. I could do my evaluation and have nothing to hide, but he sure couldn't do his part.

Packed red blood cells were running in by noon and Eli did well with the transfusion. At dinner time, Lynn Parsons, nurse of Dr. Landon's group, delivered medication master sheets to me for my use both here at the hospital and for use at home with Eli.

When Dr. Landon came in, we talked for about thirty minutes. The kind doctor was optimistic and felt that all was not lost regarding the most recent MRI results and there was a lot to hope for.

Ryan, another cancer patient in 5D, and Dina, his mom, stopped by Eli's door. Dina said she had some important things to tell me and that she would do so tomorrow as it was getting so late in the evening. I said okay although I had no idea what she wanted to talk about.

Eli fell asleep about 9 p.m. Matt phoned an hour later and we talked for about an hour. Matt thought I should be optimistic like Dr. Landon was. I fell asleep by midnight in my chair bed.

June 7, 1990 – Thursday

This morning was like most mornings except that Eli seemed to have gained a better appetite. He drank a full four ounces of apple juice and ate some Fruity Pebbles breakfast cereal, which was the favorite of my two boys. They would have gladly had it for breakfast, lunch, and dinner if I let them. That's how much they loved the stuff. As a mother though, I made sure they also had my fine servings of pork chops, fried chicken, pot roast, meat loaf, bacon, hash browns, homemade pies, and much more. I always did my best at making sure my boys had plenty of juice and milk to drink as they loved juice and chocolate milk.

Seeing what Eli ate this morning gave me renewed faith that he would be okay. And to prove me right, his HGB was 9.2 this morning and that was certainly an improvement. His platelets were still hanging at 70,000 and no differential was run as his WBC was 7.8 so obviously Eli's immune system was holding its own right now.

Ardy called me around 10 a.m. and told me that Henry wouldn't be here this Friday night or Saturday morning. So, Henry wouldn't be visiting his son, nor would Eli and Noah have a chance to play together. Ardy also told me that Henry picked up Noah about 8:30 this morning, which made me afraid knowing all too well that Henry would be messing with Noah's head and my mother most probably would, too. I must arrange more counseling for Noah because of this

Around 1 p.m. Eli's VAC (chemo) was completed. He received one IV bag of cyclophosphamide, and both his vincristine and dactinomycin were infused using large syringes.

Eli was on a test; a controlled study of different central nervous system depressant medications, medication combinations, and placebo interchange. I prayed something positive would come out of it

At around two in the afternoon, I was able to chat with Dina. I immediately liked her as she was an amazing woman and did cares for her son, Ryan, just like I did for Eli. Dina told me that over at the Ronald McDonald House, Gavin told her many things about me and my boys that she knew weren't true, as she witnessed how I cared for Eli. She was concerned about some occurrences over at the Ronald McDonald House, too, she confessed to me. She said that Gavin probably needed professional counseling for anger management. She had seen how angry he could get, and conversely, how easily he could fall into sobs. Dina had witnessed much so I told her I had to tell my lawyer and the EU police, and she agreed.

After leaving a message with my lawyer, I let the charge nurse, Janell, know I wanted the EU police as soon as two of them were free to come up here and take down reports.

On the other hand, my sister Riley called and informed me that she went to the police station and filed charges on Matt as he had told her to back off or else; and she took that as a threat. Officer Montrose said that it was illegal to make threats on the phone and that Matt would need to deny the threats so he wouldn't be in trouble.

Riley wanted to know why I talked in riddles to her on the phone, although to me it was downright obvious. Riley was out for number one and the purse string my mother controlled. I didn't believe one word of what Riley ever said to me and I would not give her more than riddles since she wanted to play dirty.

Right before dinner the EU police showed up and they spoke with Dina and me and took down reports. Dina's testimony was the best, as she heard and saw the bad things that went on at the Ronald McDonald House, while mine may be categorized as simply hearsay from Dina.

After everyone had left, Eli woke up sick to his stomach and he threw up once and then I cleaned him up. I know full well that Henry would never do this for either Eli or Noah. It simply was not in him to do these cares for anyone.

After Eli fell asleep, I phoned Matt with updates on everything and then I got off the phone when Eli woke again throwing up. This time Eli threw up repetitiously and it was horrible. I cried inside to see my son so sick.

Eli fell back to sleep and next awoke two hours later throwing up badly again. I called Kristy Patterson, Dr. Landon's nurse practitioner, and she ordered Thorazine be given to Eli and he received IV Thorazine immediately.

Eli woke up again about one hour later suffering from the same fit. When he was done, I cleaned him up and changed his bed linens like before. I placed a cool cloth on his forehead and rolled him on his side hoping that he would not aspirate emesis. Then he fell asleep.

Ardy called an hour later to tell me that Henry had returned Noah earlier in the evening. I breathed a sigh of relief. I talked with Noah and he told me that he still felt sick. I told him I loved him and that we would have the doctor order medicine to make him feel better. I then told Ardy I wanted a return doctor appointment made for Noah and she said she would do so in the morning.

By 11 p.m., I was so deeply asleep.

June 8, 1990 – Friday

At 1 a.m. Eli refused to take his oral Decadron and then he fell back asleep and so did I, only to wake up as usual around 6 a.m.

After Eli's cares and needs were met, he was placed on sedation this time and then chemo was initiated. Dee Hardy came in while Eli was receiving chemo, and we did some serious discharge planning. At one point, Henry called wanting proof that I would be at Horizons Mental Health, in Harper, at 10 a.m. on Monday. Dee told him, yes, that was the plan. Henry went livid. I told him to knock off the crap, which only incensed him further, so I hung up on him.

My lawyer phoned at noon and said he was going to call Dina after lunch. Dr. Landon came in around noon and pushed Eli's vincristine slow

IV himself, while we talked about discharge for my son. Dr. Landon was still optimistic and he proved his concern for his patients and their family by taking the time to push the vincristine in slowly and talking with the family.

New England Critical Care came right after lunch and we went over the use of the IV pump Eli would have at home. I was fully competent in the usage of the pump and the tubing, and how to do Eli's TPN and hydration fluids. After they left, Homecare USA came in to show me the set up for Eli's suction pump and the correct usage. I was competent in this as well. Eli was still sedated so I left and went to Cancer Action for the supplies Eli would need for home care. My car looked full and I was not sure how much more would fit in. I went back to Eli's room after parking and I was surprised to see Eli was retaining fluid. He was third spacing fluid more than he had in the past. Third spacing fluid is when fluid leaves the blood vessels and seeps into the tissue causing swelling. Eli's body was swelling and puffy looking. After weighing him, we found out Eli had retained four pounds, six and a half ounces of fluid. Dr. Landon was notified right away even though Eli's electrolytes were stable.

Eli's nurse and I kept a close watch on Eli. We wanted to make sure the fluid didn't go to his lungs. We also decreased the IV rate. Eli voided 1 oz. by 8 p.m.

Then, Eli voided a tiny bit more thirty minutes later. They decided to run Eli's TPN at 50 ml per hour. Eli fell back to sleep, so I napped while keeping an eye on Eli. Matt called around 10 p.m. and I told him what was going on with Eli, and also what Officer Montrose of the Durango Police had to say. I was listening to the news and found out that Donald Duck, one of Eli's favorite stuffed animals, had raised $5,000 for Dream Factory in a rally.

June 9, 1990 – Saturday

Eli was wide awake at 4 a.m. and so we played, but we had to be quiet as the other children were sleeping. Eli fell back asleep at 6 a.m., which was my normal waking time.

By 8:00 a.m., Eli woke up and I attended to his morning cares. Eli voided pretty good this morning and he was not as edematous as yesterday, which was great. I thought he may receive a small dose of IV Lasix before the day was out. With his TPN running at 50 ml. per hour, Eli was nowhere close to having received it all, but Dr. Landon came in at 10 a.m. and said to stop it, so I did just that and flushed Eli off. Eli ended up receiving about one half the bag of TPN.

In reviewing Eli's morning labs, I figured his ANC was a good 2436 although he was now starting to trend downward. HGB was 8.7 and platelets were good at 76,000 and holding. Eli was watching TV and I told him I needed to do more laundry down the hall where the washer and dryer were kept for family use. It did not take me long before I was back again with Eli, who was having a great time watching *Superman* on the VCR.

Dr. Landon wanted Eli's normal saline hydration fluids removed as well, so we did that. Eli ended up napping until about 6:30 p.m. and I felt edgy like something was going to happen, but I just didn't know what it was going to be. Needless to say, I was not able to nap when Eli was napping. Eli voided really good when he woke up. That excess fluid was coming off him and I was so glad.

Henry and Gavin showed up to Eli's room at about 8 p.m. without warning. They walked into the room and had the nerve to *ask me for money as they did not have much*. That was really rather ludicrous of them as they knew I was here with Eli all the time and that I could not work until I got Eli back home. They left about an hour later and I was thankful. Matt called me around 10:30 and we talked for an hour at least before I fell asleep.

June 10, 1990 – Sunday

I woke up at 4 a.m. again and Eli was sleeping so I was not sure why I woke up. My body clock was so messed up these last few months. I would never take back my time with Eli here for anything. My boys were my world and I would do all I could for them.

Eli awoke around 8 a.m. and I did his usual cares. Eli refused break-fast this morning and I did not push him on this as I trusted Eli on knowing when he could and couldn't eat. I was looking at the antibiotic that Eli's nurse, Mitch, had started half an hour ago and I noted that Eli was receiving IV Thorazine by mistake. Half the bag was already infused, and not only that, but the bag was also outdated more than eight hours. I stopped the infusion immediately and called Mitch into Eli's room. Mitch removed the tubing and the remainder of the IV Thorazine, and when he came back in, he had new tubing and the antibiotic, clindamycin, Eli was supposed to receive.

I still liked Mitch a lot as he was so good to Eli, and I knew Mitch was torn up inside on this medication error. Errors happened on busy nursing units, more dangerous for newborns, infants, children and the elderly. I was thankful that it was Thorazine and not something worse. I was upset that this happened, but I calmed down real fast when I realized how much worse it really could have been. The wrong medication could have killed Eli.

Around 10:30 this morning Henry and Gavin showed up. Henry started bitching at me for almost an hour, and I was not able to leave as Gavin had the doorway blocked. I was unable to call out for a nurse or help as Henry controlled the phone and call button. I just had to listen to them complain about every little thing. At this point I was glad Eli had received the Thorazine by mistake and that he slept through all this commotion. They both hustled me to give them money as though I had any. Then Gavin jumped down my throat, and said it was all an act over at the Ronald McDonald House for Dina and that nothing bad was meant by it at all.

So that was what the fuss was about. But Gavin did not fool me one bit! Dina and I both knew what he did and what he said. It was his problem if the police or SRS were coming down hard on him. Henry and Gavin came here because they knew I had been at Horizons Mental Health in Harper tomorrow morning. At 2 p.m. Henry wanted me to sign a piece of paper stating when I would be back, what I was going to do, who I was going to see, and when I would be picking up Noah; and a whole lot more crap.

Henry did this in front of the assistant head nurse at the nurse's desk. The man was being a DICTATOR, but of course, he never was able to get me to sign a paper for him. I just laughed at how ridiculous his demands were.

In the afternoon, Eli and I played Mario Bros on his Nintendo for almost an hour, and then he was tired again so I told him I had to go to Durango, but that I would be back as soon as I could. I left for Durango at 5 p.m. and arrived home around 8:45 p.m. I called Ardy and talked with her and Noah and told them I would be over as soon as I made a complaint at the Sheriff's office on Henry and Gavin. It took until 10 p.m. for them to see me as the officers were busy in other areas. I still picked up Noah though and we went to bed as soon as we reached home.

June 11, 1990 – Monday

I was up by 6 a.m. and after eating, Noah and I left for Horizons. We arrived around 9:30 a.m. and I signed all the releases needed for my lawyer and for court. After our appointments and testing, I took Noah out for lunch in Harper and then we went back to Durango. We arrived at around 2 p.m. and Noah changed into his swim trunks and I brought him to the pool. Then we had a supper break, after which, I brought Noah back to the pool.

We both missed Eli as it was always the three of us at the pool and things were just not quite right without Eli. After the pool closed, we went back home and I did laundry and Noah had his bath. He was tired from all the swimming and my son fell asleep in no time. I spoke with Matt on the phone and he reported that he had rented a house in Kiowa and had given his thirty-day notice to the owners of his house in Durango. Durango and Kiowa were five miles apart. Then I fell asleep.

June 12, 1990 – Tuesday

I was up by 6 a.m. and packed with clean clothes for Denver. If Eli had been here it would have been an almost normal morning. After calling

EU and finding out how Eli was, I prepared for court and the myriad of things I had to do today. I knew Mother would have Ella in court and poor Ella would feel retribution from my mother if she did not say just what my mother wanted her to say. It was a sad situation all around.

Ella was subject to my mother's abuse every day. After stopping by the SRS office and speaking with Zoe Penson about court today, I went to pay my electric bill and then on to my lawyer's office. Things went well overall with court at 1:30 with my mother, and basically all was still on hold for now and my protection order on her remained. The judge knew Noah and I did our mental evaluations yesterday in Harper, as did my lawyer, of course, and the SRS and Zoe Penson; then I went over to Ardy's house and left for EU from there.

Today was another busy day. I was in Eli's room at EU by 6:30 p.m. and found Henry with Eli. He started in on me right away so he must have spoken with my mother and found out she didn't get her way all the time. Eli was awake and Henry was yelling at me and then after upsetting me he had the nerve to take four or five photos of me trying to hide my face. Then Henry made threats on Matt saying *I'm going to get him. I'm going to get the bastard.*

Those words would get Henry in more trouble and I couldn't care less except that his behavior was affecting Eli. After Henry left, things became quiet and I played Nintendo with Eli. We had a rather normal evening here at EU afterward. When my son became sleepy I checked him for urine. He was dry so I let him sleep. I had done so much running around today getting things done, preparing for court, preparing for Eli to come home, etc. that I fell asleep as soon as my body hit the chair bed. If Matt had called, I never heard the ring. Life was muted for me until the following morning.

June 13, 1990 – Wednesday

I was up at 6 a.m. and both Eli and I had our usual morning routines. During Eli's bath, I found a yeast infection in his groin. Worse, I found open areas, two of them, on his coccyx. These were both Stage II bed-sores and preventable. Henry didn't have Eli sleep on his side, just his back, and if his bed was raised Henry didn't get the fact of shearing force on the skin caused bedsores, or he didn't care. When I was not here the nurses weren't doing their jobs, either, in preventing bedsores. I was rather ticked off about this as they knew Eli was susceptible to skin breakdown and infections. I had Eli's nurse come in and see the yeast and the bedsores. Skin treatment orders for Eli's coccyx were done and some nystatin was ordered for the yeast infection.

After looking at Eli's labs I saw his ANC was 736, platelets were 61,000 and his HGB was 8.1. Both Henry and Gavin arrived and they were just nit-picking everything. I was not sure why they must be this way. I knew, though, that I couldn't let them know that Eli was going home or they would cause trouble and prevent that from happening. Everything was planned and set up perfectly. Arrangements were made through Dee Hardy for Eli to go home tomorrow. I was ecstatic for Eli, and Eli was thrilled to say the least. He wore a big grin knowing he would go home tomorrow.

Dr. Landon came in at 5 p.m. and more arrangements were made for Eli's discharge. Then I found out that about one-hour earlier Henry had heard about the plans to take Eli home, and all the arrangements, which were made in Durango and Denver. Henry took Gavin with him straight down to administration for yet another visit with them, trying to cause enough trouble to prevent Eli from going home. All I could do now was to wait and see what happened as far as Eli's discharge.

Dr. Mason pushed in Eli's IV vincristine and we chatted some more about Eli's condition. Henry popped inside Eli's room at about 8 p.m. and loudly stated that he was of the opinion Eli shouldn't be going home.

Upon hearing this, Eli cried. I comforted Eli as much as I could, as Henry left right after voicing his opinion. That bastard intentionally hurt Eli by what he just said, and then left. He was such a cruel person. I did not think Eli would go home now. The social workers would see Henry as a threat to Eli and they would make him stay in the hospital for safety reasons.

Ardy phoned close to 9 p.m. and I talked with her and Noah. Eli was already asleep so I just crashed again as I felt worn out from all the struggles.

June 14, 1990 – Thursday

I woke at 5 a.m. this morning and Eli had slept all night long. I had all of Eli's cares completed by 8 a.m. and Henry arrived thirty minutes later. I could just tell by his demeanor and the look on his face that he was intent on causing trouble and my heart sank.

The EU social workers came in and a discussion was held while Eli was receiving some packed red cells before going home. Social Services deemed it was not safe for Eli to go home due to Henry; they said they could not ensure Eli's safety therefore they would not allow Eli to go home. After the hospital staff left Eli's room, Henry just looked at me and sneered, then he walked out of the room leaving both Eli and I crying. I held my son in my chair bed and just soothed him the best I could, and then when Eli quieted down, I phoned Ardy and we both spoke with her and Noah. Then I called my lawyer to let him know what had happened.

After touching up my makeup, I took Eli down to the gift shop to pick out a couple toys. I did not have the heart to leave Eli to go to my car and retrieve some of the items I had packed earlier, so Eli chose two new toys and we went back to his room. Eli and I were both depressed at not leaving, but he played and watched movies until he was tired and sleepy. I was literally cursing Henry before I fell asleep.

June 15, 1990 – Friday

At around 1 a.m., I woke up with a start. The fire alarm was going off on 5D and a code red was being called overhead. The code red was on 3D unit and it was an intentionally set fire. I took Eli off his TPN as I knew we could not take the IV pump down the stairs when evacuating, should we need to do so, and the nurses were doing the same with the other children on the unit. We were all prepared to evacuate to the South and 5F unit (adolescent unit), and then to go down the stairs at the southernmost stairwell when at about 2:30 a.m., it was announced that it was all clear.

I put Eli back to bed as he was so tired and he fell asleep before I even had his TPN running again. Between the fire fighters, the EU police and staff, the fire was put out pretty fast and the area was secured, but much had to be done for safety. I was not sure what had happened, but safety was important. So, I was not too upset for having to be up for an hour and half waiting. I knew if danger was coming our way, we would have been evacuated.

I was up again at 5 a.m. and Eli was up at his usual time, and I did all of his cares. At around 9 a.m., Social Services came into Eli's room and they said that Eli could have things worked out. I was not holding my breath on that one, nor would I tell that to Eli if it was prevented yet again. I called both my lawyer and Dr. Landon and each stated they would do all they could so Eli could go home. We would see.

Henry called into Eli's room three times this morning and I had to hang up on him each time. It got bad when Eli saw me upset and he knew his father was on the phone. Eli told me, his mother, to just hang up on him. At age five years, he understood the meanness and sadness in the world, in a way that most five-year-olds would never know. This was not the first time Eli had told me to hang up on his father, and I feared it would not be the last time, either.

At 3 p.m., I went down the hall to do laundry while Henry was in a meeting with New England Critical Care to learn the IV Pump and I was told to leave the room. No problem as I did not want to see nor hear Henry's failures in all of this. I was back in Eli's room by 4:30 p.m. and only Eli was there. Julie, a nurse I chatted with on occasion from 5F, came by and asked me to go down to dinner with her. Henry returned and looked at both of us and snickered.

This was the first time I had ever gone to have a meal in the cafeteria with any staff person, and I went as Henry still had one hour of his time left with Eli. I was back by 8 p.m. and Henry had already left. I was sure though, that he went down to the cafeteria and took pictures of Julie and myself for whatever devious purpose he could think of. Dr. Harmon, together with Dr. Landon's blue team, stopped by Eli's room as I was putting Eli to bed for the night. He waited and then we quietly talked as Eli fell asleep. I asked Dr. Harmon what chances both my boys had of literally surviving their father. Dr. Harmon said, "Not good at all. He is a sociopath." Then he left the room. This was not a comfort, but I had asked for this answer.

I felt horrible. I was selfish; I wanted my babies, my boys, so badly. It was devastating to see them hurt. My selfishness in wanting children only gave them pain in every conceivable way.

Matt called later and we talked about all that had happened and what Dr. Harmon had to say. Matt was positive on the phone, and I did believe Matt would do what it takes to ensure the safety of my boys and myself. Matt was my solid rock to lean on, and I loved him so much.

June 16, 1990 – Saturday

I was up at 6 a.m. like usual. Eli was sick to his stomach and had been ill during the night as well. I had cleaned him, changed his bedding, and positioned him on alternating sides so that his coccyx could start healing.

Henry showed up at 12:50 p.m. today during my appointed time with Eli. I left for a few minutes so he could see Eli and then went back to Eli's room. Gavin showed up after I arrived and finally both he and Henry left.

In the middle of the afternoon, Henry showed up at Eli's room with his father, Carter, and his sister. They were told they had to leave as my time with Eli was until 4 p.m.

At 4 p.m., they all came back to Eli's room. Due to Eli's ANC being so low, I asked for temperature checks on everyone, including me. Eli's ANC was 120 and Eli already had a temperature of 37.8 C or 100.04 F with conversion. I requested the temperatures taken as two of them had been on a plane in a closed and confined space and could have come in contact with sick people. Carter, Grace, and I were afebrile (no fever)–no temperatures, but Henry had a temperature of 37.8! Henry did not want to wear a mask so I told Eli's nurse and she got a doctor involved. It came down to the fact that both Eli and Henry were told by the doctor to wear a mask, and Henry was quite livid with me over his wearing a mask. Did this man want Eli sicker? Henry was such an jerk. I then left the room as it was his time with Eli. On my way out, and for the eighth day in a row, Henry had taunted me by calling me a "whore dog." Neither Carter nor Grace cared that Henry was treating me in this fashion.

I was back at 8 p.m. and prepared Eli for bed. I was so tired I just fell asleep really fast.

June 17, 1990 – Sunday

I was up at 6 a.m. and it was a usual morning where I did all of Eli's cares. By this time, most of his baths were bed baths, which allowed me to see his skin easier and monitor for any bed sores or rashes.

Eli had two large loose stools after I did his cares, and I thought they were IV antibiotic related. After being cleaned up both times, he then had four large liquid stools before 10 a.m.

Henry and Gavin showed up then, so I left to get shampoo and other assortments I needed from the store. Eli's ANC was 30 this morning and I prayed Henry wore a mask. I was back to 5D nurse's station by 11:15 a.m. and I informed Eli's nurse I would return again at noon for my time with my son.

At noon, I was at Eli's door and Henry left. Eli and I played together, and while doing this, I was sorting out information inside my head for when Eli would be home with me. At 2 p.m., Eli was moved to a new room, 5091. I called Ardy to let her know the room number and Noah answered the phone. Both Eli and I spoke with Noah and Ardy. Right before 5 p.m., Henry and Gavin arrived and they stated to me that they wanted to leave around 6 or 7 p.m. this evening, so I left and then returned back to Eli's room at 7 p.m. Henry then ordered me in a loud voice to not come back until 8 p.m., which was ridiculous considering what he asked of me earlier. Then, Henry started calling me a "whore dog" again. Thankfully, Eli was asleep and did not hear what Henry said.

I ignored Henry, and after he left, I settled down in my chair bed and tried to sleep.

June 18, 1990 – Monday

Today, Eli's tobramycin antibiotic was discontinued. By midmorning, Jimmy from maintenance had a clown come in to see Eli, and Eli was delighted. Jimmy was a nice old man.

Dr. Landon was here before lunch and said that he was also stopping the Fortaz antibiotic and we would just have Eli on clindamycin for now and see how it went. Dr. Landon said we might have to change the amount of chemo drugs Eli was receiving. Eli's ANC was zero this morning – nothing to fight infection with.

Ardy called and said that Henry picked up Noah to take him to the Bear Diner to meet Carter and Grace, and that he would be keeping him overnight. That would be his overnighter then for this week. On the other hand, Eli and I had a peaceful evening with just the two of us talking and playing while watching TV. When Eli fell asleep, Matt phoned and we spoke for an hour. This time we talked about how much closer we had become.

June 19, 1990 – Tuesday

Eli was up twice during the night, but he didn't throw up. After our usual morning routine, I gave him a Tylenol suppository for a temp of 102 F. By midmorning Lucy Stone with Social Services at EU came by and asked me for Henry's lawyer's name and address. EU was stepping in regarding the issue on Eli and his going home. Henry was not home when I called him.

Dr. Landon walked in at lunchtime and changed Eli's TPN caloric intake to see if Eli would then eat more orally. Eli's resistance to infection was slowly going back up as his ANC was 60 this morning.

Ardy phoned me at 6 p.m. and said that Noah was not back yet, nor had Henry called her either. Instantly, I became worried, and phoned Ardy two hours later to check if there was an update regarding my son. Ardy told me that Henry called her and that he was going to keep Noah overnight again.

Henry had him since 12:30 p.m. yesterday, and I was worried that I wasn't able to reach Henry at his place by phone. After getting off the phone with Ardy, I called the Durango Sheriff's Department and spoke of my concerns. They were going to go out to Bow Mar and perform a welfare check on Noah. They did not find either Henry or Noah though. Finally, at midnight, Henry answered the phone and stated that both he and Noah were home together. For some reason I did not believe that Noah was with him as he refused to let my son get on the phone. I spent a restless night worrying about Noah.

June 20-1990 – Wednesday

Eli was up twice during the night throwing up. Having the emesis on top of the radiation burns in his esophagus was not a good combination, and my heart sank at knowing how painful this was for my son.

Eli drank four ounces of apple juice for breakfast and managed to keep it down. Eli's ANC was 70 this morning. Platelets were okay at 124,000 and HGB was 9.3.

My lawyer called to say the deposition was changed to July fifth.

By midmorning, Eli wanted watermelon and cantaloupe. I went to the store as I knew he would ask for some at times when the kitchen was closed. After lunch I calculated Eli's oral intake to be about ten ounces of fluid and a few bites of the fruit. In the middle of the afternoon, Henry called and ripped into me about the sheriff's department doing a welfare check on my son. I just hung up on him. There was a meeting set for tomorrow on discharging Eli. Due to Henry causing problems, New England Critical Care would not provide service for Eli due to safety reasons and that asshole did not care. I swore he wanted to make sure Eli never went home! Eli fell asleep early and Ardy phoned and my son was there. Finally, I was able to speak with Noah and he was just so sweet on the phone.

June 21, 1990 – Thursday

Eli was sick to his stomach early this morning and then he fell back to sleep. After his morning cares, Eli drank four ounces of apple juice and kept it down. Eli's morning ANC was 66, platelets 152,000, and HGB was 9.4. I took Eli to the eye clinic, and he could now see twenty feet with his left eye and five feet with his right eye which was encouraging.

Dr. Landon stopped by to see Eli and said he was stable, but that there was yeast found in his stool samples. That was a downer.

At 12:30 p.m. Henry showed up and I left for a while. Then at 1 p.m. a meeting commenced. Present in person or by speaker phone were Lucy

Stone and Frida Bales of EU Social Services, Zoe Penson of SRS in Durango, Henry's lawyer in Silverthorne, Dr. Harmon from EU, Henry and myself. It was decided that we had to come up with a plan together that would work for Eli's going home and that both parents needed to work with the provider of medical equipment, meaning that Henry must attempt to learn an IV pump and Eli's cares. I initiated the phone calls to start the process of Eli going home even though Henry said he would, but he never did.

Eli received his vincristine chemo IV push while we were all in the meeting. Total Pharmaceutical Care arrived about 4 p.m. to arrange for new IV pump training and said they would call in the morning.

In the afternoon, Eli broke out in hives and for this he received IV Benadryl. I wondered if Eli was allergic to vincristine. I prayed he was not as that was one chemo medication he certainly needed.

Eli and Noah got to speak with each other around dinner time, and the smile on Eli's face was such an illumination to my sorrowful heart.

Henry called from the Ronald McDonald House and yelled at me, saying, *"I would rather see the SRS place our boys into foster care than go home with you."* That bastard cared not one bit about Noah or Eli, and I loathed him.

When Ardy called in the late evening, I spoke to Noah on the phone and I also informed Ardy of what Henry said about foster care. I cried about what that man was trying to do. How could one man be so cruel to his children? My heart broke with things looking hopeless. My faith was receding again, and I cried myself to sleep.

June 22, 1990 – Friday

Eli was up three times with loose stools in the night. I cleaned him up fast as I knew the stools would be hard on his skin. Eli's ANC was 66, platelets were 166,000 and HGB was 9.4 and holding. At around 10 a.m., a home care supply company came in, and I did not know them nor were they the ones I had called. I listened though and accepted their packet of information. Total Pharmaceutical Care came in an hour later and we went over their pump and the services they provided. I don't know about Henry, but I knew I was going with Total Pharmaceutical Care.

I told Eli after lunch I was going out to buy him new tennis shoes and he was happy about the new shoes. He liked the ones I bought him and they fit just perfect. After I had placed them on his feet, Eli wanted his nurse to come in and see his new shoes, and Rita made a big deal out of them with Eli smiling the whole time. Rita loved Eli as if he was her own child. Henry called after that and informed me on the phone that I had just lost both boys. I immediately hung up on him and he left for Durango sometime after that. Eli and I were able to speak with Ardy and Noah for a long time after supper and it was so good. I knew I had to have been smiling broadly just like Eli was doing, and he was sure a chatterbox on the phone. Henry phoned around 10 p.m. and said he was home; then he started yelling at me so I hung up.

June 23, 1990 – Saturday

I was up as usual this morning and thinking that maybe the third time Eli was discharged, he would actually be allowed to go home.

Henry called and said that he wanted Noah, because Ardy received money, from the State of Colorado, in caring for him. He had stated this off and on for over two months now. I was thinking that since Henry had no income, he wanted Noah so he could receive benefits from the SRS.

Ardy loved my boys and she was a great protector. She called into Eli's room after lunch, and both Eli and I spoke with her and Noah. It was just so good to see Eli talking actively with both of them. It was like part of Eli's personality had come back, and I was so glad to see this. I noted this afternoon that Eli's right nostril was running clear fluid from his sinuses. Now this was a really big deal as this was the first time in over three and a half months. This also meant that more pressure had been relieved, which meant that more tumor was GONE! Eli and I had a normal afternoon and evening free of stress from Henry. Should I worry? Maybe, as he was being too quiet.

June 24, 1990 – Sunday

I was up at 6 a.m. like usual and all cares were done by me. After breakfast, I found out from Eli's nurse that the night of the Code Red being called (06-15-1990), Gavin had come up to 5D at 3 a.m. to find out if I ever left at night. He was told "No, Sarah does not leave at night" more than once and was finally ordered to leave.

Eli and I had a great morning, and at lunch time, it became apparent that he had developed a liking for iced tea.

Eli's ANC was 108, platelets holding at 161,000, and HGB of 8.8.

Eli also napped for a second day in a row; the normal kind of nap children do and not medication-induced. Eli and I watched some of his favorite movies on the VCR after being seen at the dental clinic. About 7:30 p.m. I caught another medication error. Eli was given clindamycin IV for the second time in two hours instead of cimetidine. I informed Mitch about the error, and it was traced back to Ava, who made the mistake.

Mitch called Eli's doctor to notify him and he also made an error report. The doctor said to just keep an eye on Eli, but that he should be okay. Had that been tobramycin, Eli would have become ototoxic, and potentially lose his hearing. Thank the Lord, Eli was okay.

Matt phoned after 10 p.m. and we had another long talk while Eli slept. Of all things, Matt found out Henry's supposed new work phone number. I wasn't even sure Henry had a job.

June 25, 1990 – Monday

I actually slept in until 7 a.m. After our usual morning routine, Eli's nurse Marci, gave Eli expired Fortaz, which had been discontinued three days ago. This made me flare. I was so pissed that my first thought was: *are they trying to kill Eli?* What if I had not been here?

Casey stopped by again this morning and checked on Eli. It was always nice to see her especially since she was from Durango, too. She visited on a regular basis.

After a basically quiet afternoon learning the new IV pump and everything from Total Pharmaceutical Care, Ardy called. While talking with Noah, he informed me that Daddy went harvesting Sunday and Monday and that he was left at Bow Mar with my mother and Ella. Ella and Lily brought him into Ardy's at 9 p.m. I thought my lawyer would find this interesting, especially knowing how drunken Henry got when he harvested with his father.

June 26, 1990 – Tuesday

I was woken at 4 a.m. by big flashes of light. We ended up having a horrible storm during the night and many fires were started because of lightning; big bolts of lightning. Eli was scared so I laid down beside him in the bed and he went back to sleep. Each really loud thunder bolt woke him, but when he saw me, he went right back to sleep.

Eli's ANC was 570 this morning. Platelets went up to 243,000 and his HGB was hanging at 8.3. Eli and I had a pretty good day, and chemo was to start tomorrow.

At around 6 p.m., Gavin called into Eli's room and Eli answered the phone. Riley got on the phone and told me, "You have no business doing any IV's at EU or at home. Only a registered nurse can do it." She just didn't get it at all. Many children left EU with home TPN and their families learned how to do the cares before they were discharged. A parent must be competent at this, and if not, they wouldn't be allowed to perform the procedure, and then a registered nurse would be brought in to do this for them. "I am not going to tell you about Mother's test results" and "that it was you and only you that caused trouble at EU." She went on to say that Henry did not cause any trouble at EU and that it was not fair for Henry, Gavin, and Mother not to see Eli at my place when he went home. Riley then stated that "I was the only one to cause trouble at EU and that Social Services had nothing to do with it." I hung up on her, irritated. Obviously, someone was lying about so many things.

How could Riley be such a blind, opinionated person like my mother? I guess living with each other made them so alike.

Later on, Ardy and Noah called, and Eli and I both talked with them; it was a great boost to my day. Today Eli and I watched *Cinderella*, *Ghostbusters,* and *Muppets Take Manhattan.*

June 27, 1990 – Wednesday

I woke up normally and all was good. Chemo was scheduled to start again today. Henry called while I was caring for Eli and he was yelling so I hung up on him. I saw Eli smile slightly when I hung up on his father. Nothing got past five-year-old Eli!

Chemo started in the morning, and Eli's second day on the study regarding emesis with chemo was initiated. Eli failed and vomited four times so Thorazine was given. I decided that Eli was done with the study. Dr. Landon did not argue the point.

Eli slept most of the afternoon, but he woke up in time to talk with both Ardy and Noah. Before bedtime I noted that Eli was rather edematous again, and with much effort, Eli was finally able to void a little bit. I alerted Eli's nurse, and his IV fluid rate was decreased so his lungs would not fill up.

June 28, 1990 – Thursday

Eli was up and down all night long; he was sick twice, and yesterday it was four times. Henry called this morning – he did not want to talk with Eli. He only wanted to know when Eli was coming home. I told him I was not sure and *I am not sure*. Henry and my mother must be planning something.

After Dr. Harmon checked on Eli, his chemo was initiated. As expected, Eli kept me worried as he became more edematous this afternoon. I made the nurse observe him more closely so she could document. I also had her listen to his lungs.

By evening time, I was able to get Eli to void twice. Eli slept most of the day because no one wanted him to throw up, and so he received Thorazine at the appropriate times.

Ardy phoned in the late evening and I spoke with her and Noah. I told them there was no way to predict when Eli would be discharged. Then in a soft voice, I told Noah I loved him so much.

June 29, 1990 – Friday

I was up at 6 a.m. and Eli had a fever twice during the night and blood cultures had to be drawn. It was probably the Cytoxan that caused it.

I was really frustrated this morning, but I did not let Eli see it. However, I did go out to the nurses' desk and let them know of my frustrations and let Eli's doctor know as well. Were they trying to kill Eli with this damn chemo? I found out from Henry that he plugged the air conditioning hoses on purpose. Why? It was a humid summer; the air conditioning was needed. I took Eli down for sinus and chest X-rays and I obtained clean catch urine on him to test for infection. The second blood culture was done in the late afternoon and Eli's fever rose to 103 degrees F. Eli received another Tylenol suppository and he went to sleep pretty easy with the Thorazine on board.

I simply crashed after speaking with both Ardy and Noah. I missed talking with Matt, but I knew he was on business in San Antonio, TX, right now and couldn't be disturbed.

June 30-1990 – Saturday

Eli and I spent another night of erratic sleeping and tummy sickness. I prayed fervently for the nausea to subside. Blood cultures were drawn again this morning, and Eli had a temperature of 102 F, so he received another Tylenol suppository.

Neither Eli nor I were happy campers this morning. By midmorning, Dr. Benjamin and the blue team came in to see Eli.

Eli's sinuses were infected so his antibiotic needed to be changed, and who knows what after that. Henry had Noah yesterday in the daytime and he picked him up again this morning to stay with him overnight.

Eli had a Panorex X-ray of his jaw this afternoon, and IV Fortaz and oral vancomycin were initiated. Vancomycin was calling out the big dog in the world of antibiotics, and Eli's fever was still spiking at 103 degrees F by midnight. To heck with sleep, I guess, for either of us. I prayed Eli's fever would subside and worry for my little boy was ever present.

Chapter Seventeen

July 1990

July 1, 1990 – Sunday

Eli and I had a great day today until his TPN was hung. I was doing my usual check on his bag and I noted Eli was receiving TPN mixed especially for a two-year old girl with cancer. Chrissy's TPN was hanging and running into Eli. Now, two nurses messed this up. Rita was Chrissy's nurse and she hung Eli's TPN on Chrissy first. Later, Eli's nurse, Susan, hung Chrissy's TPN on Eli. Two nurses had a chance to make sure they had the right bag of TPN and they messed up big time. This time I blew my top as this should not have happened. I stopped the wrong TPN on Eli and flushed him off. Rita did the same for Chrissy. New bags for each child had to be mixed in the pharmacy and then sent up. This process was not a fast one, and I was unable to sleep until about 3:30 a.m. While waiting for a new bag of TPN for Eli, Henry popped in at about 11 p.m. He didn't care about the mistake I caught and he left abruptly after saying snidely to me, "You mean you aren't out whoring around?" Then, he left to go to the Ronald McDonald House. Damn the man to hell!

July 2, 1990 – Monday

I was up early as usual and performed the scheduled morning care. Eli's ANC was 700, platelets 66,000 and HGB 7.3. I saw packed red cells in Eli's near future.

Henry came over and I showed him the process for a Hickman dressing change.

We had a meeting with Kristy Patterson and Dr. Benjamin today. Dr. Benjamin said that if Eli was to go home now, it would be like serving him with a death warrant due to low ANC. When Eli's ANC was elevated, the germs in his sinuses at the base of his brain were kept in check by natural immunity. When Eli's ANC dropped or was low, the germ becomes rampant next to his tumor, and Eli's brain became susceptible to germs and possibly death.

This meant we had to wait yet again for Eli's ANC to be on the rise. After Eli fell asleep, I had a long talk with Matt. He tried his best to encourage me, but sometimes the situation just seemed totally hopeless.

I found I was writing less in my journals now and sometimes I wrote in a code, afraid that Henry or Gavin might steal my journal somehow.

July 3, 1990 – Tuesday

After our usual morning routine, I was exhausted. I kind of dozed in my chair by Eli's side. He had been up and down again all night long.

Henry popped in at noon to shower and leave for Durango. I was glad to see him go and I never even saw him tell Eli goodbye.

After taking Eli to the dental clinic this afternoon, he received a Platelet transfusion. Around 9 p.m. I asked the doctor on call, Dr. Monroe, for a light sedative for Eli. IV halcyon worked for three blessed hours of sleep for Eli.

Eli's blood was too thin so he had to have a shot of Vitamin K. He received packed red blood cells at midnight. I know it sounds strange for blood transfusions to be done at that hour. But Eli had O Negative, CMV (cytomegalovirus) negative blood, and that was rare and difficult to obtain even in Denver. Essentially, Eli has one dedicated local Denver donor only. I wish I had Eli's blood type, but I didn't, and so I couldn't help my son. Henry had O Positive blood and they didn't match either.

July 4, 1990 – Wednesday (Independence Day)

Come 3:30 a.m., Eli was up and down the rest of the night as was I. When Eli's doctors made rounds this morning, more platelets were ordered for Eli. His little body was just not making them at all now. I was so sad for my son. I wanted to stay here with him, but I knew I must give my full deposition tomorrow morning in Durango.

Eli's ANC dropped fast to 90, platelets were 38,000 and HGB was 9.5—thanks to having received the packed red cells yesterday. I found out that Joey, another child with cancer at EU, died yesterday. This was so sad. Had I known yesterday, I would have gone to his mom and given her hugs and let her cry. I took Eli down for another X-ray of his chest after the platelets were infused. Eli was tired and he laid down for some sleep. I told him I had to go to Durango tonight for court things in the morning, and that I would be back as soon as I could. Eli whimpered for just a bit, but then he said he knew I would be back.

I called Ardy to talk with her and Noah, and I finally left EU at around 8 p.m. After arriving home at midnight, I phoned EU and spoke with Eli's nurse, Rob, and he told me Eli was sleeping.

July 5, 1990 – Wednesday

I spoke with Eli's nurse, Maci, at 6 a.m. and Eli was sleeping again. Then, I prepared myself for the deposition.

I went over to a friend's house, Theresa's, and watched a demo deposition tape so I would know what to do and expect. At 9 a.m., I was in the process of doing my full deposition for Henry's lawyer. By lunchtime, I was done and so I went over to Ardy's to pick up Noah.

My son was ecstatic to see me and we fell into a tight hug. After feeding Noah lunch, I called EU, and Eli's nurse told me he was watching a movie in his room. I felt so wiped out and totally drained by this time. Much later in the afternoon, I went to SRS and told them I had done my part of the deposition so that they could now obtain that material for use in court.

Then I took Noah out to supper. After arriving back home, I called Eli's room and he answered the phone. Eli talked with both Noah and

I, but this time Eli was different – he wanted me back tonight. I could hear fear in his voice, but his nurse said Eli had a good day. I told Eli I loved him and would be back as quick as I could tonight. I then called the charge nurse, Emily, and she said Eli was really okay, but that she would watch him extra, since he was so different on the phone. I took Noah back to Ardy's at 8 p.m., and then I fueled up my car. Anna drove by while I was fueling up and she saw how I almost fell over out of exhaustion.

Anna made me follow her home and lay down for a nap on her couch. I told her I must only sleep two hours. After a couple of hours, Anna woke me up and I phoned EU to tell them I was headed back so they could tell Eli if he woke up. Anna went with me to EU to make sure I would not fall asleep driving. Real friends did this kind of thing for each other and I was grateful.

July 6, 1990 – Friday

Anna and I arrived at EU early so we stayed quiet so Eli could sleep. Eli's ANC was zero; platelets were 28,000 and HGB 10.1. Anna slept part of the morning and early afternoon in my chair bed; as I told her, she was not leaving to go back to Durango without some sleep.

When Dr. Monroe came in, he told me that Eli's body had rejected the platelets he was given and that his bone marrow wasn't making any at all. Platelets were one thing I could give to Eli if I was CMV Negative. Dr. Monroe arranged for me to be cross-matched for single donor plate-lets at the blood bank in Denver, so I went and had that done. Henry was angry to find out that Anna was here today, and he called every EU social worker he could to cause trouble. He would rather create a ruckus than think about Eli's predicament regarding platelets. I informed him that it would be advisable to get cross-matched for Eli this coming Monday. Then I hung up and Anna left shortly afterwards.

Social Services informed me late this afternoon that the time arrange-ment made back in March was for that weekend only. Why were they saying this now? What had Henry done? I guess I would know the answer soon or by Monday at the latest since he was coming back then. At around 9 p.m., Henry and Noah came into Eli's room. This I did not expect at all. They looked at Eli sleeping and then they left after I gave Noah some hugs and told him I loved him.

July 7, 1990 – Saturday

Eli was up and down again all night long with diarrhea and dry heaves. I had his nurse give him Thorazine for the dry heaves and that helped. Eli had an ANC of 80 this morning with platelets at 32,000 and HGB at 9.6.

At about 8 a.m., Henry phoned Eli's room and asked me where I was last night, and then he just hung up fast. That jerk knew I was here all night with Eli. Everyone would be much better off if that man just never opened his damn mouth.

By midmorning, the phone rang, and when I answered it, it was my mother. She asked me what I was doing in Eli's room during Henry's time with Eli. Well, Henry was not here for one thing! Annoyed, I hung up on Mother. Twenty minutes later, Henry, Noah, and Gavin showed up in Eli's room. I did not leave except for a bathroom break.

Later in the evening, I found out that Gavin came to the hospital last night to see if I was with Eli. I found out after Eli's night nurse came on duty and told me about it. Oh well. He saw I was indeed here. I am sure that angered both him and Henry.

I called Eli's nurse back to his room after he told me his head was hurting really bad, so she could get him pain relief. The Tylenol did not work and Eli told me, "You gotta make me feel better." It was all I could do not to cry. I wished I could perform miracles, but I could not, so I prayed and told Eli we would ask the doctor for stronger medicine for his headache. Eli had not complained of a headache since the middle of March—why did he have one now, and a bad one at that? I prayed to God for relief.

July 8, 1990 – Sunday

At 9 a.m., Eli was still asleep and this may be attributed to the morphine he received for his bad headache.

Eli's ANC was 60 (still dropping), platelets of 31,000, and HGB of 10.3.

At 11 a.m., Henry, Noah, and Gavin came into Eli's room. I took Noah to the Denver Zoo at around 2 p.m. I knew he must be bored at the hospital when he had to stay there for an extended time. I informed Eli I would take him, too, when he felt a little better and he gave me a weak smile.

Noah had a great time and I took photos. When we arrived back to Eli's room, he was receiving four units of platelets and was sleeping. It was always three or four units more, nowadays. I went looking for photos that I had taken of Eli and Noah at EU and found out they were stolen! Henry had to have done this while Noah and I were at the zoo. I would never get those photos back, and I knew he would never admit to taking them. I was so terribly hurt.

Eli and I spent a quiet evening before falling asleep.

July 9, 1990 – Monday

No change in Eli's ANC today, HGB hanging at 8.7 and platelets at 31,000. Eli would need more platelets. The only way to get Henry to have his blood cross-matched was for me to take him to the blood bank. Good thing it wasn't far away and I did not have to listen to his crap for long.

After getting back to Eli's room, I took him to the ENT clinic and the Eye clinic for checks. Henry left Eli's room at 7:30 p.m. and showed back up at 11 p.m., drunk with beer on his breath. That was not allowed at EU nor at the Ronald McDonald House so I was not sure what he planned to do for tonight. Gavin would probably let him back in at the Ronald McDonald House though. Thankfully Eli slept through all of this while the nurses made Henry leave. I hoped they documented this in Eli's chart.

July 10, 1990 – Tuesday

Eli's ANC was only 80 this morning, platelets at 32,000, and HGB 8.1. Today was different. Eli slept off and on and watched movies on the VCR. I mostly read as Eli slept. On the other hand, Henry asked for Eli's medical chart and he spent hours reading it. I had never read anything in Eli's chart, but then why would I? I had the reports and scans. I was not afraid of what staff members wrote about me. I knew what the doctors thought as I was so involved with Eli's care.

Henry asked me once or twice what a medical term meant, and both times I referred him to Eli's nurse even though I knew what they meant, so he stopped asking me. I didn't know what Henry was looking for, and I didn't really care. I was sure he would be angry to see I did so much and see whatever was charted on him. After he left, I went to sleep.

July 11, 1990 – Wednesday

After having a bad night with Eli and me not sleeping and feeling sick, the morning turned out to be pretty good. Eli was content to watch his favorite movies – he never seemed to tire of them and he asked for them by name. When I came back up at noon, Eli told me that Henry slapped Noah across the face to get him to shut up. Eli never lied! I made sure my lawyer knew about this incident.

Eli's ANC was 144, HGB and platelets holding. Casey poked her head in the door and we briefly chatted. She was refreshing to see. The day seemed so long for both of us, and yet I was afraid of what each consecutive day would bring as there always was something. I found my journal notes were getting shorter and I had less energy, but I would persevere for my son. Eli sensed the anxiety in me although he never said anything; he knew his mama loved him dearly and would fight for him and his brother with each breath I took. Sometimes it seemed like the days were one big blur and that neither Eli nor I had a life prior to EU.

We both went to sleep restless later in the evening.

July 12, 1990 – Thursday

After our usual morning, Henry phoned into Eli's room. Within a couple of minutes, Henry hung up on Eli. I did not get the chance to tell Eli I was sorry that his daddy hung up on him when Henry called again. A couple of minutes passed and once more he hung up on Eli. Now I was angry. There was no end to his hatred and abuse. I was so tired of all this yet I knew Eli must be even more so.

Eli's ANC was 208 this morning so he was slowly going upward. By midmorning I went over to the Ronald McDonald House; after picking up Noah, we went to Eli's room. On the walk over, we chatted and my son told me what his father had said to him and how he had slapped him when they were inside Eli's room. My heart just broke yet I knew that for the moment, both my boys were safe with me.

Chemo started around noon so Eli was relegated to his room for a while. The boys played until almost three in the afternoon and it was a joy to see them having fun together. Henry picked up Noah around 3 p.m. and they left for Durango. I worried for Noah and I dreaded tomorrow as it would be eight years since Joshua earned his angel wings.

Eli went to sleep early tonight, and after I spoke with Matt at length, I fell asleep.

July 13, 1990 – Friday

Eight years ago, Joshua was born. I must stay focused on Eli today and not allow sad memories to pull me down, or Eli would sense them and be sad too. I didn't want that to happen. So, for the moment, I shelved thoughts of Joshua.

Eli's ANC was 320 so he was headed up, even with chemo running into him. I knew a blood transfusion was just around the corner. Platelets and HGB were holding but it was only a matter of time before they dropped. After our usual morning routine, I took Eli down for a chest X-ray and a CT scan of his chest. Eli slept most of the day.

I went over to the University of Greenwood in Denver, and to the dental clinic there. Not having much money and with one tooth hurting, I knew my cheapest choice was to have a dental medical student pull my tooth. No way could I afford a root canal. The student wasn't so bad, but it did take a long time since his work had to be checked often by a dental professor.

The evening was quiet, and Eli went to sleep early. After speaking with Matt on the phone, I simply crashed. As I was falling asleep, I wondered how Noah was doing.

July 14, 1990 – Saturday

After our usual morning routine, I got down to business, writing notes for my lawyer. The last two nights, Henry had Noah out at Bow Mar. Henry was ignoring the one overnight rule the judge ordered. I was upset, more so as I was unsure how Noah was or how he had been treated.

Dr. Benjamin came in this morning and we discussed the effectiveness of Eli's antibiotic, Ceclor, as Eli had been on it for such a long time, even before admission to EU. I phoned the Durango Clinic to get a complete run down on all the medications Eli had been on, for Dr. Benjamin to review.

Right before one in the afternoon, Henry, Noah, and Gavin showed up in Eli's room. I was so glad to see Noah, yet I worried he was under the control of Henry and Gavin, both abusive persons, and quick to anger. They stayed for about forty-five minutes, left, and never came back for the rest of the day.

Eli and I went to bed at around 9:30 p.m. I worried about Noah and how he was doing, knowing that Henry and Gavin were so mean to him.

July 15, 1990 – Sunday

The days ran together and my worries built up on top of each other. My stress headaches were worse, yet with all the pain I felt, in so many ways, Eli's pain must be so much worse. More than I could even begin to imagine. Eli's HGB was 7.1 this morning, so a blood transfusion would occur soon. Henry would not leave me alone most of the day and nurses had to intervene at times. This was not good for Eli. I both hated and pitied Henry in a way.

In the late afternoon, Ella and Riley phoned into Eli's room. I knew they taped the entire conversation, they always did and it never ended. They tried to upset me, but their plan backfired. Towards the end of the conversation, I found out that Henry, Noah, and Gavin had gone back to Durango. This meant Noah was at Bow Mar, and fear rippled through my whole being.

I fell into a restless sleep tonight with Eli at my side. He and I gave each other comfort; my little boy living a hell of a life extended comfort to his mom, while she, with feet dangling toward the pits of hell, tried so much to share with her son a taste of Heaven on Earth. If only it were that simple.

July 16, 1990 – Monday

Another chest X-ray was done on Eli right after our usual morning routine. The doctors hoped Eli could go home for a few days, but I was not counting on that to happen, and I refused to let my boys down again if it didn't occur.

At mid-morning, Frida Bales (EU social worker) came in and she wanted to talk with Henry to check if he would cause trouble if I took Eli home for a few days. We spoke in low tones so Eli didn't hear us and then she left to call Henry.

Eli's ANC of 504 was still on the rise, platelets were fine at 134,000 but the HGB of 7.1 caused packed red blood cells to be ordered for my boy.

In the late afternoon, another MRI was done on Eli's head and neck. I prayed improvement was found on this scan. I was still trying to keep arrangements made and business taken care of in the hopes that Eli could go home for a few days. There would be a meeting at the hospital tomorrow; Eli's safety was of utmost importance.

Frida Bales must have upset Henry. It was apparent in the way Henry came into Eli's room at around 10 p.m., bitching up a big storm, keeping Eli and I awake until the nurse told him to leave. I knew this bastard's plan. If he caused enough trouble, (just like last time) Eli would not be allowed to go home. I so hated this man – not that he was a real man! After Eli fell asleep, I did too, but my mind couldn't rest because of the troubles Henry was causing all of us, including the hospital staff.

July 17, 1990 – Tuesday

Eli was up and down again last night. He sensed anxiety coming from me and the hospital staff. Eli's ANC was 540 today and climbing. I tried to remain calm as I knew Total Parenteral Care Home Health is coming to train Henry on Eli's home IV pump. I wondered if my sister Riley would complain about that one – that Henry needed to be a registered nurse to do that for Eli. She was ignorant of the fact that parents needed to know these things to care for their long-term sick children at home in a safe manner. Of course, I would never let Henry touch the pump at home. But the staff of Total Parenteral Care needed to document that both parents had been trained on their equipment.

EU required this documentation as well. They knew that I was more than proficient in this, but be that as it may, Henry also had to show proficiency. Otherwise, I would lose it and probably cry in frustration.

Mid-afternoon found Henry, the social workers, doctors and I, in a business meeting, in the hopes of getting Eli home just once for a couple of days. Eli had stayed 136 days here in the hospital, and he needed to be home and be a little boy again for a couple of days at least.

The staff took Eli down for another chest CT scan while we were in the meeting, and I found out that Eli needed a new set of sinus X-rays.

Eli ate little for dinner and though I was disheartened by that, I was lifted upon speaking on the phone with Noah and Ardy.

Right before 9 p.m., Henry came back to Eli's room stating that he was staying the night with Eli. I left and went over to the Ronald McDonald House, directly to the basement, and laid on a couch down there. I refused to sleep in a bed Henry had slept in, and I did not trust him not to come back during the night and rape me. A person should not feel fear in a safe house such as this. My whole body shook with terror until I fell asleep on the couch in the basement recreation room with my coat over me.

July 18, 1990 – Wednesday

I woke up around 5:30 a.m. and found I had actually slept for five hours straight! After tidying myself, I walked over to EU and Eli's room. Eli's ANC was over 600 today and I was so relieved. Eli and I had a good day, which began with his usual morning cares. Henry never even tried, and he slept most of the day over at the Ronald McDonald House. Evidently, he now knew sleep in a hospital setting wasn't easy by any means; yet he had never been there when Eli was sick to his stomach.

Total Parenteral Care came to the hospital and I signed the papers. I might, just might be able to take Eli home tomorrow. I kept my emotions in check as best I could as I really didn't want to let Eli down yet again.

Late in the evening Eli and I spoke with Ardy and Noah like it was a beautiful routine we had established. I tried not to let Noah have high hopes of Eli coming home, but that was not easy with a six-year old boy who missed his mother and brother.

Later, Matt's voice on the phone helped calm my nerves. I fell asleep anxiously, after Eli was asleep, knowing that we still had many hours to go, and that taking Eli home could still be put on hold if Henry caused any trouble.

July 19, 1990 – Thursday (HOME!)

I was up early and Eli and I did our usual morning routines. Eli was smiling and I knew he was thinking of going home, but I was anxious knowing anything could still come up to prevent that from happening. Eli's ANC was 812 this morning.

Henry came into Eli's room around mid-morning and he had such a temper. He was attempting to prevent Eli from going home. I shattered inside as all my hopes for today diminished in just two minutes.

EU social worker, Frida Bales, wanted to be notified at extension 7060 if any problems arose so I called her. Frida and Henry didn't get along at all. Frida was onto his outbursts and she had come to the conclusion that Henry couldn't prevent me from taking Eli home, and furthermore, the SRS in Durango as well as the police would take care of Henry. I would also keep my doors locked at all times, as I always did in the past. I finally got my car loaded down, and it was rather a harrowing day as Henry was of no help, but, I did have a nurse help me.

By 10 p.m., I finally arrived home with Eli. I had to unload his IV pump and supplies and get Eli hooked up to his TPN and get him settled. After Eli went to sleep, I unloaded the rest of the medical stuff from my car, alone, with no help. Henry never came over to bother me and I was thankful.

It was way too late to have Noah come over, but I did call Ardy to let her know I had Eli home in his own bed. I fell asleep, exhausted, but with a wide smile plastered across my face.

July 20, 1990 – Friday

I awoke just like clockwork and went to Eli's room to turn down his TPN for one hour. One-hour titration was required when both starting and stopping TPN, so blood sugar doesn't go out of kilter. After his sponge bath, Eli and I went over to Ardy's and we chatted with them all before taking Noah home with us. It was amazing to have both my boys in my car for the first time in over 145 days! After arriving at our apartment, Eli and Noah played and a home health nurse phoned to say she was coming over for a visit. The day was just perfect, even when some siblings stopped by to see Eli. My mother and Henry never visited, and I am sure Henry was drunk since it's a Friday night. Eli's midday normal saline hydration went well. Later on, Eli became angry when he could not be in the bathtub with Noah when he took his bath. But Eli's Hickman couldn't get wet. I asked Noah to hurry with his bath while Eli started chattering about Teenage Mutant Ninja Turtles and his favorite one, Donatello. Eli also loved the color purple so that may be the reason he liked Donatello, aside from the fact that Donatello was the youngest and smallest among the four Ninja Turtles. It was so hard to get the boys to go to sleep tonight. They were so happy to be together. I could not break their hearts by telling them that Eli would need to go back to EU for more care. Instead, we spoke of seeing Mickey Mouse and Donald Duck as Eli had decided that his wish (for the Make-A-Wish-Foundation) would be for us to go to Orlando, FL and Disneyworld. Both boys were so excited at the prospect!

July 21, 1990 – Saturday

I was ecstatic upon waking up as this was the second full day at home with Eli. We now had a new normal routine, and the TPN was going well.

Both boys rode their red dirt bikes, with training wheels on them, for a while on the sidewalk. They were being little boys again and my heart just melted. This was like a dream come true, even if Eli had no hair and he was much thinner.

In the afternoon, before Eli's daytime hydration of normal saline was completed, his Hickman caught on some furniture and he obtained a small tear in the tubing. I immediately took him to Frisco Hospital for the ER doctor to repair. The ER doctor was not sure what to do really, so I actually helped him along in the procedure, having seen it done at EU while Eli was there. After the repair was complete, I told the doctor that heparin needed to be flushed in slowly, but he refused. I think he was scared of doing this. So, I took my boys back home and once there, I called the EU pediatric oncology nurse who told me to flush heparin slowly, which I did, and then I clamped off the affected port so it would not be used for twenty-four hours.

What would have happened if Eli had not been with me? I don't think his father would have done anything really. We had a lazy rest of the day. Jacob came over and tossed a small football around with Eli. I could see his heart breaking for little Eli. He played with both boys equally just like old times. This was so good to see and I took many photos of them. More of my siblings stopped by for a while and they brought Henry. Henry did not make a ruckus and for that I was glad. However, he did throw many pointed barbs my way and many sexual innuendoes. I really wished he would just grow up, but I doubted he ever would.

The boys had chicken nuggets with honey for supper and Eli did eat a few bites. Noah ate all of his supper. Just knowing Eli could tolerate a few bites was wonderful. This evening, instead of having Noah take his bath first, I hooked up Eli to his TPN and then he lay down on the couch with his stuffed Ninja Turtle, Donatello, while I had Noah take a quick bath. This seemed to work out better that Eli did not see his brother in the bathtub and want to be in it with him. Overall the day was tiring for all three of us, and we went to sleep early.

After my boys settled in for the night, I spoke with Matt on the phone to let him know how things were going. Matt and I had decided that he would not come over while Eli was home. As I fell asleep, I wondered how long I would get to have Eli here with his brother and their toys and friends. It was a rather disconcerting thought.

July 22, 1990 – Sunday

All three of us had a great morning and afternoon, and then I knew I had to take them out to see their father and that my mother would be there. I tried to ignore much of the commotion at Bow Mar, and of course, Mother made supper that Eli could not eat so he was forced to watch the others eat, and it did not bother her at all. I chose not to eat and to play with Eli instead. It would be nice to say there wasn't any arguing going on, but that I cannot say as arguments happened day in and day out around my mother and she must be the center of attention.

When it was almost dark, the boys shot off a few fireworks. They had a lot of fun and got dirty playing. They were tired and had a full day, so we went home around 10:30 p.m. I gave Eli a sponge bath first and hooked him up to his TPN for the night, and then Noah had a bath. Both boys fell fast asleep, so I took my own shower. Then, Matt and I spoke on the phone for over an hour. We missed talking face to face, but for the boys' sakes, it couldn't happen during this trip. Our love kept on growing and I felt safe and secure in our relationship; totally not like with Henry. With him, he was only a way out from my mother. I fell asleep knowing that I was loved by Matt, and that Eli had just spent his third day at home, out of the hospital.

July 23, 1990 – Monday

Today was Eli's fourth full day at home!

The morning went great and Eli tried to eat some Fruity Pebbles for breakfast like Noah was doing. After breakfast, I took the boys up to the local hospital as Eli was scheduled to have lab work done for EU doctors. The lab tech wanted to poke Eli, but his veins were poor and I told him I would draw from his Hickman like I did in the hospital. The lab tech looked at me with doubt, before he gave me the needles and syringes I wanted. I drew off waste blood, then the blood for the tubes which I handed to the tech, and then I immediately returned the "waste" blood back to Eli. This was how EU liked to do it with the children since they needed the blood. If one was good and quick with drawing labs, there was no reason not to give the waste blood back.

The boys went with me to see my lawyer, Mr. Troy, and it looked like the divorce was not going to be anytime soon. My lawyer bill was huge, but it seemed like Mr. Troy had taken a personal interest in Eli and all that had happened. He had not asked for any payment of any sort yet, and for that I am grateful.

After arriving back home, the home health nurse came to check on Eli. By then, I had Eli hooked up to his normal saline hydration and she just listened to his heart and not much else as I had already done everything. At least she was able to document the good care I gave to my boys and the clean home environment I had for them. She saw that my boys had all they needed and more.

Henry had the gall to call my landlady, Jill, this morning to harass her and she let me know what he did. I wish I had known sooner so I could have told my lawyer.

But I did call and left a message for him so he would be kept in the loop. It was a beautiful day out and the boys rode their bikes on the inner sidewalk adjacent to my front door. They were such a joy to behold. Joel, of the Durango Reporter, stopped by for a story on Eli and he also took a few photographs; some with Eli riding his bike and some of him sitting next to me on the couch, exhausted.

In the interview, I told Joel about the type of cancer Eli had, its rarity, and what his treatment plan was. I also told him of the planned trip to Orlando, FL, and Disney, which Dream Factory was gifting Eli with. The article would be on the front page of next week's newspaper. After Joel left, I found out that I was being checked on as far as gentleman who had been visiting. Henry was still too damn jealous! This paranoia was getting so old!!

Henry banged on my front door at 5 p.m. for a visitation with both boys, but not for overnight. I had to let him have a couple of hours with them. After they left, I called Matt and said maybe now would be a good time to try and repair the oil leak on my car.

Spencer and Matt got my car in the best shape possible, so I would be able to take Eli back to Denver when the time came for me to do so. Later on, Henry brought Eli back to me, but he had left Noah at Bow Mar with my mother. I was not a happy camper about that, but I had to get down to caring for Eli, so I did. We both fell into a troubled sleep since Noah was not home with us.

July 24, 1990 – Tuesday

Eli and I did our usual home morning routine, but without Noah it was not the same. I was sure Eli worried about him as much as I did, and we fretted for reasons of our own. Eli knew things I did not and maybe it was best that way. I didn't know what I would do if more abuse came to light. Yet, I felt I should know more, but Eli remained mysterious.

After breakfast, I packed my car for a return trip to Denver. The home health nurse stopped by and did the required exit review from services, since we went back to Denver today. Nothing was ever required from the local home health service except for charting. I knew copies would be sent to Total Parenteral Care and I hoped SRS received them as well.

Henry harassed me on the phone while I was trying to pack my car. That bastard had the nerve to do this to me when he had overdone his entire allowed visitation the last few days. By 2 p.m. the creep was still harassing me with phone calls. Then, Henry told me that my mother had cancer and had been at the doctors all day long in Silverthorne. He was so full of crap. I knew he was lying yet again. My mother did not, and never had cancer of any type. Then, he informed me that our tax refund checks were in, and they were held in Silverthorne pending our divorce.

I left with Eli to pick up Noah from his father after fueling my car. All hell broke loose at Bow Mar as they refused to give me Noah, and I ended up crying so hard for my boy. He wanted to go with me as well. I went to Ardy's and called my lawyer, Mr. Troy, and Zoe Penson of the SRS to make them aware of what had just transpired. I had no choice but to go ahead and leave for Denver with Eli.

I made it to Johnsonville, but my car was having problems. After having it looked at, it was determined I would not have any air conditioning for the trip, and because of time constraints no fix could be done. July in Colorado was really hot, yet we were back on the freeway to Denver.

Eli and I were to stay at the Rosewood Inn at 95th and I-25, in a double room by the pool and playground as the Ronald McDonald House was full. I had no money for the hotel, but the American Cancer Society stepped in to pay for the bill, and I was grateful. Total Parenteral Care home health called and they brought over more filters for me to use with Eli's TPN.

After giving Eli his meds and hooking him up to his TPN, I got him settled in nicely in one of the beds and made him quite comfortable. Eli had faith in his mommy, and he was not afraid of being in new surroundings.

Henry called twice and I just hung up on him. I phoned Ardy to let her know that Eli and I had made it, and we were okay. Then I laid down in bed with Eli and cuddled with him until I fell asleep. I just knew that after all the trauma he endured today, he needed me next to him…and I needed him, too.

July 25, 1990 – Wednesday

The next morning, after packing my car, Eli and I went to EU for CT scans of his chest and head areas. After that, we were able to go over to the Ronald McDonald House since they had a room for us for the night. I readied our room and unpacked the supplies Eli would need. Food was brought in for the families staying at the house. I realized then that Henry actually liked being in this air-conditioned house, and being fed delicious homemade food with nice entertainment, and the ability to do laundry when he chose to do so. Eli played Nintendo for a while this evening. He was so calm. I could tell by the relaxed way he interacted with the other ill children. I knew Eli felt safe that I was there to protect him.

When we got tired, we went to our room and I readied Eli for bed and his TPN. No sooner had I done that, I fell asleep, too.

July 26, 1990 – Thursday

It was a treat to have coffee before Eli woke up. Our morning was quite normal as far as it could be, and Eli was sick to his stomach once. A short while later he took his oral medications and didn't get sick again.

One of our Denver friends, Dennis, was driving by and noticed Eli and I in the parking lot of the Ronald McDonald House. He pulled up to check on Eli before going on his way. So many people loved and cared about him. My son had an impact on people and affected them in many ways I couldn't count.

Mid-morning, I took Eli to the pediatric clinic at EU as they wanted to check on his white port. Things went well, so Eli and I took a short drive in the car so he could see a little of Denver before going back to the Ronald McDonald House. Total Parenteral Care called early in the afternoon and they delivered more TPN and medical supplies for Eli. I was so glad that Frida Bales (EU social worker) kept Henry from messing things up with this home health care company, or Eli would never have gone home, even briefly.

Henry didn't fool Frida Bales one bit! Denise Simms (nurse with Pediatric Oncology) called around dinnertime and said that the plan was to hold off tomorrow's scheduled IT medications until we knew what the CT scans showed and we saw the reports. Henry phoned later in the evening and had Noah get on the phone.

My son asked me if he could go to "Yellowstone" with his cousins Ava and Emily. It broke my heart that I had to tell him no. He left the phone crying hard. The last thing I wanted was for Noah to get stuck in a hellish vacation with my mother. Her unbridled abuse would have terrified my son. I could not allow that to happen, nor could I let him be gone that long with Eli so sick.

Eli's friend on 5D, Ricky, finally went home with his mom today. These horribly sick children were in the hospital for such long stretches. The other parents and those whose children were also at the Ronald McDonald House shared root beer floats with Will (another child with cancer). It was his birthday and he would be going home with his parents tomorrow. Not much later, Eli and I took the elevator up to our room on the third floor, and I readied Eli for bed and hooked up his IV TPN. I don't think I was even done when Eli was fast asleep.

July 27, 1990 – Friday

I was up early again this morning and did our usual routines and though the morning went well, I can't say the same for the early afternoon.

In the morning, Eli and I waited three hours in the Pediatric clinic for his IT therapy, before finally, the spinal tap was done and chemo injected in his spinal fluid. Afterwards, both Eli and I got his pre-admittance cleared for the coming Sunday.

After cleaning our room, I loaded my car and Eli and I left for Durango. Boy, was it hot out!

We arrived home by 7:30 p.m. Shortly after, Henry brought Noah over to my apartment. Gavin was with them.

Although we talked, inside I was seething to know about the abuse he inflicted on Noah. Henry and Gavin watched as I put the TPN in the refrigerator, set up Eli's IV pump and tubing, and did all the necessary work so I could hook up Eli to his TPN. Although they remained quiet, I knew Henry and Gavin thought I did a damn good job of doing Eli's cares! They also knew that Henry could never have done what I just did. It seemed like forever before they finally left.

My boys loved being together again. Had I allowed Noah to go to Yellowstone, he would have missed this time with Eli and I knew he would have regretted it later on. I did the right thing all around.

Eli fell asleep; Noah took a bath and fell asleep. I phoned Matt later and we talked for a long time. Before I put down the receiver, I uttered a brief thanks to God again for giving Matt to me. I know that without Matt's ongoing support, it was not certain whether I could have handled everything as well as I did. Blessed—this is what I felt every time I remembered Matt. Although tired, it still took me some time to fall asleep.

July 28, 1990 – Saturday

I was up early with both boys. Emma and Ardy called to check on Eli. He got on the phone and was full of smiles as he chattered with them, which in turn lit my face.

Ardy brought over Noah's bike so he could ride it at the apartment, and the boys had a great time all day long. Again, I was thankful my boys could play like this and have this precious time together.

Mid-afternoon, Henry came by with Gavin. Again, Henry put off trying to fix the air conditioner on my car. Henry decided he wanted his visitation done in my apartment! I told Henry and Gavin to take their visitation elsewhere because I could not keep up with their nosing around my apartment and I had to get my car fixed. They finally left. I phoned Anna and she told me that both Spencer and Matt were in Spencer's garage and they fixed my car's air conditioning. They also did much needed muffler and exhaust work. I was so grateful and after thanking them, I went home. I called all over and could not reach anyone at Henry's, Gavin's, my mother's house, or Ella's. Finally, I reached them at my mother's house. Apparently, Henry was using her house while she was in Yellowstone as she had air conditioning and his trailer didn't.

Just as I had finished some salad for supper, Henry brought Eli home. I had to clean Eli up before I could get him ready for his TPN, and I then put him to bed as he was tired and worn out. Before Eli fell asleep, he told me it felt cool in our apartment and how much he liked it.

After a long phone call with Matt, I fell asleep listening to country music playing softly on the radio.

July 29, 1990 – Sunday

Just like the usual, I woke up early and packed my car. I always did this chore alone and my family never cared to help with packing or unloading. *I had such a caring family*, I thought sarcastically. My family was extra special as no one else I know would have put up with the craziness of the family I have. Matt would help me, but then I would be held accountable in some way; and my boys and I would receive retribution of some sort from my mother and Henry.

By 10 a.m. Eli and I were on the road back to Denver and EU. When we arrived at the Ronald McDonald House parking lot, we saw that both Henry and Noah had already set up house there. Upon arrival at EU at around 2 p.m., I found out that both Dr. Cole and Dr. Moran had decided in the middle of this morning that Eli was not to be admitted. Dr. Moran wanted to meet with radiology one more time, and they didn't want to do a biopsy on Eli's right lung unless necessary. After that, I had to take Eli down to the ER so that he could have labs drawn – it was decided that if his labs were okay, Eli didn't have to be admitted to EU. Eli's lab work was okay.

Henry and Noah took Eli back to the Ronald McDonald House while I went to the outpatient pharmacy to refill three of Eli's medications. While doing so, I worried how this arrangement was going to work out over at the Ronald McDonald House with Henry in town.

After returning with the medications, I set them up and gave them to Eli. I added all the IV medications and IV multiple vitamins to his TPN and hooked him up for the night. I securely taped the needle to the port used, as there was no way I was staying in that room with Henry, and the house didn't allow for families to have two rooms. So, Henry, Noah, and Eli stayed in room four, while I slept half the night in the library and half the night in the recreation room. I prayed Henry would come down if Eli's IV pump beeped during the night. Henry did come down, but only to harass me. I told him Eli could not be left alone on the third floor and he finally gave up on me and went back to room four. I called Matt late in the evening to wish him a Happy Birthday. His special day was tomorrow.

July 30, 1990 – Monday

Last night was restless for me as I had to sleep alternately on chairs and on the carpet. I couldn't find a blanket to stay warm. Regardless, my situation was nothing compared to Eli's.

I had been worried about surgery on Eli's lungs since he was diagnosed, and my worry had only grown stronger. The morning went well with both boys and I kept them in places where all the people in the house congregated, such as the kitchen or recreation room so that Henry would be hard pressed to cause trouble to my boys or myself.

I had been told by the pediatric oncology nurses at "Cancer Action" yesterday that I could get more medical supplies for Eli. So, later in the morning, Eli and I went to Cancer Action and picked up disposable supplies such as blue pads, small Depends, dressings, and the like. They were not a supplier of IV type things, but I was able to get Eli a quilted lap robe to put on whenever he became cold. The lap robe had blues and purples in it and Eli liked purple; the blue brought out the blue twinkle in Eli's eyes. Both Eli and Noah had blue eyes, a gift inherited from me through the grace of God above.

Dr. Cole phoned around 4:30 p.m. to tell me that Dr. Moran had not met up with radiology as yet due to a medical emergency of some sort. I had been waiting to find out all day long if the spots on Eli's lungs were artefacts (shadow type things) or not.

Dr. Cole called back around 5 p.m. to have Eli admitted to EU as the spots were artefacts except for the big one. As I took Eli over to EU thirty minutes later, my heart was just pounding in my chest and I was terrified for Eli knowing he had to have yet another major surgery.

Eli was admitted to room 5022 for tomorrow's surgery. The cardio-thoracic surgical team planned a biopsy on the big spot in one lung only. I was not sure how much Eli could sense from me, but I was positive he was sensitive to my anxiety.

I tried explaining to Eli while I did his medications and TPN, but Eli seemed uninterested in what I had to say. The nurses charted that all meds and TPN this evening were performed by me.

After Eli fell asleep, I did, too. Restlessly, I would wake up from nightmares, from the littlest sound inside our room, with my heart thudding in fear... afraid for my son.

July 31, 1990 – Tuesday

I woke up to a loud bang down the hall from Eli's room at around 2:30 a.m. Then, I discovered Eli had not been given his midnight and 2 a.m. pre-op IV antibiotics, which the doctors ordered. Needless to say, I was pissed. After giving Eli's nurse a piece of my mind, she handed the antibiotics to me and then brought me new tubing. I did the rest as she wanted out of Eli's room as fast as she could go. Eli had a fever spike by this time of 102 degrees, and he threw up twice later in the morning. Eli had to take his medications twice since he brought up his first doses in his emesis and we could see them in it. With some anti-nausea medicine on board, Eli was able to keep his second set of morning medications down.

So many people at EU had read Joel's story about Eli. Joel was the one who wrote the story for The Durango Reporter newspaper.

The staff loved Eli's photo of him riding his red bike with training wheels. One nurse commented that they didn't see this side of the children they took care of, and that this reinforced their beliefs that sick children needed to have some time to be children and not just patients in a hospital. It was true, and my conviction about this belief held even stronger.

Eli and I went down to the surgical holding area at 1 p.m. Eli started asking me lots of questions then and was talkative. Only the pre-op nurse and I were with Eli. He said he knew yesterday that the doctors were going to go into his right lung in surgery. Eli also stated he knew he was going to ICU (Intensive Care Unit) after the surgery.

Then, Eli asked me the question I dreaded the most. He looked into my eyes and said, "Am I going to die?"

My blood froze. The nurse stopped what she was doing and became as still as I was.

"No!" I said a little too loudly. I didn't know how to explain it to him. How could I explain to this little boy that what he asked broke me apart?

Before I could even begin to open my mouth, he asked again, "Am I going to go to Heaven where Joshua is?"

Although my throat was blocked with a huge lump, I somehow managed to tell him, "Only if God really needs you right now."

"I want to go to Heaven, Mom," he said innocently. Behind those blue eyes, I didn't see a speck of fear. And for a while, I wondered where he got the concept of Heaven.

I wanted to cry because I didn't want him to go just yet. Not now. Not in a few months. Certainly, never before me, not if I could help it! So, I told him softly, "We don't always get what we want in life. So, you might have to stay with Mom for a while."

I knew not what to say next so we prayed together. I kept praying while Eli was given light sedation before surgery. They finally wheeled him away to the operating room at around 2 p.m. I lost my chance to ask Eli what he knew of Heaven. *Why didn't I ask Eli? Why didn't I ask Eli what he knew of Jesus?*

My heart broke as I cried. Eli wanted to go to Heaven! How did my five-year-old little boy know of Heaven when I refused to tell him much of Heaven? Talking about heaven made the possibility of Eli dying too much of a reality. I wanted Eli to know of God and Jesus, but I was terrified of Eli dying… so I said little to him about Heaven. Somehow, Eli knew though. He knew of Heaven and he wanted to go there. Who was I to tell Eli, "We don't always get what we want in life and that he might have to come back to me." Was I selfish to not want to give Eli back to God?

Dr. Moran came out of the operating room at around 3:45 p.m. He told me that they removed the entire large tumor mass (it was rhabdo-myosarcoma), as well as some surrounding tissues. Eli was okay and was taken to ICU at 4 p.m. One hour later, I was in ICU and Eli was in so much pain. The nurse gave Eli a lot of morphine and I couldn't stop crying inside, or outside for that matter. Seeing Eli this way, going through hell and horrible pain, I wondered if it would not be better for Eli to go to Heaven like he wanted to.

And yet, I was selfish!

Eli had a drainage tube in his lung and he was on a heart/respiration monitor as well. He wore a pediatric oxygen mist mask and the nurse told me I could only stay thirty minutes with him. Right before the time was up, I went outside to call Henry who was in the waiting room, so he could see Eli. He stayed for a couple of minutes, left, and went to the Ronald McDonald House. Henry was never in pre-op holding and never heard the thoughts and wants Eli voiced during that time. Only his nurse and I heard them. Henry and I never spoke while Eli was in surgery.

While Eli was in the operating room today, so was little April, a young girl who had to have her leg amputated as her treatment for osteosarcoma had not worked. This was the same thing that happened to young Roni.

Little Chrissy's mom was told today that Chrissy had only limited days left.

Little Diane (diagnosed two days apart from Chrissy two years ago) coded on 5D today. She was in PICU and was not expected to make it through the night.

Why did so many children have to die?

Why are so many in such pain?

I asked the Lord why. But either He did not speak to me, or my ears were so deaf that I didn't hear His response.

I returned to Cardio-Thoracic ICU again before 9 p.m. I was able to get Eli to swallow some of his medications, but not all; and not all medications were sent to ICU from the pediatric floor.

I stayed with Eli for more than an hour and a half until his nurse said I had to leave for a while. That was the only time I went back to the waiting room. Half an hour later, I was back in the ICU with Eli. He had required a straight catheter but only 180 ml. of urine was obtained.

Eli's extremities were so edematous. His nurse and I helped my son stand up in bed so he could pee—five hours after coming out of surgery!

Sometime after midnight, I finally left the ICU and stayed in the ICU waiting room for the rest of the night. The ICU staff and Eli's nurse knew where to find me.

Henry stayed at the Ronald McDonald House all night, sleeping in a nice bed with blankets, clean sheets, and pillows.

Chapter Eighteen

August 1990

August 1, 1990 – Wednesday

Ichecked in on Eli off and on during the entire night. I was so tired yet restless, knowing Eli was in pain. It tore at my heart.

Eli's nurse let me into the ICU just after 8 a.m. I gave my son his oral medications, then flushed and placed Heparin in the white port of his Hickman. Afterwards, I gently changed Eli's Hickman dressing. The chest tube drainage system was removed by the doctor after I completed the Hickman dressing change. Eli hurt and was given some morphine. Then, we moved Eli back to 5D and the west step-down unit on 5D. Even though Eli wasn't in a regular room on 5D, at least he was in the step-down area and receiving good nursing care. Overall, Eli had a fairly good day and required less morphine. Or it could be that Eli was no longer reacting to some of his pain since he was so used to it. What an awful thought.

Eli received a gift today—something he had wanted for a long time—a *He-Man Power Sword*. Eli was given the thirty-dollar kind and batteries to use with it. Eli loved watching *He-Man* cartoons on the television just as much as he liked *Superman*, *Spiderman*, *Batman*, and *Ghostbusters*. Although Eli couldn't really play much with the power sword, he kept it at his side. Now and then, he would turn on the button to light up the sword, even though he could not swing it around in play. Eli kept both the power sword and Precious next to him in bed. This evening's asthma treatment only helped minutely, and Eli received more morphine. I called both Ardy and Matt with updates on Eli before I tried to get some sleep. I figured Henry had already phoned my family.

August 2, 1990 – Thursday

Eli had a fairly good night in step-down, receiving morphine as needed, and I slept fitfully. It was good to see him sleep more than usual. I gave him the morning medications, dressing changes, and a sponge bath. Eli was weaned down from the oxygen and it was going well.

Midmorning, I went over to the Ronald McDonald House to shower and wake up some more with coffee. I was back in Eli's step-down room by noon. Then, I got to hold Eli for the first time since yesterday when I held him long enough to transfer him to step-down. I kept Eli in my arms for an hour and after placing him back in his bed I went to check on his lab work, which all looked pretty good. His HGB decreased somewhat, but most likely due to dilution related to the additional IV fluids he had received.

Henry hadn't really bothered me the last two days, but I'd made sure to be around other people at the Ronald McDonald House. He didn't put up much argument with ICU either. It would be nice to think he was finally realizing how critical Eli's situation really was, but I seriously doubt that he did.

By mid-afternoon, Eli was moved to room 5081 on the regular 5D pediatric unit. The afternoon went well, and I had both Eli and Noah to myself all afternoon and evening. This was so nice, but I wondered about Henry and if he had left Noah stranded again in Denver.

I walked Noah over to the Ronald McDonald House around 8 p.m., and Henry was still there. Henry said all was okay, and that he had been "a handy man" over there, "fixing" little things for the house. I guess that was more important than visiting your ill five-year-old son who had just gone through major surgery.

After kissing Noah goodnight, I went back to Eli's room and looked at his pulse ox, noting he was staying in the 90s which was good. Eli fell asleep quickly. Before I made up the chair bed next to him and fell asleep, I phoned Ardy, and then Matt with updates.

August 3, 1990 – Friday

Eli needed morphine twice during the night. He still had lots of pro-
nounced respiratory stridor. Respiratory stridor was a high-pitched musi-
cal breath sound resulting from turbulent air flow in the larynx or lower
in the bronchial tree. Stridor was a physical sign caused by a narrowed or
obstructed airway. Children with croup had this, but Eli's was related to
his lung surgery, and being in bed so much after the lung surgery. After
his sponge bath, Eli sat up in a chair for half an hour. Sitting erect would
help Eli get better. He surprised me by taking two steps as well. These
were small things, but after what Eli went through, these were big steps
for my son. When Dr. Cole came, the decision was made to hold off on
chemo treatments until after Eli received sixteen low-dose radiation treatments; two each day for eight consecutive days, on his right lung area.
The radiation treatments would commence when Dr. Moran declared
that Eli was healed enough to receive them.

I felt so bad for Penny and her little girl, Dot, who was transported by
an ambulance today to Fort Zarah, so that she could die in the hospital in
her hometown. I told Penny goodbye. I loved little Dot, such a precious
little girl. Only three years old and she had acute myeloid leukemia (AML)
for over two of those three years. AML was a worse form of acute lym-
phoblastic leukemia (AAL). I was thinking back and remembering that
many of us moms here with children with cancers came from an area
within a hundred-mile radius of Fort Zarah. Fort Zarah is located in
North Central Colorado, along the Colorado River.

Fort Zarah, Home of the Big Red One (First Infantry Division), was
known for its excellent training, abundant recreational opportunities, rich
history, and tremendous relations with surrounding communities. We,
parents, wondered why children within a hundred-mile radius of the fort
became ill with rare cancers. When Eli was admitted to EU in March of
1990, the hospital averaged twelve new cases of children with various
cancers each month, and by August 1990, that number had doubled. Fort
Zarah did so many training missions and they flew day and night. What
could our children have been exposed to? I wondered if the Colorado

River was contaminated as well. Every time this subject was brought up by parents at Fort Zarah with children who had cancer, their concerns were brushed aside. These thoughts had troubled me since March of 1990. Mrs. Edward's baby girl died today. She was in the same ICU as Eli. The little girl had been in a coma, on life support. Sadly, this little girl had been hit by a stray BB that was shot off by an eleven-year-old neighbor. This boy had his life altered forever as well; such a tragedy to have happened.

Eli sat up for one hour this afternoon and he drank a total of six ounces of apple juice in between several bites of clear Jell-O. Afterwards, Eli took eight steps before he returned to bed. Eli was sick to his stomach around 9 p.m.

August 4, 1990 – Saturday

Eli and I both had a good night's sleep. That was hard to come by nowadays.

Eli got out of bed by himself this morning and walked over to the chair and sat down. He also rotated himself in bed last night off and on without complaining of pain, although I knew he must have pain related to his surgery. Midmorning, Dr. Moran came in and removed the painted-on bandage from Eli's incision, leaving just the staples in place. Dr. Moran said that Eli could resume radiation on Wednesday. As Dr. Moran was leaving, Dr. Cole came in to see Eli. Eli's HGB was 7.2 and if it was still low tomorrow, Eli would receive another packed red blood cell transfusion. The plan was to resume chemotherapy after the radiation treatment. Eli wouldn't be receiving chemo this week.

Eli's oxygen was decreased to one liter per minute, and we were weaning him off the oxygen. Gavin showed up around 12:30 p.m., something that I had not wanted nor expected.

Eli got out of bed by himself in the early afternoon and walked along sixty-square floor of tiling (sixty feet) before he stopped. It boosted me somehow, knowing that my son had energy to do this now.

Eli had received 2 mg. morphine ten minutes before taking this walk. Around dinnertime, he received an additional 2 mg. of morphine, and about ten minutes later, I managed to convince him to take another walk. Eli walked from his room by the 5F elevators, through 5D unit and into the pediatric step-down unit. Then, Eli turned around and walked back through all of 5D and ALL of 5F, up to the south end window. Eli didn't stop there! He then walked back through all of 5F and 5D to the 5D nurse's station, before returning to his room. That was a good three hundred yards plus more, and I was ecstatic.

If I were Eli, I don't think I could have managed what this little brave boy just did. Eli was truly amazing. Noah was amazing, too, plus he had been a trooper without having his mom (260 miles away) with him all the time. Mike and Pam Warner sent balloons and candy to Eli today. They were nice people who gave gifts to the children at EU in hopes of cheering them up. At 6 p.m. Eli's oxygen was discontinued as he was doing so well. Eli's diet was restarted, even though he was eating Jell-O and drinking apple juice earlier. He was started on codeine for pain with morphine available as back up if codeine was ineffective. Little Dot died today. God had another angel child in Heaven. So many children were dying from various cancers; and this left me all the more afraid for Eli. Gavin and Noah never returned to EU, so Eli and I crashed early. I fell asleep after a long talk with Matt and we prayed together for Eli and Noah.

August 5, 1990 – Sunday

I drew Eli's morning labs and the codeine was supposed to be working for his pain. However, I was not sure my son was being honest about how much pain he might be experiencing. We judge it by his grimacing and groaning, and then we asked Eli directly if he didn't come forth on his own.

I took Noah to Swope Park and the Denver Zoo. He walked all over and up and down the hills and he still wasn't tired. We rode a single hump camel together while at the zoo and it was a rough ride! I loved my precious time with Noah and took snapshots to keep the memories.

After arriving back at the hospital, Henry, Noah and Gavin were leaving EU for the Ronald McDonald House, and then Gavin would be departing for Durango. As the elevator doors closed, the nurses and

I heard a hand hit Noah before we heard him scream. I followed them down in another elevator and caught up with them and saw the red marks on Noah. I hugged my son. I prayed for his safe delivery back to Durango and I gave Henry and Gavin hell! Noah had done nothing to deserve this abuse! I would inform my lawyer tomorrow. I was troubled by this incident and thought of Noah while Eli watched movies on the VCR. We both fell asleep early this evening. Not too long after, Eli woke up and drank six more ounces of apple juice and ate a few bites of applesauce.

August 6, 1990 – Monday

I awoke from a nightmare at around 3 a.m. after hearing Noah scream loudly in my dreams. I was so upset that Noah wasn't safe with either Henry or Gavin. I prayed my son would suffer no more abuse, but I was terrified for him. And yet, there was nothing I could do about it right now. I prayed Ardy could help soothe my son when I could not. I was so angry at Henry! I heard that asshole's voice as the elevator door closed and heard him smack Noah on his little head. Three nurses nearby heard him do it, too.

Eli was sick to his stomach around 8 a.m. I hated seeing him suffering so much. An hour later, when the episode passed, Eli wanted to go for a walk and he demanded that I fill his squirt gun with water, so I did. Eli walked without effort, and several nurses and passersby received a dose of water from him. He was having fun and I loved seeing him this way. Eli's bleeding time was bad during his morning labs, and we weren't sure why this was so. He received Vitamin K in his IV because of this.

Right after lunch, I phoned my lawyer and told him what happened in the elevator with Noah. He advised me to report it to SRS. I also told my lawyer that H & R Block in Durango prepared our tax forms and that I didn't want Henry to have access to them until I received either the originals or copies of all documents. Then, I phoned SRS in Durango and was informed that Zoe Penson would return my call tomorrow morning.

Mid-afternoon, Eli and I went down to Radiation Oncology and Eli was platted for all the radiation to his chest. Eli would have External Beam Radiation on his lungs as well as his heart, liver, stomach, and spinal cord. The extent of the field bothered me greatly, and I prayed Eli would survive what he was to endure next. I took two full loads of belongings from Eli's room out to my car before dinner using Eli's wheelchair. Henry and Gavin didn't help with these things of course. They could care less. They're only good with hurting people.

Eli and I watched *Teenage Mutant Ninja Turtles* on TV, and when Eli tired, I prepared him for bed. As he fell asleep, I was on the phone talking to Matt. He was such a rock for me. I knew we were both comfortable with the direction our relationship was going.

August 7, 1990 – Tuesday

Like clockwork, I was up at 5 a.m. The morning flew by as I took everything out of Eli's room. By 11 a.m., he was discharged. At noon, Port Films were done in Radiation Oncology after which Eli and I went over to the Ronald McDonald House where Noah and Eli played Mario Brothers on the Nintendo for a while. At around 4:30 p.m., both Henry and Noah left for Durango. I prayed for the safety of my son while in his father's care.

Eli drank juice and ate applesauce for dinner, but chose not to try anything else. I didn't want to push Eli to eat – he needed to do this at his own pace, with his radiation ravaged throat. After setting things up in our room here, I noticed that the wrong filters were sent, so I couldn't set up Eli with his TPN. More than an hour later, the right filters arrived and I set up Eli for the night. I think we both fell asleep instantly right after that. Truth be told, I sure had no recollection of falling asleep.

August 8, 1990 – Wednesday

I awoke to Eli throwing up around 3 a.m. After we went through our usual routine he fell right back asleep so I went back to sleep as well. I was up by 6 a.m. and was able to take Eli to Radiation Oncology before 8 a.m. Eli received the first of sixteen radiation treatments. On our way back to the Ronald McDonald House, we stopped by the EU police office. All the paperwork I did had been sent to the Denver County Attorney's office. After lunch, I wheeled Eli back to Radiation Oncology, and he received his second radiation treatment for today. He had fourteen treatments to go.

Earlier, I had been busy in the kitchen at the Ronald McDonald House making Eli's favorite cookie– chocolate chip. I really wanted Eli to take just one bite of one cookie, but he said no. I know he smelled the cookies, but he couldn't eat any. I felt just awful for Eli. The radiation was probably causing problems with his poor little stomach. We played together outside today on the playground at the Ronald McDonald House. Right before we went back inside, Eli took one piece of a Sixlet's candy and planted it in the sandbox. Eli said he was "going to grow a bunch of candy." I guess that made sense to a five-year-old. Eli always watched me work in our vegetable garden at home, so evidently he thought he could grow candy. I wasn't about to tell him otherwise.

For dinner, Eli had some juice. Then I cleaned him up for the night––he was tired so I let him go to bed early, and I hooked up his TPN. It was nice that the Ronald McDonald House allowed TPN to be kept in the refrigerator. Then out of tiredness, today became the second night in a row that I had no recollection of falling asleep.

August 9, 1990 – Thursday

For the second consecutive night, Eli woke up at around 3 a.m. throwing up. It could be the damn radiation causing this. I cleaned him up before he went back to sleep.

Later in the morning, we had our usual routines except that after I flushed Eli off his TPN, he didn't want to get up and out of bed. I told my son he had to have a radiation treatment, but he didn't want to go. In the end though, he sat down in his wheelchair waiting for me to take him over. Looking at my son, I wished once more that he could just be a little boy doing ordinary things that little boys do. And none of this crap.

Eli received his third radiation treatment this morning, and afterwards we went over to the M. C. Mueller building on the EU complex and labs were drawn from Eli's Hickman. Then we loafed around at the Ronald McDonald House. Neither of us felt like doing much so we just relaxed watching the TV in the recreation room. I lay down on a couch and Eli lay next to me, looking at cartoons. At 2 p.m., Eli received his second radiation treatment, and now he was down to twelve treatments left.

After arriving back at the Ronald McDonald House, Total Parenteral Care (TPC) called and then one of their nurses, Brenda, came over to see how Eli was doing and to see how the TPN was going. She was happy with our setup and how Eli's cares were being performed by me.

Ardy phoned to say she was taking Noah to his annual dental appointment so the dentist could put protective sealant on his teeth, which is normally what I had done for both of my boys.

This time though, Eli didn't get to have this procedure. I would take care of that later this year as the dental teams at EU were keeping an eye on his teeth. Then I called Social Security as they needed to know that Eli was out of the hospital. Eli's benefits changed when he was not inpatient. If not for my notes and journals, I would not remember everything I needed to do.

Around dinnertime, Kristy Patterson, a Pediatric Oncology nurse, called and informed me that Eli's labs were great. HGB and platelets were both up, and his glucose was okay, as was his bleeding time. She went so far as to say Eli's labs were the best labs she had seen since March, which was the first time Eli was admitted at EU. I felt good and quite optimistic upon hearing this. Volunteers brought supper to the Ronald McDonald House this evening. It was really nice of them and they provided so much food that everyone would be able to partake of leftovers for a day or two. I met Ken and Betsy Canter, two of the volunteers, and we had a nice prayer for Eli, all the children, and all the families, on the back porch this evening. My wavering faith was renewed, and as though the prayers were heard, Eli and I fell asleep soundly.

August 10, 1990 – Friday

My body clock had me up at 6 a.m. After morning cares, I left with Eli in his wheelchair for Radiation Oncology, which was scheduled at 8 a.m.

Afterwards, I cleaned up our room at the Ronald McDonald House and loaded up my car, as Eli's doctors said I could take him home following this afternoon's radiation treatment. Eli was ecstatic, and his joy was contagious. I was excited to go home, too. Eli's excitement didn't stop him from falling asleep while I cleaned and loaded our bags and medical supplies into my car. We checked out at 1:30 p.m. then went over to Radiation Oncology and Eli received his treatment. Only ten treatments left. It was a cause for celebration.

By 2:30 p.m., Eli and I were on the road to Durango, and by 6:30 p.m., we were home. I called Henry, but he didn't answer. Then, I called my mother's. Ella answered and told me that Henry was working with his father in Lincoln, which was really code for saying, Henry was busy being drunk.

Noah was with Grandma, and this pissed me off although I had to keep calm so Ella would bring my son to me, which she did at about 8:30 p.m. She took two hours to go ten miles. Gavin stopped by to check up on me, then he left and Riley called me twice. I think they just wanted to harass and upset me. I must concentrate on not falling into their trap and having them tape me while I lost my temper. By 10 p.m. I had both boys fed, bathed, and in bed. It was so sweet to have them together with me. This had been such a precious time for all three of us. Right before I went to sleep, I called Henry and sure enough he didn't answer. This meant that Noah would have been with Grandma all night long, until who knows when, if I had not intervened. I made a note to inform my lawyer of these facts.

August 11, 1990 – Saturday

Eli and I woke up at 6 a.m. while Noah slept on. By 8 a.m., I had Eli flushed off his TPN and he was playing with Tinker Toys, building something I was not sure of. All this time, Noah slept.

Henry phoned me at around 9:30 a.m. and he sounded quite drunk. He said he was calling from his brother Spencer's in the country. That he got drunk and stayed there last night. Mid-morning, Gavin showed up and played with both boys. I monitored him closely. Gavin asked to take both boys out to their father's just after lunch. I allowed it since he was due his visitation. I simply stopped Eli's saline hydration early so he could go. Thirty minutes later, Henry showed up drunk at my front door. The man had all sorts of photos for me to look at, and then he fell on my sofa and passed out. Obviously, Gavin knew all along that this man wasn't home, yet. Equally obvious to me was that my boys were with my mother. I called my sister, Riley, to come and get Henry or else I was going to do something "drastic" to get him out. She knew I meant I would have the police remove him, so she came right over. She managed to get him up, out my door, and into her car all by herself. She would do anything to help poor Henry nowadays, otherwise known as "keeping the gravy train" with my mother intact.

I had supper at Prospector's Restaurant by myself, and I was home before 7 p.m. when Riley phoned me. I pretty much ignored her and got off the phone. Then my favorite aunt, Lucy, phoned and we talked for some time. Lucy was wonderful to talk with – smart, intellectual, and overall nice. Then, I went outside to roll up the windows on Henry's car and I found a check from Carter to Henry in the amount of $370 for "labor." I should have just left the car to the elements and if it rained, then some damage inside the car would just happen. But I tried to do right although the jerk didn't appreciate it! Evidently, Henry sobered up with some coffee from my mother, and my boys came back in with Henry and Riley. After cleaning them up and hooking Eli up to his TPN, I carefully took his IV pump and pole out to my car, so we could go out to my younger sister Michelle's home, for her oldest son's birthday party. Henry said that he spent the night with Mark Woodrow in Linville last night. I really didn't care where he stayed. His actions only gave me more ammunition to use against him in court to keep my boys in my custody. Eli played with his cousins on the living room floor at my sister's. Many photos were taken, but no one would give me some of these shots.

Eli chose not to have cake or ice cream at the party, and I took the boys back home right before 10 p.m. Eli was tired and fell asleep immediately and Noah not long after that. Around 11 p.m., Henry called and sexually harassed me. He said he *wants* me. There was no way in hell this was going to happen, and so I just hung up on him. I spoke with Matt after that and he calmed me down. We had a special and precious talk as I fell asleep on the phone.

August 12, 1990 – Sunday

I was up by 5 a.m. as I knew I had a lot to do this morning. I loaded my car up with most of our things. Eli woke up around 7:30 a.m. and I did his morning cares. After that, Ardy, her grand-daughter, and finally Jacob stopped by to see Eli. Jacob tossed around a small football with Eli. I took a few photos and Eli was so happy. Later on, after they left, I finished loading my car up and Henry phoned me simply to sexually harass and be emotionally cruel to me again. How I hated that man! I ended up leaving for Denver in Henry's car as it was so hot out and my air conditioner stopped working. I think the high was around 110 degrees. Henry refused to let me take Noah back into Ardy's, and this was upsetting. Eli and I arrived at the Ronald Mc Donald house around 5 p.m., and then one hour later Henry called me. He wasn't as abusive on the phone, but I didn't stay long on the line either. I got off fast saying Eli needed something and I had to go. I was worried about Noah and his safety physically, emotionally, and mentally. Eli and I had a quiet evening in the recreation room watching a *Batman* movie. We lay next to each other and I cuddled with Eli—I was not sure who needed the cuddles more—Eli or me? Then we fell asleep.

August 13, 1990 – Monday

Eli woke up around 5:30 a.m. and so I got up, drank some coffee, and prepared both of us for the day ahead. Eli received radiation at 8 a.m. By now, there were only nine radiation sessions left on his lungs and organs. Then, we went over to M. C. Mueller, and labs were done to see where Eli's counts were at. Afterwards, I gave Eli a big surprise – we went to Swope Park and the Denver Zoo! I put Eli in a zoo stroller since he had no strength to walk the zoo hills, and off we went. Eli was absolutely delighted and didn't care that he was in a zoo stroller at age five years. I took many photos of Eli riding a Shetland pony with a real saddle, and he remembered how I always took both him and Noah to the rodeo each year in Durango where they saw cowboys on horses with genuine saddles.

Upon leaving the zoo, a boy who was with his friend commented loudly after Eli took off his baseball cap, "He's an alien! Look at the alien!" To my horror, Eli heard and understood what the child meant. I was angry and really protective of Eli then. I held my baby son as close as I could all the way back to my car while I talked to him about the giraffes, and all the animals we saw inside the zoo, and his pony ride. I couldn't take away that moment when he heard those horrid words in reference to Eli having no hair, but I could distract him by telling stories of the animals we saw. The teacher sponsor never said one word to the older child, nor mentioned what he yelled out to his classmates even though she heard. I wasn't about to stay and have a conversation with them about the student's lack of empathy and his harsh comments.

I had Eli back to EU for his afternoon radiation treatment, and now he was down to eight sessions left. As we were leaving they told me to bring Eli in half an hour earlier in the morning. Amazingly, Eli was so tired from his zoo outing that he slept all the way through his afternoon treatment. Later, Eli and I had a quiet evening and Kristy Patterson called to tell me that my son's counts were starting to drop. After I had Eli in bed and set his TPN running, I lay down and worried about how much his counts would drop with the radiation as I fell restlessly to sleep.

August 14, 1990 – Tuesday

Eli was up three times during the night with horrible emeses and it just wouldn't stop. I cleaned my son many times and held him as his little tummy hurt due to all the radiation he was receiving and its cumulative effect. I felt so helpless that there was nothing I could do to take away his pain, and it hurt me even more watching him vomit and dry heave so much. This was just not right. I prayed so hard for Eli and this just kept happening.

I brought Eli on time for his first radiation of the day at 7:30 a.m. The morning went well and Eli spotted a Denver police car near the Ronald McDonald House. Eli started chatting up Officer Ken Carson and his partner. Then, Eli made a thorough "inspection job" of the inside of their patrol car. Eli received his afternoon radiation treatment early. That totaled ten treatments and six left to go. I prayed Eli got through them all. We spent a quiet evening playing with toys, playing Nintendo, and watching cartoons and talking about a zillion things. Eli went to sleep early this evening and thankfully was asleep when Henry phoned. Henry started a verbal sexual abuse without even asking how Eli was. To stop his harassment, I hung up on him.

August 15, 1990 – Wednesday

A loud thunderstorm woke me up early. After getting Eli ready, we huddled together under my umbrella and ran to my car. After arriving at Radiation Oncology, I was informed that Eli's normal machine (6 MV) was down and that we should go back to the Ronald McDonald House. So into the storm we went and arrived wet but safely. Then by 9 a.m., I was informed that they could do Eli on COBALT! Lord – why did things keep changing? I was angry. Eli was fighting a killer disease and he couldn't even use the regular multi-million-dollar machine that was designated for his treatment. At least they provided the use of Cobalt although the radiation was different than the 6 MV machine. Eli would still have external beam radiation with the Cobalt machine, but this was not what his protocol called for. After calming down, I took Eli back for his treatment at 10 a.m. on the Cobalt machine. While having his treatment, I updated several people including Reverend Raymore's secretary, lawyer Huggins (a lawyer who was a partner with my lawyer), as well as Ardy. Eli received another treatment on the Cobalt machine around 4 p.m. While Eli was in Cobalt, I heard them page for Dr. Trowbridge to proceed to Cobalt. I didn't know what was going on and I was afraid – no one would tell me anything! I couldn't just walk into the Cobalt room. Finally, Dr. Trowbridge came out and told me the machine had a "glitch", but that Eli was able to receive his treatment. I didn't know if I could trust them with all this, as things didn't seem quite right to me. Maybe it was due to Eli being on Cobalt. The evening passed by quickly and we both crashed early as we had a long day. The days were running together again, but Eli liked being at the Ronald McDonald House and not an in-patient, and so did I.

August 16, 1990 – Thursday

I woke at 6 a.m. and found that Eli's TPN tubing had come apart and blood was backed up in the tubing, despite my taping. It must not have been for long as his Hickman flushed easily. The Lord had kept Eli's Hickman safe.

After receiving his morning radiation treatment, Eli only had three sessions left. We went over to M. C. Mueller for lab work and then to the outpatient pharmacy so that Eli's cimetidine could be refilled. Cimetidine helped promote the healing of stomach and duodenum ulcers. Eli had a nap, and then we took off with him in his little wheelchair to the hospital. Paperwork was left in the Pediatric Hematology Oncology office per request of my lawyer, and then Eli had his afternoon radiation treatment. By this time, only two treatments remained.

At the Ronald McDonald House, I called the grade school and SRS. I set up school needs for both my boys. I had been so upset the last few days. I wanted Eli to be like a normal child. I was SICK of people asking, "How do you do it?" or simply saying, "I don't know how you do it." Both of these comments really angered me; it was not like Eli, or I, or anyone else had a choice! Why did Eli have to be robbed of his childhood? I had so damn many questions! I prayed Eli healed fast and had a happy time after treatment was complete.

Denise Vogue from Dream Factory called. I told her that the doctors would let them know about Eli's wish trip to Orlando and Disney World as soon as possible. Eli was excited to know he would fly on a big plane and see Mickey Mouse and Donald Duck with his brother. I spoke with Patsy (ward clerk) on 5 D. Little Chrissy passed away at 3:20 last Friday afternoon.

Why all the innocent children? I so wanted these kids to be kids. Why so much pain and suffering and why did they have adulthood thrust upon them? Eli and I had another peaceful evening before going to bed except for one phone call. I ended up hanging up on Henry again as he was abusive to me on the phone. I answered his calls so he couldn't tell his lawyer I was denying him health information on Eli, although he never asked how Eli was doing. At least I was able to document that I answered the phone and the reason why I hung up. Of note, both bars in Kiowa (Timothy's and Ronson's), held a joint fundraiser some weeks ago (I am not sure when this was actually held); it was a dart tournament and the financial proceeds were for Eli and his medical expenses. They collected more than $1200 and the money was given to Henry directly in cash. Henry was noted to say, "We can party down tonight," when he was given the cash. I am sure much of it was spent on alcohol, as nothing went toward Eli's medical bills. Henry didn't make any deposits into the bank-controlled account, which was used to pay the bills I submitted to them. Eli had many expenses and Henry didn't care about helping.

Henry's priorities were never how they should be, and he just didn't give a damn.

August 17, 1990 – Friday

Eli was up at 4:30 this morning sick to his stomach with emeses and dry heaves again. It was difficult to begin the day with optimism at this point. Eli and I were both tired as I wheeled him over for his morning radiation treatment. Afterwards, I told Eli he had just ONE MORE SESSION LEFT! The morning passed swiftly as I cleaned our room and loaded the car. After Eli received his LAST radiation treatment in the early afternoon, we left for Durango and arrived home around 6:30 p.m. Henry arrived with Noah about an hour later. I was shocked to see Noah's face. Prior to bringing him in, Noah fell off his new bike at *Grandma's* house.

Ella had been *watching* him. Noah's face was smashed up badly. Henry asked me what I thought of Noah's face, and I said he must be seen by a doctor, and so Henry followed me with both boys to the Durango Emergency Room. Noah's forehead, eyes, nose, upper lip and chin were just one large smashed abrasion! His upper lip was quite swollen and the skin under his lip and jaw was split open as well. His two front teeth were loose. I made this assessment prior to saying that he needed to be seen by a doctor. I worried about a head injury, as obviously this was something to consider in the consultation. Noah was seen by the doctor and his dentist, Dr. Oliver, also came up to see him and wanted repeat X-rays in three weeks. Afterwards, I was "allowed" cuddle time with my hurt son before his father took him back to Bow Mar.

I was upset that both my boys weren't able to stay with me as Henry said this was his "visitation" day. I was unable to physically keep my son with Eli, and so I just wrote in my journals to give to my lawyer so that maybe we could get visitation enforced, and Noah back to Ardy's care. My son had been at Bow Mar with my mother for about four weeks now.

Eli was hooked up to his TPN and asleep by 9:30 p.m. I was missing Noah badly and just wanted both boys together. Visitation must be enforced ASAP. I fell into a restless sleep.

August 18, 1990 – Saturday

I was up early with Eli this morning and he liked his sponge bath. I had Eli in the bathtub, and although I let him play in the water, I made sure he didn't get wet from the chest up to avoid infection to his Hickman. Eli had fun and I washed his little bald head with a soapy washcloth, which was the same thing I did to the rest of his body. It was better for Eli to play and for me to give him his bath this way so he could save strength for quality time being awake this morning.

After drying off and helping Eli dress, I changed his Hickman dressing and then we went downtown to the bank. The bank had called and said the medical expense account had about three dollars left in it and they wanted to give the money to Eli. He was given the money directly and put it in his little Batman child's wallet. I thanked the bank for handling the medical expenses that I had submitted. After we left, Eli wanted to spend his money so I took him to the dime store across the street and he took his time choosing a new toy for three dollars. Then we went over to Ardy's house to visit, and we were still back home by 10:30 a.m. to wait on Noah.

After we arrived home Gavin stopped by. He wanted to know where Eli and I had been and who we had been with. I told him to ask Ardy, the bank, and the dime store, then I slammed the door shut, and so he left.

Henry never brought Noah to me and that got me upset. The boys needed some time together. I took Eli out at 1 p.m. to see his father and Noah. Henry had to give me abuse through his damn jealousy over what I was going to do while the boys played. He even lifted my skirt up to my waist as I left his trailer. Damn him! If I had stayed, I would have endured abuse during the entire visit and the boys wouldn't have gotten their quality time. Right after Noah had dinner, I went back out to get both boys and this time, I was able to get Noah as well. That was great as things were going to change real fast with Noah, his safety, and who cared for him while I was at EU with Eli. On the way in, we stopped off at Jacob's home, and the boys and I had a great visit with him. It was a joy to see and make more precious memories.

The next item on my itinerary was the park in Kiowa. The boys played so well together and it was precious to see. Eli really tried to keep up with Noah playing – he tried hard, and Noah even waited at times for Eli without saying anything. Why did my boys have to be so grown up? Why couldn't they just be little boys at play with no worries?

Afterwards, Eli was tired, so I took them to the Dairy Queen for another supper which mostly consisted of chicken nuggets. Eli just licked at the honey and rested. Then it was home, baths, and bed. Both boys fell asleep as I was hooking Eli up to his TPN. I spoke on the phone with Ella for about two hours, and I was pretty sure she was taping the conversation. I told her what Henry did with my skirt as I wanted that on tape, and of course my lawyer would be given this information. Then, Matt and I spoke for a long time. We were even closer than ever. This was real, true love.

August 19, 1990 – Sunday

I was up early and the boys woke when Eli's IV pump beeped that his TPN was complete. I made them both breakfast, and Eli only nibbled a little, but he managed to drink a small amount of chocolate milk. I dropped off Noah at Bow Mar while Eli and I went to Silverthorne for groceries, after which I picked up Noah on the way home. Noah had wanted to ride his new bike. He knew I would be back to get him, and he said he would be okay. Noah was right. After arriving home, Jacob came over to see both boys. He loved my kids like a grandfather would love his grandchildren—my sons and I had many visits with Jacob over the years living next door to each other.

I put Eli to bed at 8:30 p.m. as he was so tired, and Noah followed an hour later. Then I lay down for some sleep but Noah came in to see me as soon as I turned off the light. He lay down next to me and for two and a half hours he asked me a lot of questions about Eli, death, and dying. I had to tell him all I knew and give him as much comfort as I could. Noah asking these kinds of questions made the reality of Eli dying too much of a possibility. I told Noah about Heaven, and he said his father had told him there wasn't a Heaven. I knew Henry didn't believe in God, but I sure did and I tried to get Noah to understand. Finally, he seemed satisfied and went to bed.

August 20, 1990 – Monday

I woke up at 5 a.m. when I heard Eli vomiting and dry heaving. I helped Eli, cleaned him up, and he went back to sleep. I just wished this would end. Eli just couldn't keep doing this as his tummy hurt so much. I had to wait awhile before I could give him his Tagamet to help his stomach as that was an oral medicine and he would have just thrown it back up. It was so wonderful to have both boys with me again for two nights in a row. I collected all my papers for the school and the hospital lab. Then I phoned Dr. Oliver, a dentist, and made a return appointment for Noah and even an appointment for Henry at his request as he was unable to pick up the phone for this kind of thing for himself. Then I phoned the Durango Hospital to tell them Eli would be up for lab work and that I would draw them. I then woke up both boys right before 9 a.m. as they had slept on while I did my busy work.

After doing Eli's labs, we went to the grade school where I set Eli up for kindergarten and Noah for first grade. I gave the school a copy of

Eli's birth certificate as they needed that, and Eli met with Mrs. Black, his kindergarten teacher. Eli loved seeing the new classroom and the entire visit with his teacher. We all talked together, and I mentioned that the woman, who tutored Eli while he was an inpatient at EU, would be getting together with her regarding his schooling. Then we went to see Miss Spearwood, who was slated to teach first grade to Noah. I set up with the administration that only I or Ardy could pick up either of my boys after classes. I gave that to them in writing. I would ensure safety for Noah when school started!

Henry came by at noon and took Noah to Bow Mar. I followed them later, around 1 p.m., as I had so much more to do. After arriving home, I called Kristy Patterson at EU regarding Eli's labs. His ANC was 940, HGB 8.4, platelets 105,000 and dropping. Eli was to be admitted again, so I left Total Parenteral Care a message that Eli was going to be admitted, and I also cancelled our room at the Ronald McDonald House. Eli would restart his chemotherapy, and it would include mesna, a rescue medicine given after chemo.

I had lunch with Anna and we had a good talk, and then I went to my lawyer's. He was still busy so I left more information for him. Then I called back to Bow Mar to see how the boys were and of course, Henry ignored that question and obsessed over what I did while alone in town. He yelled so loudly to me over the phone. I hung up on him and called Father Stevens at the church rectory. We spoke about faith and the baptism of both my boys, as well as the anointing of the sick for Eli. Father Stevens was uncomfortable doing this for Eli and Noah against Henry's wishes. One way or another, it would be done. Henry brought the boys in around 7 p.m. After baths I hooked Eli up to his TPN. I restlessly fell asleep around midnight.

August 21, 1990 – Tuesday

I had my car loaded by 7 a.m. I really didn't want to go back to EU. I wanted Eli to recover and get well. No more living hell. Eli didn't deserve all this shit, this pain and suffering. No More of Being Robbed of Childhood! No More of Death Hanging Over His Head!

Then, things just started preventing me from getting Eli to EU. First a phone problem. Then I had to wait for my lawyer. Then I had to pick up some things from Ardy and tell her the plan to get Noah back again. Then, I had to stop by at Bow Mar to tell Noah goodbye, and for the boys to say their goodbyes. Henry royally gave me hell for what I did last night, saying I was out having a party, which was totally a lie. But this upset me and I ended up crying. Both boys saw me and cried with me just as hard. This torment MUST stop.

I left for EU after Henry refused to hand over Noah. Right before I hit State Street at Silverthorne, a highway Patrol Trooper stopped me for doing 69 in a 55mph zone. He saw I was upset, Eli was sleeping, and I told him I needed to get to EU. He told me slow down and take it easy and to stay safe. I got Eli admitted by 3 p.m., and two hours later, Henry phoned to give me hell yet again, so I hung up on him. Little did he know the plan in place for tomorrow when Noah got out of his first day at school. No one but Ardy or I could pick up after his class day ended. The school, my lawyer, and SRS were all in on the plan. Eli slept all night long, but I had this nagging feeling that Eli wouldn't be back home again for some reason, and this premonition bothered me greatly. I tried to be positive and I prayed frequently, but I somehow knew Eli wouldn't be going home again. Tears coursed down my face until I finally fell asleep.

August 22, 1990 – Wednesday

The early morning went fine and Dr. Landon came in with his team to see Eli. He said that mesna would be given with this Cytoxan chemo series, because they didn't know what damage was being done to Eli's bladder. They would like to prevent hematuria, blood in the urine, a condition Eli had in the past, and I was in full agreement. They screwed up Eli's first two series of Cytoxan. His counts had dropped some more and so he may not be able to receive chemo yet. I spoke to Kristy Patterson and she talked with Dr. Landon. The protocol said that Eli's ANC must be 500 or more to do Cytoxan, and so Cytoxan was initiated. Eli received Ativan and Thorazine before chemo started, and Eli was a little sleepy during the day. Later in the afternoon, Eli watched *Ghostbusters* on the VCR while his chemo was running, and I caught up on paperwork and chatted with Eli when exciting things happened in the movie.

At around dinnertime, Eli received his IV vincristine slow push. The vincristine was increased in dosage to 1.1 mg. total. Mesna followed Cytoxan, and it was a three-hour infusion and completed with three small mesna syringes. Dr. Moran stopped by to see Eli around 8 p.m. His assessment showed Eli had a resting heart rate of 170, so he was placed on telemetry and it measured 169. This was NOT a normal numerical figure for a five-year-old. Eli should not be in tachycardia! The typical resting heart rate for a five to six-year-old child was 75–115 beats per minute. Eli's oxygen saturations were 94 percent so that wasn't a concern. I cornered Dr. Moran out by the nurses' station and asked him why Eli was having tachycardia. Dr. Moran said, "Who knows?" Then, he said Eli would be monitored during the night, and if necessary, he would be treated for his rapid heart rate. Dr. Moran saying, "Who knows?" was rather disconcerting to say the least.

August 23, 1990 – Thursday

Eli had tachycardia all night long. I caught Eli's nurse, Sheila, in the hall this morning and she had already contacted Dr. Mattioli about this situation. Eli would have an EKG and an echo of his heart. I was worried that the chemo was taking a toll on his heart. Total Parenteral Care stopped by to pick up Eli's IV pump, pole, and sharps container. At least those items wouldn't get stolen from my car. Dr. Landon came in and said Eli's HGB was 7.3, so Eli would receive some packed red blood cells. Platelets were now 80,000. Dr. Mattioli was aware of Eli's blood counts.

At noon, Eli's saturations were 95 percent and his pulse was still 170. This bugged me. Maybe Eli would improve after he received packed red cells. Right after lunch, Eli received his Cytoxan over thirty minutes. I read up again on Cytoxan (cyclophosphamide) and found out that this chemo drug could cause heart issues. The medicine to save my son was killing him. Eli then had an EKG done followed by mesna, to infuse over three hours.

Dr. Donald Wagner, otolaryngologist, came to see Eli as did Dr. Mattioli. Dr. Mattioli suspected the Adriamycin (doxorubicin) chemo was damaging Eli's heart. The ears, nose and throat doctor came in and fiber-optically looked at Eli's nose and throat. Eli's epiglottis wasn't functional. When function was normal, the epiglottis prevented food from getting into the trachea. Eli could aspirate anything now. Eli was restless and decided to watch *Superman* for a while and I simply reclined in the chair bed crying softly for him. Damn Cancer to Hell! Damn the Killing Treatment! It was looking more and more like a tracheotomy may be necessary. Eli was started on packed red blood cells as he slept, and Henry arrived at EU late in the evening for a few minutes and then left. He stated that my mother said, "Go ahead and go," as she was planning to do something to keep Noah. On the other hand, she was unaware of the plan we had in progress. Eli stayed up until 2:30 a.m. At one point, his nurse took him out to the nurse's desk and he played with toys while I crashed on the floor of the consultation room.

August 24, 1990 – Friday

I awoke at 6:30 a.m., went out and got Eli, and put my little boy in bed. What a day yesterday and last night had been, and today was yet to be seen. Mid-morning, Eli had a CT scan of his head and neck. Henry was checked but he was unable to donate platelets for Eli because he was on an antibiotic. So, he came to EU sick, with Eli's counts going down. What an jerk. Another single donor was found in the Denver metro area and they graciously donated specifically for Eli. The platelets would be ready by tomorrow.

Eli's heart echo was done in the afternoon with Dr. Mattioli present. First measurements showed 24 percent and overall 28 percent heart muscle damage. Dr. Mattioli wanted to use an isotope on Monday to further check Eli's heart. The nagging feeling that Eli wouldn't go back home again hit me full force after hearing what Dr. Mattioli said about Eli's heart.

Kristy Davis, the EU school teacher, stopped by and things were set up for Eli's schooling. She would work in conjunction with Eli's kindergarten teacher in Durango. I found out from Roni's mother that the Adriamycin (doxorubicin), the chemo that damaged Eli's heart, wasn't given by IV push anymore as it was too damaging. Guidelines said that it should be dripped in over one hour at least, and mesna should have been given with Eli's first two chemo series! We were all killing Eli with the drugs he was receiving – not just the cancer! Eli's eye doctor stopped by and his assessment showed that Eli needed more eye lubrication now. Eli received more packed red blood cells.

Eli stopped breathing for about twenty seconds. I hit the call button and then I noted Eli to have stair step inspirations, and then nothing! I shook Eli's shoulders and managed to get him breathing again. I literally saved my son, yet what did I save him for except more pain and hell? In less than five minutes, Eli had apnea for six seconds and then in a couple minutes, he stopped breathing for five seconds. Respiratory Therapy drew blood gas (arterial blood) from Eli's wrist. He never felt the stick and could not be roused.

Eli was taken to ICU Step Down right away. His nurse and RT staff left me alone with Eli. When his oximetry (pulse ox) dropped to 52 percent, I would oxygenate and bag him so he would have better saturations. I used the call light but no one came! Then, I pushed the "code blue" button as I was bagging Eli for the third time, and RT finally came in.

Henry had stepped in while this was going on, and he made no effort to help me with Eli. He just sat in a chair. We ended up moving Eli to the PICU, and Eli was bagged the whole way there. Dr. Landon was made aware, and a portable X-ray of Eli's chest and neck showed some airway constriction in his neck. I stayed by Eli's side the rest of the night and prayed. Eli never "woke up" during that time. Henry had gone back to the Ronald McDonald House for the evening, never calling to check on Eli.

August 25, 1990 – Saturday

I had to leave PICU at 7 a.m., so the staff could do their bedside report with open rounds, and I would not overhear another patient's status. I was able to go back in at 7:30 a.m. Eli's heart rate would periodically drop, but not like last night. About an hour later, Eli sort of just "woke up." No warning, no movement. Eli simply opened his eyes and blinked at the bright lights, moved his head, and then focused on me. I was so happy, but I didn't say too much as I wasn't sure how Eli really was, and I wanted him to get his bearings before too much stimulation occurred.

Henry arrived at PICU around 9 a.m. If he had cared, he would have been over sooner. Mid-morning, a CT scan of Eli's head showed no change in his main tumor mass. I was sad, but Eli was maintaining his oxygen saturations and alert. Such a change from last evening! At noon, Eli was off oxygen completely! Throughout the day, Eli's personality was slowly returning. I was amazed for God answered my prayers at the best time. The doctors, nurses, and I had no idea why this happened to Eli, nor did we have an inkling as to why this occurred. He was coming out of it now, but I knew God had a plan.

August 26, 1990 – Sunday

Eli stayed the night in PICU and his saturations dropped twice to the 80s range, but he came back up on his own pretty fast. For an average morning, I guess one could say it was as "normal" as possible for PICU and Eli. His arterial blood gas looked pretty good, and a little later, he was transferred back to 5D and into room 5019.

Eli now wore only a pulse ox and had been off oxygen since yesterday. After what happened the day before, I found it ironic that now, it felt good to be back on 5D and have Eli acting almost like the little boy he was a week ago. I prayed so hard for Noah and Eli this evening. Eli had become accustomed to wearing the pulse ox, and of no surprise was the fact that after Eli was moved back to 5D, Henry never came back to see him and just stayed at the Ronald McDonald House. He really was a heartless man. Eli and I just watched cartoons on television, and I spoke with Ardy and Matt, giving them both updates on the day's events. Eli's eyelids fluttered before he finally fell asleep. With that, I decided to obtain some rest and slept, too.

August 27, 1990 –Monday

Eli's oxygen dropped to 70 percent saturation one-time last night while sleeping. We did our usual morning routine and I was ready to see what would happen today as I knew Eli had a problem somewhere. Eli had two neck X-rays to check on his "epiglottis" which showed some edematous swelling, which would cause airway issues. Afterwards, Eli had a Multiple Gated Acquisition Scan (MUGA Scan) done on his heart muscle. The compilation of which should be ready this afternoon.

MUGA Scans were useful non-invasive tools for assessing the function of the heart. A MUGA scan produced a moving image of the beating heart, and from this image several important features could be determined about the health of the cardiac ventricles (the heart's major pumping chambers). Improper as well as proper cardiac function could be measured from the MUGA scan. If a patient has had a heart attack, or any other disease that affects the heart muscle, a MUGA scan could locate the portion of the heart muscle that had sustained damage and could assess the degree of injury.

But more importantly, a MUGA scan gave an accurate and reproducible means of measuring and monitoring the ejection fraction of the cardiac ventricles. A common clinical situation, in which repeated MUGA scans were useful, was in following a patient's cardiac function during the delivery of chemotherapy for cancer. Some chemotherapeutic agents (Adriamycin being the most notable) could be quite toxic to the heart muscle.

By measuring the MUGA ejection fraction periodically during chemotherapy, oncologists could determine, on an ongoing basis, whether it was safe to continue with the therapy, or whether certain medications needed to be stopped. A MUGA scan was accurate and reproducible enough to detect subtle, early changes in cardiac function that might easily be missed by other techniques. It was a highly effective, non-invasive means of monitoring one of the worst side effects of chemotherapy and allowing that therapy to be delivered more safely and effectively than would otherwise be possible. After the MUGA Scan, I took Eli down to the ENT Clinic as Dr. Wagner wanted to check on Eli while he was still partially sedated from the MUGA Scan. Dr. Wagner found that Eli's epiglottis' swelling had decreased considerably with the use of steroids for the inflammation. Eli would continue the Decadron until the swelling was gone.

Eli had a sleepy but good evening just resting and playing with Precious and watching cartoons. Eli slept well tonight and his saturations dropped to 89 percent just once, and his heart rate (at one point during the night) rose to 159.

August 28, 1990 – Tuesday

Eli had a fairly good day today and he received a card in the mail from his friend, Logan, which had a five-dollar bill enclosed. Eli demanded that he must go to the gift shop to see what new items they had, so we went. He found one toy to buy and kept the remainder of the money in his little Batman wallet.

Eli had a new double lumen put on his Hickman by Cerese Bregman, so this meant that Eli was off all IV's for the day. Eli ate seven cheese crackers and drank some 7-up. He even ate a little chicken noodle soup. I knew it was too much to hope that all would be well after seeing him get some of his appetite back, but I was still elated to see Eli eat more than his usual portions.

At around 7:30 p.m., Eli was taken to the Sleep Disorder Clinic, and wires were hooked up to his head, and an EKG monitor, as well as a pulse ox. After he was hooked up, I went back to 5D and picked up his medications and TPN. I gave Eli his medicines and hooked him up to his TPN down in the Sleep Clinic. I carefully flushed and heparinized his Hickman ports per instructions from Cerese Bregman. Eli's new lumens had sealed nicely.

Eli woke up at 10:30 p.m. While calming him down, I changed his clothes and told him all would be okay with the wires, and he could just sleep through this test. I told Eli the test was not painful and he trusted me.

August 29, 1990 – Wednesday

Eli had a mostly okay day, but experienced a temperature spike of 102 degrees Fahrenheit. Dr. Mattioli called me and said the MUGA Scan showed little damage to Eli's heart. I prayed Eli would not receive more damage to his heart as he fought this quest to beat the "bad guys" in his little body.

Come evening, Eli did have some problems. He had abdominal pains as well as back pains (UTI or Cytoxan?). Eli was crying so his nurse gave him one half dose of Codeine to take the edge off his pain. Eli desaturated on and off all night down to 70 percent. Eli was sensitive to so many medications. His pulse ox was set to beep when he went below 90 percent and I took notes of the time and how far down Eli went, so I would have the information for his doctors. The days and nights were running together yet again.

August 30, 1990 – Thursday

Eli was up at 7 a.m. and it looked like he may have a viral illness going on as well. He now had fever blisters and cold sores on his lips, around his mouth, and along a facial nerve on his right side. It was hard to say what the cause was, but I suspected shingles as Eli had chicken pox at age two years.

I was sad I couldn't give Eli a kiss, but he was chipper this morning. He was almost his old self and that was nice to see. Preliminary results came back from his sleep study. Eli did have moderate sleep apnea during Rapid Eye Movement (REM) sleep in favorable conditions. I wasn't thrilled to hear that at all.

Eli needed the pulse ox on now any time he napped or slept. Eli had to stay in his room due to his potential viral disease so we played and watched *Superman* on the VCR. We both crashed early for the night. Henry hadn't been around for a couple days now, which was just as well.

Back in Silverthorne, school was going well for Noah and he was now under the care of Ardy since school started. I spoke with both of them again tonight. I missed my son, but I know Ardy took excellent care of Noah. My notes were getting shorter again.

August 31, 1990 – Friday

Eli and I both had another so-so day. I took Eli to the eye clinic, and his right eye was looking better and healing well. I was glad the medicine I put in them all the time was working. Denise Vogue of Dream Factory called again. Plans were now being made for Eli to have his wish to go to Disney World. Henry wasn't here and I managed to convince Father Spencer to baptize Eli this evening – this was done in Eli's room on 5D. He wanted to know the wishes of Henry regarding baptism and I just said Henry wasn't in the "picture" right now. Later my mother phoned and was a little bitchy about not having Noah now. I just hung up on her.

When Eli fell asleep, I saw him desaturate to 71 percent ten different times in thirteen minutes. This troubled me. I fell restlessly to sleep at some point, but woke up with each beep of Eli's monitor.

Chapter Nineteen

September 1990

September 1, 1990 – Saturday (7th month at EU)

My internal clock must have been broken as I woke up later than usual, and I was rather sluggish in doing our morning routine. I knew the doctors would be rounding soon so I did all I could before they arrived.

After the doctors' rounds, it was decided that Eli may have Herpes Zoster (shingles) as the rashes followed a facial nerve and not just around his mouth. Eli's history of having chicken pox and his depleted immune system meant that he was susceptible to a break out anytime. I was right in my suspicions about the virus. Eli was moved to a room with strict isolation as he was contagious to others who haven't had chicken pox as well as those with poor immune systems.

By noon, Henry showed up and told me in front of Eli that I was "flashing my panties for the doctors and that I wanted it hard in the rear". Damn that abusive and jealous man! I didn't flash my panties! I didn't want it in the rear from him either! I would rather he just went away and never came back! He then left as he wanted no part of the shingles.

Eli hated being in isolation yet again. He told me he felt tired so we just watched his favorite movies on the VCR. I cuddled him, but I had to be careful not to kiss him. It felt strange embracing my baby son yet not being able to give him a loving peck. Eli didn't understand why we all wore gowns and gloves, but I made sure he knew his mama would still snuggle and hold him.

When Eli fell asleep this evening, the apnea monitor showed him doing some desaturating. He did this eleven times in ten minutes. He would drop to 62 percent then go to 65 percent, then to 62 percent and then back up to 96 percent. This was nuts! I was watching him closely and his apnea monitor never went off. Obviously, this wasn't going to work out, and Eli would require his pulse ox back, and that is what was done. I think I fell asleep around midnight after a phone call with Matt and some prayers.

September 2, 1990 – Sunday

Eli woke up around 2 a.m. and he stayed awake the rest of the night. We played and watched television, but it seemed like he never tired. Eli was still going strong at 10 a.m. when Dr. Cole came in to see how he was doing.

It was then decided that Eli needed Contact Isolation instead of Strict Isolation. The herpes zoster was changed to Human herpesvirus 1–a cold sore virus running rampant in Eli's body. Herpes simplex 1 caused sores around the mouth and lips (sometimes called fever blisters or cold sores) and could spread through kissing or sharing objects such as toothbrushes or eating utensils. Attacks could be brought on by general illness (from mild malaise to serious conditions), fatigue, physical or emotional stress, immunosuppression due to medications such as chemotherapy or steroids, or disease.

Symptoms usually appeared as a blister or as multiple blisters on or around affected areas—usually the mouth leaving tender sores. Although there was no known cure for this, treatment can relieve the symptoms. Eli would require 7–10 days of IV acyclovir (anti-viral). The blisters and cold sores could cause tingling and burning just prior to their breakout. The pustules themselves could also be painful. Since there was no cure, the virus remained in the body inside nerve cells, and would come out if something should trigger it to be active again. Herpes and shingles were clinically distinct diseases, with different symptoms and modes of transmission. However, they were both caused by members of the herpes virus family. Upon completion of the IV Acyclovir, Eli was to receive a five-day hard chemo series. It looked like Eli would be an inpatient again for some time. That strange feeling that I would never take Eli home again came back to me, and I just feared for my little boy. A five-day hard chemo series must be done to save Eli's life, yet the chemo almost killed him. It was so damn difficult to see this happening. I hated cancer!

Henry had come over to use the phone in Eli's room this morning. He called my mother and she wanted to know if I would be back for the court date this coming Thursday. I gave her no answer and then I asked for Ella. I informed Ella that she was going to start taking Noah to the Catholic Church on Saturday evenings in my absence and that Henry couldn't deny this to my son – especially when Ella taped everything I had just said to her. Funny how Henry, who didn't believe in God, now couldn't do one single thing to prevent my son from going to church like he did in the past. It would look bad for him in court if he tried to say no. Finally, Noah got to know more about God, the Lord and the Holy Spirit and I was so happy for that. Henry, Ella and my mother were informed by me, that I had Eli baptized by a priest here at EU, and also that Eli received the sacrament and anointing of the sick. Although no response from Henry, the rest said it was the right thing to do.

Ella said that Ava would go to church as well and Emily if it worked out. It seemed funny how they wouldn't deny this to Noah now, and then I called Father Stevens and left him a message regarding my plans for Noah. Anna called and we spoke for about twenty minutes. Anna had been updated on Eli and she knew now how Matt and I felt! Eli and I did a lot of cutting shapes and gluing today since he was so determined to stay awake. Henry said he was going back to Durango tomorrow, and I was sure he would so that he could be present for court. Unfortunately, he also said that Gavin was coming to EU today. I didn't need Gavin around!

I left to mail a letter around 3 p.m. (EU Post Office) and Henry was so damn jealous that he actually tried to follow me. I wished he would just leave me alone! Gavin showed his face around 7 p.m., but not for long as he took one look at Eli and left. Gavin made Eli feel like a leper! More spots appeared on Eli's face so I guess we would wait and see what happened now that Eli was being treated with the anti-viral.

Eli finally went to sleep around 9 pm. He had been up since 2 a.m. during the night—nineteen hours since he slept – and I wondered if the zoster or whatever was causing internal nerve problems, and such pain that he couldn't sleep. Eli just isn't telling me about it though, and he never looked sleepy. Eli could be stubborn and not give me direct answers sometimes; I think Eli just didn't want me to know certain things, like he was trying to protect me. I fell asleep exhausted.

September 3, 1990 – Monday (Labor Day)

Eli was on his pulse ox last night and his saturations dropped often while his heart rate went up. No one knew what caused this, and the nurse documented these occurrences. I thought that the damage to his heart was making it work harder to get oxygen-rich blood out to his body and organs. Upon further reflection, I believed we were seeing his heart damage manifest itself in this manner. That scared me more knowing that Eli was coming up to a five-day hard chemo series soon. Last night was a bad night for sleeping, with the pulse ox frequently going off, but I knew that I would wake up to its sound and would help him when he dropped down. I would do everything I could for my son.

We had our usual morning as far as isolation went. Dr. Cole showed up midmorning to see Eli. He said that he couldn't say for sure what Eli really had until the culture came back and that it would take a while. Not knowing hurt. How could they not know if my son had shingles or simplex!

Eli loved Dr. Cole and enjoyed talking to him. This time, it was Dr. Cole who initiated the conversation with Eli. He said that his own kids had a pet turtle at home. Dr. Cole really liked Eli, too. You could just see how much they appreciated each other.

Later, Gavin showed up with Henry right behind him. Henry accused me that my car wasn't in its usual parking stall at the Ronald McDonald House. That was a blatant lie! Perhaps he thought he could use this tack in court on Thursday. Sadly, for him, all the nurses knew that I had been at Eli's bedside both day and night. My God – the nurses and I watched Eli's saturations and heart rate all night long! Henry was more nuts than I thought. He had no clue as to how sick Eli really was, or maybe he didn't really care. He may just be following the gravy trail of my mother. I couldn't stand his verbal abuse so I had to leave the room. The man left to go back to the Ronald McDonald House.

Eli's ANC was at 250, which was not good at all. Yesterday it was 256. I was worried for my son, and I loved him so much! When he took a nap, I tried to get one, too. But Henry would either intentionally pop into the room or call me on the phone just to wake me up. I guess he thought he was the only one who needed sleep, and to hell with Eli and me!

Eli woke up at around 4:30 p.m. and Gavin came over about the same time. He told me that Henry had already left for Durango, and then Gavin went back to the Ronald McDonald House. Eli seemed a little perky after his nap and we watched *Superman* on the VCR. Eli fell asleep again right before the movie ended so I went and told his nurse that I wanted to go to the hospital chapel for just a little bit. She said that she would watch my son closely.

I spent some time praying in the chapel and then went back to Eli's room. He was still asleep. I looked out the west window of the room and it was just getting dark at 8 p.m. The season was changing yet again and it was getting darker earlier now. Eli had done part of winter, spring, summer, and now he was spending fall at EU. We were both tired of living in the hospital day in and day out, season after season. Noah was growing up and I was missing out. I missed Noah so much!

September 4, 1990 – Tuesday

Eli desaturated several times during the night (down into the 50s), but his heart rate was mostly normal. Around 7:30 a.m., Eli woke up and started screaming loudly in pain, which was emanating from both his feet and ankles. He cried out and asked for a doctor. I knew that he had to be in horrific agony to be screaming like this. My son knew how to put up with pain, often without complaint. They gave him 1.8 mg of morphine and took X-rays of his feet and ankles. Dr. Cole was at a loss as to why Eli was experiencing this pain. He said it may be because of the anti-viral medication, or maybe metastasis of Eli's cancer. Damn all of this! I wanted Eli back to his normal life!

Visitors stopped by Eli's room today. Kristy Davis, Eli's teacher, brought some school work. Later, a man from the Denver baseball team came in with George Gunner and they gave him an autographed photo and baseball in a protective case. That was sure nice of them. I took a few photos. After Eli fell asleep, he dropped to 48 percent saturation and his heart rate shot up to 179 beats per minute. It was another long night. I was drained from worry, and prayed as tears flowed freely down my cheeks.

September 5, 1990 – Wednesday

Morning went like usual. Eli received his chemo treatment, a vincristine IV slow push. He was now halfway through his entire protocol of treatment. I feared that he may not be strong enough to get through the second half. Eli was also due to receive packed red blood cells today.

Kristy stopped by to see Eli's progress on writing his name, and she gave Eli fun activities to do. It was funny to see Eli try to write his name. His "E" was mirrored backwards and I felt so proud that Eli could now write his name!

The blood transfusion started around 1 p.m. At 3 p.m., Kristy Patterson came in to inject 1 ml. of urokinase into the red port of Eli's Hickman to see if they could de-clot that lumen. No one knew why it clotted off. I talked to Kristy for a while, and I couldn't stop myself from crying, even in front of Eli. I shared with her my concern for both my boys and she took the time to listen to me. By the time I was done, she checked on Eli's red port and the urokinase worked! Now he had two good ports again.

I found out that Eli's ANC early this morning was at 80, which meant that Eli was susceptible to more infections. To think he just had vincristine today! Had I known it was this low, I might have refused today's vincristine until Eli was stronger.

Using crayons, Eli drew me two different drawings today and I taped them up on the wall of his hospital room. I told him he was getting really good at drawing houses and people, and he gave me the biggest smile he could give. My poor little boy! He cried so much when I told him that I had to leave the hospital tonight because of the court hearing tomorrow, and that I was working hard to save both him and Noah. He told me he really didn't want me to leave him tonight. He said he wanted me to save both of them, but he said that I should do it over the phone. He didn't understand why I had to go. I hated the thought of not being with him, knowing that he could desaturate. But the court date couldn't be postponed, and I had to be there. I loved Eli so much and this just broke my heart. I finally left for Durango around 8 p.m. and got in around midnight, just crashing in bed for my much-needed sleep. I kept my phone next to me in case EU called me for any emergency.

September 6, 1990 – Thursday

The Durango Police called me around 2 a.m. saying I needed to call EU immediately. At about the same time, my mother and Henry both knocked on my door. What was odd though, was that Eli's nurse never called me. So, I figured they were just trying to cause trouble. I called Eli's nurse to check up on him. She told me that Eli was doing okay. Then the phone rang and it was my mother telling me that she was worried about me. I know that was a lie as she had never cared about me one bit.

I called EU again. Eli's nurse reassured me that Eli was okay, that he had desaturated once thus far tonight, and that they had staff sitting with him at his bedside. I was confident that the CNA (certified nurse aide) they had sitting with him would take care of him. My son liked this girl, too. Should they need me, they would call. But for the rest of the night, my mother and Henry kept me from getting any sleep before the court hearing tomorrow.

I phoned EU just after 6 a.m. and spoke with Eli's nurse again. She said that Eli desaturated two times last night, both of which were hanging around 50 percent. Shelley, the CNA sitting in with him, gently shook his right shoulder as he failed to come back up on his own. After that, he was fine again. Shelley did exactly what I would have done. They took great care of my son. They also moved him to room 5012 so he could be closer to the nurses' desk as well.

Eli's nurse told me that Henry had called EU at 4 a.m. asking questions about me, about what I was doing and who I was with. He never once asked about his son. Eli's nurse didn't tell Henry about Eli and how he was doing since he never asked. She didn't feel like volunteering any more information. The staff knew him too well.

I phoned Henry around 7 a.m. He said that Eli had a good night at EU and that I hid from him in a garage so he couldn't find me. Obviously, Henry didn't know how Eli's night was, nor mine for that matter. I thought that he might be nervous about court today, so I informed him about Eli's night, which he ignored, and instead he kept asking questions about me. Henry stalked me no matter where I was. No one did anything about this. I finally hung up on him. The phone rang, and it was him once again. He had the nerve to phone me right back just to see if I would answer from my apartment number and to be sure I didn't call from a different number. As soon as I said hello, he started in and I hung up.

I phoned EU again around 9 a.m. and spoke with Eli's nurse, Rita. She said Eli was up, watching *Sesame Street* and drinking iced tea. He loved Rita. Even though I had no doubts about his care, I still worried for his health overall.

I met my lawyer at 11 a.m. and we discussed recent events. We were in the courtroom by 12:45 p.m. The court hearing started at 1 p.m. and we had a different judge this time, who, rather than doing anything on our custody and divorce, postponed court until October 4, 1990, at 10 a.m. Had I known this, I never would have left Eli. I went to the county attorney's office and we were set to meet at 9:30 a.m. tomorrow.

After that, I went up to the club to talk with my friend Anna and then my mother showed up. She had a camera in her hand and I was sipping on a glass of sun tea.

My mother said she wanted to get a photo of me in my "natural habitat." I raised my glass of ice tea and told her to make sure she got a good photo of me and my "drink." I knew she wanted to show that I was drinking alcohol. My mother left to take photos of my car outside the club while Anna, Lucy, and I had a good laugh. My mother stalked me, too.

I picked up Noah from school about forty-five minutes later. I also gave the school a copy of Henry's visitation letter so that they knew no one but Ardy or I could pick up my son from school. Then I took Noah to see Dr. Oliver for a follow up on his teeth. He had a bike accident when he was with Ella, and Dr. Oliver said Noah was okay but that two front teeth would come out soon.

Noah and I went to see Ardy. It felt great talking with her. Noah and I had a nice evening together. We went out for supper since I didn't have fresh food in my refrigerator and because I needed to go back to EU tomorrow. But, I made sure our meal was nutritious. I loved Noah so much!

I called Eli's nurse, Mitch, three times this evening to ask how Eli was doing and he said Shelley was again sitting with Eli all night.

September 7, 1990 – Friday

Matt phoned me before midnight last night and we had a lovely talk on the phone. After I fell asleep, I suddenly woke up from a nightmare! I remembered Eli being in my nightmare, but I couldn't place where I was. I thought about it for a while and then realized that I was at EU, but in an area I had never been before because it was not part of the real EU. I also felt really horrible in this nightmare and was totally frightened.

I was afraid for Eli, and so I called EU. I spoke with Eli's nurse, Lisa, and she said Shelley stayed with Eli all night and made sure that he was okay. I think my mother and Henry brought on this damn nightmare, but at least, I didn't wake up Noah.

I got Noah ready for school. He loved his breakfast of Fruity Pebbles and milk. At the grade school, I spoke with Noah's teacher about how he was doing. I had to say goodbye to Noah, Eli's kindergarten teacher, the school nurse, Mrs. Menninger, Mrs. Fernery, the secretary and the principal. Everyone was on the same page now concerning Noah. Afterwards,

I met with the county attorney, the sheriff's department, and the police department. All of them were on the same page now as well.

Then I called Henry and informed him that only Ardy could pick up Noah from school. I hung up right after so as not to hear his abuse. Then, I phoned EU back and Eli's nurse, Rita, said Eli was out behind the nurse's desk, on a blanket, having fun with toys and the nursing staff. That brought a smile to my face. I didn't want to rock the boat and cause Eli to cry, so I told them not to put him on the phone, but that she was to tell Eli I would be back in a few hours before bedtime. I ate lunch early at Prospector's and then went to Ardy's and told her all that was accomplished. Then, I was off to Denver once again.

Eli was awake when I arrived, and I was informed that Ardy had phoned and that I should call her back. I called Ardy back after hugging Eli, and Ardy was full of news. There was a big deal going on at the grade school when school was dismissed. Ella was screaming and yanking hard on Noah's arm and Miss Spearwood was trying to keep her hold on my son. Officer Gordon showed up, and then both Officer Gordon and Miss Spearwood took Noah over to Ardy's to make sure my son was safe. I thanked the Lord for Miss Spearwood's perseverance and Officer Gordon's presence. Ella backed down fast after the police arrived. The sheriff's department called Ardy and told her that Henry had spouted off that I was an unfit, drunk mother. Yeah, right! I never had a DUI, and yet in the time I had known Henry, he had received more than twenty of them. I informed Henry that if he wanted visitations with Noah, he should do exactly what was stipulated by the judge. Then, Henry and Gavin went over to Ardy's house and they both saw that Noah was indeed happy staying there. Gavin held out his arms to give Noah a hug, but Noah simply walked past him. I would have done the same thing if Gavin had abused me like he did to Noah this year. They left and Noah couldn't have cared less about them leaving. That says a lot, I think.

As soon as Eli and I got off the phone after talking with Ardy and Noah, Henry called and argued with me about the grade school occurrence. I heard Henry click the tape recorder button through the phone, and I just hung up on him. Eli loved talking to Noah, yet he never asked once about his father. Eli knew! Both my boys knew so much beyond their years.

I went out to check on Eli's lab results and found out that his platelet count was low at 8,000. I asked the nurse why there wasn't an order for transfusion yet. After I got upset, she placed an order for the platelets. Eli could have bled out with all the chemo sores inside his little body. He received some random donor O negative platelets. Eli's ANC was now 200. Things quieted down after that, and Eli and I fell asleep.

September 8, 1990 – Saturday

Eli had to have oxygen put on at 10:30 last night due to his desaturations. I talked with Dr. Cole for a long time this afternoon about preparing the "plan" for Eli having a tracheotomy. That was exactly how Dr. Cole put it. We would see if that came to pass.

Henry picked up Noah at 9:30 a.m. from Ardy. She had been keeping notes on everything. I found that interesting as I never asked her to do that, and yet she had been doing it voluntarily. Ardy said her notes could be used in court. What would we do without her! Ardy was truly a gift from God.

A clown from *Ringling Brothers Barnum & Bailey Circus* came to both 5D and 5F. Eli had to wear a mask for protection, but he had a great time with the clown. I took a few photos.

Later, Henry called and Eli picked up the phone. But when his father started yelling at him, Eli hung up. On his own father!

Eli's ANC was now 252 and platelets were up to 43,000. We both took a nap today. Eli crawled into my chair bed and I cuddled my son close to me, told him I loved him and we both fell asleep. After he woke up, I placed a protective mask on him and he was allowed to ride down the hall one time in the new "car" for the children—a pedal car. Then, I took him back to his room.

Eli asked me if he could go back to Radiation Oncology. He told me that radiation killed a lot of cancer ghosts and that he wanted to go back and kill more cancer ghosts. My baby wanted to live! Eli's statement tore at my heart strings. Eli's nurse, Lisa, and I told him that for now, chemo and sleepy medicine would kill the cancer ghosts and he said okay.

Dr. Cole informed me that Eli's platelets needed to be at least 200,000 for a trach and 50,000 for a nasal tube. He also said that high dose radiation might have caused some brain damage when Eli received it at the main tumor site. When it was time, I heparinized Eli's white port, however the port was still sluggish. The platelets may have partially clotted it and we had to de-clot it. Urokinase was then placed into the port. Eli went to sleep and I finally fell asleep around midnight after a long talk and much praying with Matt.

September 9, 1990 – Sunday

At 12:30 last night, I woke to Eli's pulse ox going off, and Eli was already turning blue. I initiated oxygen via a nasal cannula, but I told his nurse Susan that it would help if Eli was allowed an oxygen mask that stayed put rather than the cannula. Susan could NOT handle Eli going down to 30 percent on his oxygen saturations, and quite frankly, I hated it, too! Something must be done or we were going to be coding Eli! Thirty percent wasn't enough to sustain Eli's organs and brain. Marci came in and she brought an oxygen mask with her, which was about time. The Urokinase did work on Eli's white port, but the night wasn't good all around. Eli and I had our usual morning, and Dr. Cole reiterated what we discussed at 11 p.m. last night. The plan was to increase platelets to 50,000 and then try a nasal trumpet. A nasal trumpet (nasopharyngeal airway or NPA) was called that because of its flared end, a type of airway adjunct, was a tube designed to be inserted into the nasal passageway to secure an open airway. When a patient became unconscious, the muscles in the jaw commonly relaxed and could allow the tongue to slide back and obstruct the airway. The purpose of the flared end was to prevent the device from becoming lost inside the patient's nose. They were commonly used by people with sleep apnea, which Eli sure had in abundance. But this was only a temporary fix. If the nasal trumpet worked, the plan then was to go ahead with chemo. If not, then the plan was to increase Eli's platelets to 200,000, do a trach, wait one week for healing to occur at the trach site and then resume chemo.

In the early afternoon, Henry called 5D and told them to "tell or call him anytime I left Eli alone." That was ludicrous! I guess he wanted to know if I would go have a cigarette or get some food. All of a sudden Henry wanted to have his name "on the dotted line" for anything that happened with Eli. Henry had every opportunity to do this before, but now I guessed he wanted to look good for the court and the judge.

Eli was in his seventh month at EU and now he wants to sign? I called Henry and reiterated to him all that Dr. Cole had to say—that Henry should get his ass down here and be in the hospital if he wanted to get involved. This didn't include staying at the Ronald McDonald House playing "handy man." Henry had the audacity to ask Eli's nurse where I was last night when Eli went blue! She informed Henry that I was the one who asked for an oxygen mask for Eli since I was in the room. Emma, Henry's aunt, phoned and we talked for some time. Emma called periodically and we get on well with each other, much to Henry's chagrin. Emma received the photos I had sent to her.

Ardy phoned before dinner, and Eli and I both talked with Noah who was happy to speak with both of us. Later, Ardy told me that Lily sat down with her at Prospector's last evening and said, "I don't know what the matter is with Sarah. I love her but that Noah should be with Henry" and that "Sarah's all mixed up." Ardy told me it was hard not to laugh at her. Gavin showed up after dinner, and he had to stay at the Best Night's motel because without Henry, Gavin couldn't stay at the Ronald McDonald House since they housed immediate family only (parents/siblings), and Gavin didn't qualify. I also informed Gavin that Eli spent his money the way he wanted to in the gift shops, and that he'd better stop pushing Eli for some of the money people had sent him in the get-well cards he received. The gall of Gavin, a grown man, asking a sick little boy for money in order to pay for his food and hotel room! Eli probably had three dollars at most anyway.

Eli's HGB had dropped to 8.8, his ANC was 210, and his platelets were now 34,000. This meant his platelet infusion was futile. Gavin left then for his motel, and I finally fell asleep around 1 a.m. as I was so edgy and worried about Eli.

September 10, 1990 – Monday (Day 21)

Thankfully, Eli had a somewhat better night last night. I managed to get his oxygen mask changed to one that actually fit his face. Then I got to fight with Dr. Butler (from England) this morning regarding sedation for Eli's MRI and CT scans. I was upset and, of course, Eli didn't get to go down as scheduled. Over the last few months, Eli had done better with the scans. I still wore lead aprons and talked my son through his CT scans on being still, or I sat at the head of the MRI, minus my jewelry, and talked to Eli, telling him stories to keep him still. I wore lead shields for his X-rays too.

I phoned Zoe Penson at Durango SRS and she got an earful from me over what occurred the last few days. Then I found out that Ardy had called her right before I did to tell her the same things. What would we do without Ardy?

Gavin popped in right before noon, and he stayed when the team came in. To sum it all up, Dr. Cole, Dr. Landon, Kristy Patterson, and ten other people on the blue team came into Eli's room. It was decided to hold off on the MRI, CT scans, and light sedation until Eli's platelets were up and they knew more. Afterwards, Gavin convinced Henry to come to Denver! I was NOT looking forward to that!

By dinnertime, isolation was lifted on Eli although his ANC was only 352 and his platelets were just hanging at 27,000. Henry showed his face around 7 p.m., and then he phoned Zoe Penson at her home and ripped into her for what happened at the school and she let him have it back! Zoe, the State of Colorado, and I wanted what was best for Noah, and that was Ardy! Then Henry left in a furious mood and I played with Eli before we finally went to sleep. As I fell asleep, I realized that Henry had showed up in Eli's room, used the phone to call Zoe Penson at her home, then left furious and he never even said hello to Eli!

September 11, 1990 – Tuesday

Today had been a busy day. Eli needed some cytomegalovirus negative (CMV) O negative platelets badly. The one donor in all of metro Denver just wasn't enough. Finally, Henry actually agreed to test to see if he was CMV negative. If I only matched, I would give Eli all that I could. Mid-afternoon, I was informed that EU doctors agreed to have potential donors for Eli tested in Winter Park, Colorado. I prayed someone in Winter Park would match Eli's needs. Once I heard that, I started making calls to beg for possible donors for Eli. I called The Durango Reporter office (newspaper), Northgate Food's in Harwood, Colorado (older brother Jim worked there and maybe some people would be willing to test), his wife Nina, Child's Play, St. James's Catholic Rectory (Durango), Lincoln Daily (newspaper), KY94 and KINA (both radio stations), Channel 12 News (KWCH), Harwood News (newspaper), and the Silverthorne Journal (newspaper). After phoning those eleven places I couldn't think of anywhere else to call to get people tested for possible donation matches for Eli. I just wished I could give him mine. My blood was A positive, CMV negative and NOT a match! I wanted to donate mine, but the doctors were scared to irradiate my CMV negative platelets. Finally, Eli received 200 ml. of CMV (cytomegalovirus negative) O negative platelets, but he badly needed more donors to come in regularly. The platelets were irradiated and given with a leukocyte filter. Then the nasal trumpet was placed. Blood sprayed everywhere, but the nasal trumpet stayed in. Eli cried a lot. I had tears rolling down my face while Eli's nurse helped me change Eli's bedding and clean him up. All I could do was tell Eli how much I loved him and that things would be okay. Henry was over at the Ronald McDonald House so he never saw any of this, not that he really cared. It was late when Eli and I finally fell into a restless sleep.

September 12, 1990 – Wednesday

Last night was a horrible night all throughout! Eli's nasal trumpet came out just after 2 a.m. and Eli lost his airway. I had prayed the nasal trumpet would work, but sadly that was not to be. Back to a mask for oxygen now, and we would see what the doctors said on rounds this morning. Dr. Landon wanted to proceed with sedation and all.

I went and saw Dr. Goodman after lunch to see if she had any bright ideas, but there were none. The Otolaryngology doctors had a new device through Orthotics, which they wanted to try on Eli. It was a brace and we would see if this will work. There was a meeting with all the doctors at 4 p.m. today.

Henry was at the meeting as was EU social worker, Frida Bales, whom Henry hated. After the meeting, he left for the Ronald McDonald House and it was just Eli and me. We played and watched *Ghostbusters* on the VCR. Eli desaturated down to 78 percent after he fell asleep. I made sure his oxygen mask was on correctly. I was so scared to go to sleep. Rest had been elusive. After speaking with Ardy, Noah, and Matt on the phone, I fell into a restless sleep dreading what the night and tomorrow would bring.

September 13, 1990 – Thursday (Day 24)

Eli was sick to his tummy four times during the night, and some of it was blood. The morning wasn't good for him either, and this was the second day in a row Eli was not in a condition to receive all his TPN. I was in a sad mood that things weren't working out like I had hoped and prayed. I took Eli down by wheelchair to have CT scans done of his head, neck, and chest, both with and without contrast. They were going to have anesthesiology come and give Eli light sedation. But after reading his chart, they refused, saying that Eli was *too high risk. No light sedation!*

Eli was ill to his stomach down in Radiology even before his CT scan started. He had a mix of both bright red blood and dark brown emeses coffee-ground type old blood. I had them save some so that it could be heme tested back on 5D for positive blood. I sat with Eli at the head end of the CT scanner, and I talked to him, telling him stories and assuring him the testing would be done soon. Eli was sick to his stomach half way through the testing, and he also developed a headache after the contrast was used.

What are we doing to Eli? Why does he have to suffer so damn much?

After lunch, Frida Bales came into Eli's room. During our discussion, Frida informed me that Henry spent all of Tuesday evening with C. Moran (EU social worker) bitching. That jerk told Moran that my intention was to harm both of my boys, and that I would "*kill them.*" After she left, Frida went to find Henry so they could talk. Eli and I didn't need this jealous crap from Henry nor my mother. Why did people go for jealousy and the gravy train and disregard what was real, what needed to be done, and taking care of one another? I just didn't understand why this crap doesn't STOP!

Eli's ANC was 832, HGB was 7.9 so I knew packed red blood cells were coming, and his platelets were 122,000. I ended up down in the 1F cafeteria most of the evening as Henry was in Eli's room, and I didn't want more scenes in front of Eli. I prayed that Henry wouldn't hurt Eli mentally or emotionally. Eli's nurse called down to the phone in 1F to let me know when Henry left so that I could return to Eli's room. Eli was happy to see me although he acted somewhat subdued. I asked him if he was okay and he said, "Yeah," so I chose not to pursue this and just cuddled my son for a while before helping him back into his bed for the night. Cuddles were one thing no one could take away from us, and they were most precious!

September 14, 1990 – Friday

Eli required no oxygen last night and his saturation stayed in the 90s. Although I was grateful for this small improvement, I was sad that he had become febrile (high fever) yet again. His temperature shot to 104 degrees F and Tylenol did nothing to help combat it. Eli's nurse and I placed cooling blankets on him around 6 a.m. He also suffered lots of emeses that evening and repeatedly wanted ice chips. Unfortunately, my son didn't fall into a deep sleep, and I was sure that was precisely why his saturations never dropped below 90 percent.

Dr. Landon came in around 10 a.m., and he wanted to try two new antibiotics. We collected a urine sample to see if Eli had bacteria in his urine. Eli had a chest x-ray, peripheral blood cultures, Hickman culture, stool culture, throat culture, and a heart echo was ordered because his heart rate was jumping up to 200 and quite often. This was totally nuts! If Eli's heart was so bad because his chemo wasn't administered correctly, then why did his heart continue to function? Dr. Landon had no answer for me. I was so afraid for Eli, and I hated seeing him like this. The radiologist said Eli's sinuses were full. We would learn about the CT scan results from yesterday later on today.

Eli's ANC today was 608, HGB hanging at 8.2, and platelets of 106,000. Frida Bales stopped by to talk with me. She said my mother had called all over Winter Park, as well as many other cities and places, saying that The American Red Cross *would not help Eli*. Mother was such a *drama fanatic!* The Red Cross people were helping Eli, by calling those who were compatible to donate blood for him. My mother interfering in this manner slowed them down in the help they were giving. Maybe that was what she wanted. I just wanted her to stop! Henry came by Eli's room to argue, and I'd had enough. He did nothing to help and only hindered what we (the doctors, nursing staff and I) were doing.

Later on, Eli desaturated again, both on his side and on his back where the brace was. His nurse, Mitch, saw this and we took the brace off Eli and put an oxygen mask back on. After Eli fell back to sleep, I spoke on the phone with Matt for a while and we talked about how Eli was doing, Noah, and a little bit about each other before I fell into a restless sleep.

September 15, 1990 – Saturday (Day 26)

Eli's ANC this morning was 780 – it was taking Eli a long time to rebound this time around. I was frightened for him. His HGB was 8.0 and platelets dropped again to 89,000 when they should have continued to rise. I was so afraid for Eli, and I tried to hide it from him. I prayed for Eli silently and often.

I called Ardy early this morning as I knew she was taking Noah to the Colorado State Fair today. I told him to "buy some pink cotton candy at the State Fair for Mom today and for him to eat it for me." Eli's heart echo came back okay, said Dr. Landon, and his chest X-ray came back good as well. Dr. Landon asked me when Eli had his last IT therapy, and

I told him it was July 17. Dr. Landon knew I wrote and kept track of things, and it was fast for me to find the answer. I spoke with Dr. Mattioli for some time later today after Henry had left. Mattioli thought Eli's problem was brain-oriented. Henry finally showed up at 4:15 p.m. for only fifteen minutes, and then he promptly left the hospital without one word. I was back to using ice blankets on Eli during the evening, and I was afraid to leave his side. All I could do was pray and give care to my son. I showered the top of his head with kisses. I had no recollection of falling asleep.

September 16, 1990 – Sunday

Eli's ANC was only 858 this morning. Eli was just not getting better, not rebounding like in the past months. I was so afraid for my little boy. I needed to trust God, yet the fear kept creeping back into my bones. HGB was 7.6 and Eli would need packed red blood cells soon. Eli's platelets took another drop down to 77,000. Something was wrong, and I couldn't put my finger on what exactly was going on. I felt overwhelmed, but I stayed with my son trying to make him a little more comfortable. I felt like I was failing Eli in his comfort, yet I knew I had done what I could do. Eli had sugar in his urine, and twice this morning his emeses tested positive for blood. Eli was losing blood and no one was stopping this. The doctors were perplexed and we were working on getting Eli the necessary blood products he needed. Gavin must have driven to Denver today or last evening as he was with Henry when Henry finally showed up after lunch today. Henry said to me that they had "slept in" today. How nice for them. They cared not about Eli. I tried not to hate them both, but I did. I just couldn't find kindness, in my body, for them at this time. Their reprehensible acts were just that! They didn't stay long and again Henry never told Eli goodbye. He was just a really big asshole! The biggest one I knew!

Eli was restless and slept much of day as he was so weak. In the evening I phoned Ardy and gave her updates and spoke with Noah. He wanted to talk to Eli, and I had to tell him Eli was sick and sleeping, working on getting better. Then Noah told me everything he did while at the state fair yesterday right down to the cotton candy. I was happy he had a good time.

Matt and I spoke afterwards, and as always he was my rock. What would I do without my support system of Ardy, Matt, Emma, the SRS—the list was truly endless. Again, I didn't remember falling asleep.

September 17, 1990 – Monday

Eli awoke a little after 3 a.m. He wanted to ride his red three-wheeler, the red *Captain Eli* he had received. I told Eli he had to be quiet as the other kids were sick and asleep, and he agreed. Eli had the energy to ride the halls twice before "parking" his three-wheeler in his room. I walked alongside him as he rode. Maybe Eli was on the mend! I prayed he was.

I took Eli down for abdominal X-rays by 8 a.m., and afterwards I took him to the Eye Clinic for a checkup. Henry never bothered to stop and tell Eli goodbye before he headed to Durango. I didn't need his abuse, and my boys didn't need to suffer either, but he could have just told Eli goodbye, and maybe make Eli feel like his father cared about him!

I hadn't received the X-ray results, if they were back, but Eli could see a little with his right eye. He wouldn't be totally blind in that eye from the intensive radiation treatments. After lunch (Eli ate little to none) he wanted to ride his *Captain Eli* three-wheeler again so I let him. I had no idea where he pulled this burst of energy from, but I and the staff on 5D were all smiles upon seeing Eli enjoy life like a little boy again, albeit briefly. We had to stop Eli for a bit as he was leaving black marks on the floor of the hall. We wrapped cloth tape around both of the back wheels as well as the large front wheel, and then Eli simply took off again riding to his heart's delight. *God was so great!*

When Eli became tired, I told him he needed to park his Big Wheels and take a break. Eli said no, but I told him he could ride again after a while and that made him happy. After lying down, he fell fast asleep. I called SRS, Ardy, and the grade school with updates and took care of business to make sure Noah stayed safe. The ENT doctors said they wanted to try another kind of neck brace on Eli, so we would see what they come up with. Eli rode on *Captain Eli* for much of the evening, and

I took many photos of him. I hoped no one (Henry or Gavin) stole any more of the photos I took of Eli. They denied this though, but after losing Eli's earlier photos, I wanted to hold on to all of his newer photographs. However, I couldn't carry everything with me when I took Eli to clinics, treatments, or for testing inside EU. I did my best to hide photos in Eli's room, under blue Chux pads.

September 18, 1990 – Tuesday

At around midnight, Eli had to wait one hour to get his oxygen mask replaced. That was just wrong! All they had to do was simply tube one to the nurse's desk, but they didn't. My little boy needed his oxygen to live! The strap had broken on his little mask and Eli kept desaturating. I had to hold the oxygen tubing to his little mouth and nose area hoping Eli was getting enough oxygen. I was so angry that no one would deliver a mask, go down and get a mask, or tube a mask to the desk. They were so short-staffed, and I just didn't understand. What if I had not been here? Eli could have died! I was so frustrated! All I could do was to hold the tubing close to his nose and mouth (when open) and offer prayers.

Eli was to have both an upper and lower gastrointestinal testing today with a Barium swallow. I took him down for the testing midmorning and they placed an NG tube down Eli for the Barium. The test showed reflux. Between chemo, radiation, gastric reflux, and his emeses issues, Eli's esophagus just couldn't heal. Yet, if we slowed down treatment too long, Eli would die! The treatment was killing Eli just as much as the cancer was. A second NG tube was placed for a gastric emptying study to be done. I had to really argue to get a pulse ox in with Eli and on his finger. I just knew he had to be dropping, and I was right. Eli had to be woken several times during the test as he dropped to the 60s! Why was it so hard to get the little things that make such a big difference?

When evening came, I found out Henry was back already (he only went to Durango yesterday). Gavin was with him, and Gavin went to the ER at EU to have his Dilantin level checked (seizure medication) as he had a "couple of spells" over at the Ronald McDonald House per Henry. This meant he really had seizures and Henry was making light of this situation. After Eli's nurse hung his TPN for the night, I went and read the label to make sure he had the right mixture and medications. The pharmacy had forgotten the double dose of cimetidine. This medication had to be re-ordered, called down, brought up to 5 D by a pharmacy technician, and then drawn up by Eli's nurse and added to his TPN bag. I loved EU and most of the staff, but I hated seeing all these things go wrong. Eli needed that medicine for his stomach so badly, and his nurse never caught the fact that none was in the bag. The safety protocols were not being followed or were nonexistent. I always had to pick my battles as both a mom and an advocate for Eli. Having oxygen (keeping Eli alive by not desaturating) and having medicine to help him not throw up and damage his esophagus even more were a few of the battles I would win for Eli!

Today, I didn't remember falling asleep. Exhaustion was taking a toll on me as well.

September 19, 1990 – Wednesday

I was up early due to anxiety. Eli was scheduled to start chemo again today. I was nervous about how Eli would fare on this round. I thought his body was already too weak for chemo, but this was no longer relevant because if Eli didn't have the chemo, then the cancer cells would take over fast. Prehydration was started midmorning. Then Henry showed up and he just had to get all bitchy. Again, this was not the place nor the time for this!

A meeting was scheduled with Social Services at 2 p.m. Henry, as usual, did his thing, telling them I was "leaving Eli alone at night while I was partying" or that I was "giving Eli the wrong medicine." Neither was true and Social Services charted Henry's words and actions. They knew I was at Eli's side for him and I did his cares correctly. The nurses on 5D documented what I did for Eli and proved I was there all the time. Both Social Services and the nursing staff at EU saw how ludicrous he was, and some had said they didn't feel safe around him more than once. Well, I knew that feeling all too well. So, did my boys.

Henry left for the Ronald McDonald House after the meeting, and of course I was with Eli. My son received Benadryl, Reglan, and Decadron, all IV at 5 p.m., and then chemo started with the vincristine IV push given by Dr. Butler, followed by doxorubicin drip over one hour, followed by ifosfamide with one bag of mesna, followed by three syringes of mesna at 12 a.m., 3 a.m., and 6 a.m. I finally went to sleep after Eli's midnight dose.

September 20, 1990 – Thursday (Day 31)

The chemo went well last night but Eli awoke around 6 a.m. sick to his stomach and throwing up. Thankfully Eli threw up only once. I prayed for less emeses and esophageal healing. The rest of the morning went well and Eli was able to attend the school in the hospital unit. Children were taught by Kristy Davis, and I must say she was wonderful. Her flexible teaching style and individualized school plan worked well with kids of all ages and varying grade levels. Eli's kindergarten teacher in Durango, shared her education plan for my son with Kristy, and that is the curriculum he has been following.

By mid-afternoon, Eli was given a new sedative and right before 3 p.m. his doxorubicin drip was started followed by ifosfamide with mesna. I was so worried about how Eli would react to this series of chemo as he didn't rebound as well the last time it was done. Eli was sleepy and content to just stay in bed, using his suction when he needed it and watching *Batman* on the VCR. I phoned Ardy and spoke with her and Noah. It was so good to hear Noah's voice on the phone. I wished I could hug him, but that's so hard to do over the phone. After Eli had fallen asleep, I phoned Matt and we talked for an hour or so. Matt was so uplifting, and we prayed together again for both my boys.

September 21, 1990 – Friday

I was up like clockwork and Eli and I had our usual morning. I gave him his sponge bath, changed his Hickman dressing, and flushed him off his TPN. Eli's ANC was 1164, platelets 85,000, and HGB of 7.2.

I saw a great need for packed red blood cells again. Eli was ready for school this morning; anxious to go. I told him he couldn't ride his three-wheeler to the classroom, then we argued over riding it, until finally he said, "Okay, Mom. We will walk to the school," and so we did just that.

Eli really enjoyed school this morning. He was working on the alphabet, writing his name, and he finger painted his hands for me – his mom – as a gift. I was so proud of him. I could see that Eli was feeling like the other children in the classroom on the unit, all without hair, with some on IV's.

In the classroom, Eli was able to have the conversation and social activity all children needed. I only peeked in a few times like the other parents did. We all loved the way Kristy Davis did things in her classroom. She was just superb!

Eli was back in his bed near lunch time and was given the new sedation again. His nurse, Rita, also gave him Thorazine, but I didn't know until it was already given. Eli was to receive only the new sedation and not the Thorazine, and now I was worried if he would breathe okay or not. Just because the Thorazine was in the medication room in Eli's name didn't mean he was to receive it. Had his nurse looked at his orders, she would have seen that Thorazine was on hold. Now Eli has basically received a double sedation dose. I was upset.

Rita loved Eli and he loved her, but the mistakes needed to stop! Eli's chemo was started, and then he started desaturating due to the double sedation issue. I placed an oxygen mask on Eli, and Rita hooked up a pulse oximeter, and we saw his heart rate was jumping high. As soon as Eli's doctor came in, I informed him of the double sedation dose and that I wanted the Thorazine discontinued completely – not just put on hold. He agreed it would be safer that way and he discontinued the Thorazine. Eli received all his chemo and mesna as well.

At around 3 p.m. Eli woke up and stayed awake for two hours. Thank goodness he was coming out of so much sedation. God answered my prayers for Eli. Our evening was quiet and Eli fell asleep pretty fast. After a long talk with Matt, we prayed for both Noah and Eli.

September 22, 1990 – Saturday

I was up with the sunrise, and Eli and I had a good morning. Eli's chemo started early and I'm not sure why, but probably it had something to do with nursing staff issues.

Eli's ANC dropped to 240, platelets to 64,000, and his HGB was down to 6.3! Eli needed packed red blood cells and they were becoming difficult to get. I really feared Eli wouldn't come out of this chemo series and get stronger again like he did after his previous chemo. I was so afraid for Eli, but all I could do was pray that my son would be okay.

Eli knew that after this chemo series, the four of us were set to go to Disneyland in Florida—thanks to the Make-A-Wish Foundation. Plans were in motion for the trip, and Eli would have a child's wheelchair upon arrival. Eli's TPN and other needs were already planned and set. Eli wanted to see Mickey Mouse and Donald Duck the most and he was so thrilled. Both boys would be able to do something exciting together, and I just had to get through having Henry there as well. I figured the hotel would help me out on that aspect, as they desired no problems. The plan was to resume chemo after coming back to Colorado. I prayed Eli would get to have this wonderful experience. However, I still sensed that Eli wouldn't bounce back after this chemo series, and I tried to stay positive, but it was quite hard to do.

After this morning's chemo, Eli was awake and wanted to play Batman. Both boys had discussed dressing up as Ninja Turtles for Halloween with Noah as Michelangelo and Eli as Donatello. Eli had spoken of being Batman and wanted a little pedal Batman car. Others on the nursing unit heard about this and some of the nurses pitched in to buy Eli a Batman costume. I helped Eli into his costume, and off we went with Eli as Batman sporting a water squirt gun and shooting at people who came near him. After Eli wore himself out, we returned to his room and I removed his costume and readied him for bed. The evening was rather quiet as Eli was tired, and he watched a *Batman* movie on the VCR again. We both spoke with Ardy and Noah on the phone, and Noah was telling me about how church went that evening. I was so happy and relieved that he was back in Ardy's care, as I knew he was safe there, and she was more than delighted to have him accompany her to church. I fell asleep while talking with Matt on the phone.

September 23, 1990 – Sunday

I awoke after 3 a.m. with Eli vomiting forcefully everywhere. His heart rate jumped high to the 170s. I cleaned him up and changed his bedding. It was so hard to try and comfort Eli when he was going through so much. I cried inside when this kind of thing happened to him.

Just after 6 a.m., Eli awoke vomiting once more. His heart rate jumped again and stayed elevated for about an hour. Dr. Landon came in after 8 a.m. and he wanted to do chemo today. The plan was to have a meeting with several doctors and discuss the treatment. Chemo was started by 10 a.m. Eli's ANC was 912, platelets 64,000, and HGB 6.4. *He needed packed red cells, again!*

Just after lunch, Eli started throwing up again, and it was all quite brown and tested positive for blood. I had a bad feeling about doing more chemo on him right now. I prayed the doctors were doing the right thing and that he was strong enough to get through this round of chemo. I went over to the Ronald McDonald House by mid-afternoon for a few minutes to take care of business over the telephone, since I didn't want Henry to overhear. Then, I went back to Eli's room. Upon arrival, I found Henry going through Eli's trash can to obtain pieces of my personal torn up mail, so that he could try and tape the pieces together. *He thinks he had to know everything!* He was such a nosy asshole!

Just after 5 p.m., one entire unit of packed red blood cells finished infusing into Eli. I prayed they would work and help him with this chemo series. He was still sleeping when I laid my head down to rest around 8 p.m.

September 24, 1990 – Monday

Eli woke up early at midnight and played football on the Nintendo until 2 a.m. Silly kid did things on his schedule and not according to what anyone else thought. I would not have it any other way – he was a little boy once again, at least for a couple of hours during the night, and it was awesome to see.

Eli woke next at around 6:30 a.m., sick to his stomach. This happened again at 8 a.m. and at around 9:30 a.m., as well. But by 10 a.m., he was already feeling better so I let him go to school at 10:30 this morning.

Dr. Landon stopped by forty-five minutes later to see me. The plan was to have a meeting with Drs. Landon, Chow, and Rosenberg to review X-rays of Eli's sinuses as well as to get new ones done. Eli's ANC was 1196, unusually high for him, but he was maintaining on the rest of his labs. Overall, he had a good day today and came off all his IV tubing for the first time in six days, due to pre and post-hydration for his last chemo series.

However, in the afternoon, Eli was sick to his stomach twice again – I so *hated* seeing him suffer so much. He fell asleep early this evening before I had a chance to call Ardy. When I spoke with Ardy, she told me that Gavin picked up Noah today and took him to the park in Kiowa for a short while. Then, he dropped him off at Ardy's afterwards. I could only imagine what Gavin had to say to my precious son, or what abuse my he endured from Gavin. Father Spencer (EU priest) stopped by late this evening and we prayed for Eli. I was not sure of the time I fell asleep in my chair bed at Eli's bedside.

September 25, 1990 – Tuesday

Eli and I had another long round again last night. He desaturated to the low 50s, and I was grateful that Emily, RN, and his RT helped me keep a close check on him throughout the night. The nightmare never ended. I did my best to try and be brave without Eli knowing or seeing my emotions, except for my love. But I suspected he knew I did this. Eli was smart beyond his years due to this experience, and I felt like part of his childhood had been robbed.

Henry just had to call and wake up everyone around 2 a.m. this morning to say he had finally decided to donate platelets for Eli today. Why he mused about this for so long, I would never understand, but if he did it to torture me, then that man was far viler than I already knew. What kind of parent would hesitate to do anything for their child?

Dr. Landon arrived midmorning and said that he wanted to head a meeting with all of Eli's doctors on Friday. He also put Eli on a strict NPO (nothing by mouth) diet due to all of the emeses issues. Today just kept getting better. Eli was taken off empiric Bactrim as Dr. Landon said it wouldn't prevent Pneumocystis, and his Rondec was stopped as well. It was looking more like Eli would require a G-tube. However, anesthesia refused to touch him and Thorazine alone was too much. Eli was to have a psychological school workup because of radiation damage to his brain stem. He just wanted to go home and be with his brother and me. I wanted to do the same thing, but too much kept on happening.

Today, Eli's ANC was 854 so he was on his way down yet again from his last chemo series, which meant a new nightmare for Eli started anew. It hurt to see him in so much pain and hell. HGB was holding and platelets were dropping just a little at this time.

Eli completely and totally broke my heart today. He told me, "I'm sorry, Mom" and I replied back, "Why?" He repeated, "I'm sorry, Mom" and I asked again, "Why?" Eli then said, "I'm sorry I want to go home." I told him we would go home as soon as we possibly could and Eli just looked at me. I wondered if the "home" he wanted to go home to might be "Heaven." Once before, Eli said outright that he wanted "to go to Heaven" and I told him "we don't always get what we want and that he might just have to come back to me."

Eli scared me. I think he wanted to go home to Heaven rather than Durango and there was nothing I could do about this. I was simply too afraid to ask him if Heaven was where he wanted to go. That was the second time I lost my chance to ask Eli what he knew of Heaven. Fear of losing my son was simply too much for me to handle.

Maybe it was time for Eli to go to Heaven and I simply didn't want to accept the inevitable. In fact, I *knew* I was not ready.

Later on, Eli and I played together all evening and we both talked with Noah and Ardy. After Eli fell asleep, he started the desaturations again, especially from midnight until 1 a.m.

September 26, 1990 – Wednesday (Day 37)

Around 7 a.m. Eli started experiencing desaturations again. This was getting so scary. He was having so many problems that didn't get resolved with treatment. I am afraid for Eli, for Noah, and myself, but I continued to pray. It was hard to keep faith in God especially when I witnessed the suffering he allowed Eli to go through. I found myself flip-flopping back and forth between the wide spectrum of faith and anger at God.

Henry was supposed to be donating platelets for Eli. I guess we would find out if he'd push through with it soon enough. Eli's oxygen levels continued to drop. He was getting worse. I ached for my little boy. I asked about Eli's labs and found out his platelets took another sharp dive. This was not good news.

Just after 10 a.m., Eli received the platelets that Henry had donated for him. I prayed the platelets "took." Although Eli had repeating incidents of stomach pain, he still managed to attend school for a while this afternoon. Eli fell asleep early before dinner as he had such a bad night, and he was sound asleep when Ardy phoned. I gave her an update on Eli and then I spoke with Noah, and we talked about his day at school. I told him how much I loved him. I missed him so much, but Ardy kept him safe. Eventually, I fell asleep.

September 27, 1990 – Thursday

Eli was febrile and quite ill during the night. I felt like we were losing ground in this fight against his cancer. But I kept on praying. It hurt to see him so sick like this. His little body was so weak and exhausted. I found out this morning that yet another child who had been battling cancer died during the night. Why? Damn it all! I was so angry about all the cancer in the world and those who suffered from it and the treatments they endured. Why? Eli went febrile again later this morning. This was *not* going well at all! Eli's doctor had a "meeting of the minds" this morning. Just as I thought, the doctors did *not* have the entire picture with regard to what was going on with Eli. The doctor's meeting took place in Eli's room, and I had to actually fill them in on some things they weren't aware of or didn't read in Eli's chart. There was a possibility of a trach place-ment depending on how Eli responded to the treatments. I had never read any of Eli's charts since I was at his bedside and I went with him to treatments. I wasn't worried about what the social workers wrote about me as I knew Eli's nurses told them what I do to help him. However, I did wonder why the doctors didn't have their facts straight, or if they even really read all of Eli's notes and tests. When results came back from a scan or other procedures, I did ask for a copy so that I could read them and understand more of what was happening; and of course, I was here when the doctors came each and every day. I saw a few parents who didn't ask for these things as mostly, they didn't understand the medical terms. I never asked for a doctor's dictation since I spoke with them each day; it just wasn't necessary. I always took notes so I could research things regarding Eli. Henry was fascinated by Eli's chart, and in particular, about what Social Services wrote in it. That was all he was interested about.

Eli was listless and tired throughout the day, and he didn't attend school. I spoke with Noah and Ardy and gave them updates, and told my son I would be back as soon as I could. I missed him so much. I knew he missed his mom and little brother as well. I then had a chance to speak with Emma afterwards and I updated her on Eli. Emma has been so supportive. As I started to doze off to sleep, Eli became febrile again. It was difficult to stay positive when things were so negative. I fell asleep praying for Eli.

September 28, 1990 – Friday (Day 39)

Respiratory Therapy wanted to try Eli without oxygen during the night, and it just wasn't a good time for the testing or the evaluation, but they *still tested him against my wishes*. Therefore, Eli had a bad night, desaturations read-ily occurred, and he vomited six times before 4 a.m.! All of that in a nine-hour period, and to add to that, he had dry heaves three times. I really had to push the issue about giving him some IV fluids due to his emeses. Eli also stayed febrile all night long with his temperature ranging from 103.0 F to 103.2 F. Tylenol was ineffective and my son was hurting badly.

Each time a Tylenol suppository would be given, Eli would have a bowel movement expelling the Tylenol. Ice blankets were useless, but used regardless. I was so angry at Respiratory Therapy for what they did all night due to an order that had been written for this test. Eli's ANC was 120 this morning, and his platelets were dropping fast. The donation Henry gave to Eli failed to help him.

When Dr. Landon came by this morning, we found out that Eli was compromised more last night than originally thought. The resident who ordered the oxygen to be discontinued was *very wrong*. All of Eli's organs were damaged to some extent during the night; how much was yet to be known.

Dr. Landon initially wanted to wait until Step-Down (pre-ICU on Pediatrics) reopened, and attach Eli to all kinds of monitors, as well as assign a one-to-one nurse before doing the oxygen testing. *That certainly didn't happen last night!* I was still angry and upset by this mess and the hurt and suffering Eli endured all night long. Eli's oxygen was restarted while Dr. Landon was in Eli's room. Dr. Landon stated that my son showed a "marked worsening" without oxygen last night. I had been so exhausted, that I didn't awaken on all the desaturations, although upon hearing Eli vomit, I woke up immediately. I wish I had been able to stay awake all night for Eli, so I was aware how low his saturations went. I could have forced the issue and placed oxygen on Eli myself. I felt like I, along with the entire EU staff, failed my child last night. Eli received a Tigan (anti-emetic) suppository around 5 p.m. Finally, he had a chance to not dry heave or have so much emeses. It was so hard to get anything done for Eli last night and today. *It felt like everything was completely out of control!*

Henry stopped by after 6 p.m. and stated he was leaving for Durango. That was fine with me as he would be one less thing to cause Eli grief, stress, and pain.

Eli's wish trip to Disney to see Mickey Mouse and Donald Duck had been scheduled for tomorrow, but I scrapped those plans days ago since he was just too ill. The Make-A-Wish Foundation told me to call them when Eli was well enough to go.

September 29, 1990 – Saturday

Eli and I were both up most of the night, as his fever jumped up even higher to 106.0 F. This was now Eli's second night of ice blankets in an effort to make his temperature go down. The lab called up to the floor early this morning. Eli had taken a sharp drop in his HGB (from 8.3 to 6.0), his HCT (23.9 to 19), platelets fell from 54,000 to 26,000 all in twenty-four hours. Eli was transfused with two units of packed red blood cells. His heart rate increased to 215 at times. I called and informed Henry of what was happening and the seriousness of Eli's condition.

For the first time, Henry didn't abuse me on the phone. He just asked questions about Eli. I told him it might be a good idea to head back to Denver. It was only after several calls with updates on Eli that Henry *considered* coming back to Denver. The Denver metro area finally found more platelet donors for Eli. He can have a platelet transfusion after the packed red blood cells complete. Eli now had six units of packed red blood cells and six units of platelets on standby. They were flown in from Winter Park around noon. Eli's specific gravity was now 1.030. This meant Eli was headed for dehydration so he would not receive Lasix. Eli needed IV fluids now, but we must cut back the amount and watch him closely. The doctors, the staff, and I worried about Eli going into Congestive Heart Failure.

Balancing this was no easy task for the doctors and nurses. I worried constantly. Eli received six units of platelets after his packed red cell infusion. This was bad. Eli must have this treatment and yet we couldn't give too much fluid. They contradicted each other! I prayed and cried silently. A complete blood count (CBC) was done following the platelet infusions; and Eli's HGB and HCT were okay. However, his platelet transfusion did not work and the level remained the same. Eli's little body ate the platelets up just as fast as they went in. His weight also increased by over two pounds in twenty-four hours. This was not good since this meant too much fluid was being retained by his body. On the other hand, this was essential for him to live.

Respiratory Therapy came in and four seconds after going for a sputum collection, Eli went *blue*! Oxygen was placed stat, and on the second try, they managed to get sputum for culture. I alerted Henry about the events several times today, but I had no idea if he would come back to EU or not.

September 30, 1990 – Sunday

Eli had a totally horrid night yet again. Although we were both exhausted, I knew he was more so. I kept on praying, frightened at the same time.

Eli's temperature spiked to 106 degrees more than once, and I was so afraid he would have a seizure and die. Nothing helped to reduce his temperature. I knew deep inside this wasn't going to end well at all. Platelets were now down to 16,000 and so Eli needed platelets badly. Every time Eli threw up, bright red blood also came out. His heart rate shot up to 200 beats per minute at times and he desaturated to the 60s. Eli needed oxygen all the time now. He was spiraling downward out of control, and all I could do was give my little boy care, love, kisses, and prayers. When Dr. Landon came in this morning he said he wanted to try amphotericin B and Bactrim, both IV, and then "see how it goes." *I said "ICU!"* He wrote the order.

Today was just one hell of a day to say the least. Eli was taken to Pediatric Intensive Care Unit (PICU) at 10:30 a.m. where he received a total of six units of platelets and two units of packed red blood cells in one day. He was literally blue and we had to place him on a full CPAP mask (continuous positive airway pressure therapy) in the hopes of holding off intubation for as long as possible, so platelets could be obtained and infused. A CPAP machine increased air pressure in your throat so that your airway doesn't collapse when you breathe in. Intubation was when a tube was inserted, as a breathing tube, into the trachea for mechanical ventilation, as a life-saving measure. An emergency room physician might intubate a patient not breathing adequately so that the lungs could be ventilated. In Eli's case, without platelets, if we tried to intubate him, he would simply bleed out and die. It was so horrible! No one in Denver could donate the platelets that were desperately needed. Eli was so badly oxygen depleted, that he was blue in his face and all extremities. Eli hated the CPAP mask and he fought it, but he needed it to survive. I stayed at his bedside and talked with him and prayed. Both Henry and Gavin had trouble seeing him so sick in PICU. Eli was blue and he kept thrashing around in his bed like crazy from oxygen depletion.

At around 10 p.m., Eli's favorite nurse, Rita, stopped by to see him, and he feebly attempted to squirt water at her with the small water gun she had brought with her fully loaded. Then the doctors and nurses from PICU came to Eli's bed side and informed us they had the platelets. The doctors didn't want me to be with Eli while they did the intubation procedure. But I damn well wasn't going to let my child be alone without his mama. Henry and Gavin left.

Finally, ten hours later (10:30 p.m.) the platelets that arrived via helicopter from Winter Park were drawn into a large syringe and simply pushed into Eli using one of his Hickman ports, while at the same time a doctor tried to intubate Eli. Bright red blood immediately gushed out of Eli's mouth and sprayed the staff, the bed, and Eli. He was turning a darker blue, and they had to take the tube out and try a different, larger, breathing tube. The second one worked and Eli was finally hooked up to a ventilator. It was so hard to see him like this, and even worse, knowing that he must have been terrified and in pain throughout the whole ordeal. Eli spent a horrid night, to go with his horrid day. At times, such as when they weighed him or did report, I would go out to the PICU waiting room and try to sleep for a little bit, but sleep eluded me.

Chapter Twenty

October 1990

October 1, 1990 – Monday

Today was a little better than yesterday or last night. Eli received five more units of platelets, multiple boluses of vitamin K, and one more unit of packed red blood cells. His little body was eating up all that he received. I was so thankful that Winter Park flew in platelets for Eli both on Saturday and Sunday. Without them, he would be dead. I feared that too many organs, including his lungs, had been starved of oxygen for over ten hours yesterday. I was afraid they wouldn't work as well now as they did in the past, due to the amount of damage.

Eli's muscles were being kept medically paralyzed with Pavulon, so that he wouldn't pull on his IV's and breathing tube. He was also on IV amphotericin B (used to treat fungal infections), as well as IV Bactrim, tobramycin, clindamycin, and Fortaz (all antibiotics). Vitamin K was still being given via IV bolus to help his blood clot, and he must be given Lasix (diuretic) as he was receiving so much fluid (still on TPN) that he was beginning to get edematous (third spacing fluid outside the vessels and into cells making Eli puffy.) An arterial line was placed when I wasn't present, and I knew Eli must have been so scared without me beside him. At least, when arterial blood was needed for blood gasses, he didn't need a deep stick into an artery now. A Foley catheter was placed around 6 p.m., which was good, as Eli wouldn't have as much skin breakdown.

Most importantly, he could be monitored and we would know how much IV fluid was going in and how much urine was being produced. Ideally, both amounts should be similar. Every hour to one and a half hours, Eli received Pavulon and either morphine or Valium to help make him comfortable.

Eli understood what was being said to him. He could feel the pressure of my hand holding his hand when I touched his body as I did some oral care, and when I applied eye drops and eye ointments. Eli just couldn't move, for his own safety. I knew he was scared and so sick. When I talked with him, I could see tears falling from his eyes. The nursing staff told me that he was not crying, but they couldn't fool me. Eli heard my voice and tears started to come out of his eyes and I *KNEW* he was crying. My son was *hurting bad*, and he was *scared*, and I couldn't do much to console him.

Everything pointed to Pneumocystis (Pneumocystis pneumonia or PCP), a form of pneumonia caused by the yeast-like fungus (which had previously been erroneously classified as a protozoan – Pneumocystis jiroveci) but we couldn't be sure. Pneumocystis was commonly found in the lungs of healthy people, but, being a source of opportunistic infection can cause a lung infection in people with a weak immune system, like Eli. Pneumocystis pneumonia was especially seen in people with cancer undergoing chemotherapy, HIV/AIDS and the use of medications that affected the immune system. Eli's lungs were a total mess.

I tried to talk to Henry about what he thought along the lines of different types of codes if it came down to that. He told me, *"You want the plug pulled!"* I had to walk away from him and let the nurses try to get him to understand. That jerk just took all of it the wrong way. But, he should think about what he would do if it came to that point. Eli required five more units of platelets this evening – his little body was just eating them up! I spent half the night with Eli and half on the carpet in the waiting room. I was thankful that Noah wasn't here to see what was happening, as I knew he wouldn't be able to handle this, and that it would emotionally and mentally scar him for life!

October 2, 1990 – Tuesday

Eli was down to 50 percent oxygen this morning. That was a good sign that he needed less oxygen than the last couple days, but was far from recovery. I hoped, I prayed, and I did the cares that I could for him. I still did the Hickman dressing changes and eye care. His nurse and I administered his bed bath together.

Eli started waking up much too often and the nurses had to increase his sedatives so he wouldn't yank at his tubes. It was so hard to see him this way. Eli was hanging on, I think for me, since he knew I didn't want to lose him. This was pitiful because it was apparent he was in so much pain. Eli received eleven more units of platelets today and one unit of packed red blood cells. How could my child survive when his body couldn't produce the blood he needed? I was so thankful for the people who had donated blood for my little boy. I wish I could switch places with Eli for the thousandth time. I spent as much time as I could with Eli again today, and when he slept, I read a book or nodded off briefly in the chair by his bed. Henry went back to Durango today, yet Eli needed more support, and he needed strength from his father, to help him hold on. *Damned if you do, damned if you don't!*

October 3, 1990 – Wednesday

Eli was still at 50 percent oxygen and I prayed that he could kick the bug, or bugs that were trying to kill him. Five more additional units of platelets were given to Eli today. Whatever was attacking his thin little body was simply eating up all the platelets as soon as they were transfused. Eli's liver and the organ's enzymes had improved, so anything that attacked his liver last Friday was now gone. I did the cares that I could for Eli, and I stayed as long as I could in PICU, but oftentimes they had so many children coming in as new patients and the staff didn't like visitors in the unit at those times. Regardless, sometimes I stayed and simply pulled the curtain to Eli's room so the rest of the unit had privacy. Those were the times I talked more with him, caressed his hands, arms, and face, hoping he would feel my touch and know that I was there.

PICU admitted a twenty-two-month old boy from Winter Park who was flown in to EU yesterday. Today, they pulled the plug on this precious baby boy since he had been brain dead upon arrival. His mother had left him in the bathtub while she answered the phone. How she must be feeling. Telephone ringing or not, I never allowed my boys to be alone in the bathtub.

At around 5 p.m., I found out that Henry and my mother were up to bullshit again. In fact, Henry actually got approval from Dr. Bamatay, that going to court was okay – except that he never told Dr. Bamatay how long we would need to be gone with Eli in such critical condition. Nor did she know how far away the court would be. No way was I leaving Eli! Right before Henry left EU, he told me, "It's your fault Noah never gets to see Eli again!" *Damn him!* He knew a six-year-old boy couldn't handle seeing these things in PICU!

First, Henry left in an attempt to sway the courts, which was asinine of him still thinking of himself and not wanting to pay child support. Secondly, he *left* Eli, while being totally aware that this child could die at any time! Third, Noah seeing the environment that Eli was in - the PICU, the tubes, all the commotion and seeing his brother suffer like this, would cause him so many *traumas* he would never get over. Post-Traumatic Stress Disorder (PTSD) stayed with one for life! Fourth, I had no place for Noah to stay and he certainly couldn't sleep on the carpet in the waiting room alone. The Ronald McDonald House was completely out of the question as well. Eli could pass away soon or linger on for days, and Noah needed the stability Ardy and his school could provide him at this time. Eli and I had another long night.

October 4, 1990 – Thursday

Eli was transfused with the five units of platelets yesterday, and by 6 a.m. this morning, the entire process was repeated again. Henry was in Durango and did not even care to donate more platelets for our son.

The medical staff had changed Eli's oxygen to 50 percent, which was good even though Eli's chest X-ray results weren't back yet. What bothered me was that Eli was in critical condition and Henry was not here to offer support to his son, but instead, chose to be in court. I fully knew Eli's father should be here, yet I was also relieved that he wasn't. Henry relished dishing out abusive and snide remarks aimed toward me and in earshot of our son, just to upset us. I knew when Eli heard this crap, the tears would start rolling down his little cheeks. Overall, it was best that it was just Eli and I at this time.

I spoke with Dr. Bamatay and Dr. Harder, head of PICU, regarding Eli. The prognosis was poor. I knew in my heart that my son would be going to Heaven, which in the past is where he told me he wanted to go. However, only God knew when that would be. Henry still wouldn't decide how far he was willing to take this, and what type of code, if any, he wanted Eli to have. That jerk was only punishing Eli the most, and me secondly. This was totally nuts! I knew four people in my life who chose to think of themselves only—Henry, my mother, Gavin, and one of my sisters, in that order.

Eli went into tachycardia (elevated heart rate) this morning, and he received some medicine to help the condition, but it was not working. I was doing what I could for Eli, and Henry just wanted to get out of child support. He wanted to try and make himself look better in court. Frida Bales, EU social worker, stopped by PICU to see Eli and we talked about his prognosis. Then we discussed what Henry planned to do in court today in Durango. She felt that Henry had sunk to a new low, and then she made a lot of phone calls to my lawyer Troy, Penny (district court clerk), the district court judge, and Zoe Green (SRS in Durango). She said that the judge was going to call her back, and for me not to worry about what Henry was trying to do and to just concentrate on Eli. That was precisely what I continued to do.

When the doctors made rounds again, Eli had to go back to 55 percent oxygen. Chest X-rays showed no change in my little boy's lungs, which was bad. They also said that it looked like Eli may have a new metastasis in his right upper arm, but they would leave that up to Dr. Benjamin to confirm. My heart sank further. When Dr. Benjamin came in, he said that it didn't look like the cancer had spread to Eli's upper right arm.

At about the same time, Carter (Henry's father) came in to have his blood tested to see if he was compatible with Eli. We found out that he was and may be able to donate after 2 p.m. today! Carter's blood was **drawn** this afternoon and the platelets would be administered to Eli this evening. I was grateful, but Carter didn't stop by so I wasn't able to thank him personally.

The early evening saw Eli's oxygen going back up to 55 percent. My heart simply ached. Just when I thought there was no more space for sadness inside of me, I found out that I was wrong.

October 5, 1990 – Friday

Eli received Carter's platelets last night. He went up to 60 percent on his ventilator, and could never get below 50 percent as he was titrated. Things looked so grim. It hurt so much to see him suffer. Eli's upper right arm was red, inflamed, hard, and hot to the touch, horrible this morning; nothing showed up on x-ray and that meant it had to be in the soft tissue of his wrist where his arterial line had been placed.

I sat with Eli, spoke to him, and caressed his left arm and cheeks. I gave him *mama* kisses and I prayed. Eli just wasn't getting any better, and all that was happening was too much for his thin little body. No child should suffer this way! No adult either!

The ICU doctors wanted to re-intubate Eli this afternoon and they wanted me to leave his bedside, which of course I refused to do. Eli was paralyzed and awake, and they finally got the new tube in on the third try. I spoke comforting words to him while they were doing this. He cried throughout the procedure and continued crying with his eyes closed for an hour afterwards. Tears kept pouring down his cheeks, and I kept trying to comfort him. What five-year-old needed this kind of pain? What five-year-old needed to be this scared? Lord, that must have been scary as hell for him, and I could only imagine his pain. Eli had to be kept at 70 percent oxygen. When they tried 60 percent, the oxygen saturation level dropped fast. Eli was to receive the rest of Carter's platelets tonight and lipids were started this evening. I heard the ICU doctors mention and discuss "shock damage" to Eli's lungs. My mind just swirled with what that meant. The few people I knew who had the same condition died from it. The Pneumocystis was no better. It was a fitful night between PICU and the floor of the waiting room.

October 6, 1990 – Saturday

Eli received the rest of Carter's platelets and his count afterwards was 43,000. He was hanging on around 65 percent oxygen on the ventilator. My son was such a scared little boy who couldn't move a muscle or verbalize anything. Yet, Eli knew what was being done to him and he heard all that was going on around him, and I saw the tears roll down his cheeks. That was when I started crying and I didn't want to for fear that such an act could only make him more scared, but it was futile to try to hold back my tears. Eli's tears abated somehow when he heard my soothing words. I hope he felt the pressure when I stroked his arm and face. *Mama* soothing strokes for a frightened child.

Eli had fifteen different tubes and wires, if I counted correctly, but at that point I didn't care how many there were. I just wanted him to feel better and not to suffer with all that was being done to his little body. Henry had called a couple times today and he had been abusive and harassed me on the phone, yet he didn't come back to EU even though the nurses and I had told him about Eli's condition. Eli was at 70 percent the rest of the day. He was restless in the late afternoon, and cried buckets. Seeing this just tore my heart to shreds.

At around 9 p.m. Henry showed up at EU. Maybe he finally realized Eli was deteriorating and may not have many days left. I didn't know.

October 7, 1990 – Sunday

Eli's X-rays showed no changes this morning and he stayed fever-free all night. This was good news as far as fever was concerned, but no improvement on x-rays meant zero improvement on the disease. The antibiotics were keeping the germs in check, but not killing them off as desired. We weaned Eli down to 60 percent on his ventilator and platelets were holding at 40,000, but he still needed one shot of Vitamin K to assist with his bleeding issues. Eli received 220 cc packed red blood cells this morning with his hemoglobin being very low. So many blood products have gone into Eli in the last 8-9 days. I was equally amazed and sad to see how his little body simply ate them all up extremely fast.

Dr. Hansen, head of PICU, and I talked at length at Eli's bedside this morning when Eli was actually sleeping. We spoke quietly and we both agreed things should be a whole lot better for Eli by now. My son had made so little progress. I knew deep down Eli would be in Heaven soon, but Henry just didn't get how serious things were. Even with more red blood cells carrying oxygen around, Eli had to go back up to 65 percent on his ventilator. He was not responding like we all hoped he would.

Eli appeared less ashen today than yesterday, and thank God he didn't look anything like he did the past few days. But that wasn't enough to get him well. The doctors had mentioned the possibility of a "chest tube" and what would be done if Eli got a pneumothorax. I prayed Eli didn't develop one.

Gavin showed up tonight and spent fifteen minutes with Eli before leaving. I phoned Ardy in the evening and updated her about Eli's condition. Afterwards, I talked to Noah. Hearing Noah's voice was like a salve to my hurting heart. Ardy and I, as well as the doctors and social workers, knew that the best thing for Noah right now is the stability that Ardy and school offered. PICU is no place for Noah.

October 8, 1990 – Monday

Eli had a lot of trouble trying to stay at 65 percent during the night and we could only maintain him at 70 percent. I irrigated Eli's eyes and administered moisturizing eye lubricant. I talked to him like I did each morning on our daily routine. The time I spend with Eli was so precious. I cleaned his ears with baby oil, suctioned him, put Vaseline on his dry cracked lips, skin care cream on his face and body, changed his Hickman dressing, and so much more. Eli listened to me as I worked. When he first heard me, he had tears in his eyes, but then he stopped crying. He knew his mama was with him, helping him out. I was afraid I wouldn't have this time with him for much longer. I was so scared, but I could not let Eli sense my fear. He spent most of the day at 75 percent oxygen. He was getting worse and I was not sure how long his little heart could keep up. I didn't want Eli to be coded. That was just too much for his frail body and I doubt it would work. When the time came for him to go, I prayed it would be an easy journey, and he could go to Heaven like he wanted to last summer.

I did full range of motion on Eli's upper and lower extremities twice today, just like the other days here in PICU. I didn't want Eli to develop contractures from being bedridden, and this gave me additional time with Eli that the staff could not deny me. Other extended family members arrived at EU to have their blood tested to see if they were a match for Eli. Henry was supposed to take them to the blood bank in Denver, but he never showed up. Later, Gavin and I searched for Henry without success. He was most likely in the bar one block away.

At around 10 p.m., we were able to get Eli down to 70 percent on his ventilator.

October 9, 1990 – Tuesday

Henry was finally found in his bed at the Ronald McDonald House at 8:30 a.m. when I went to take a shower. I never asked him where he had gone, and I didn't care. All I knew was he had been in a bar, instead of being with his sick son. I didn't need to know the details.

Eli continued to slowly deteriorate today. More X-rays were done on Eli's lungs, and abdomen, in the hopes of finding out what is causing his liver issues again. I believed all the medicine being thrown at Eli was taking a toll on his liver. What scared me though, was that the medicines were inevitable.

I spoke for a long time with Dr. Ardinger, a PICU specialist, while I did full range of motion exercises on Eli, and he said the outlook for Eli was not good. I knew that already, so I didn't understand why different doctors came and told me this. I wished instead that they would tell this to Henry and make him understand that Eli was sicker than he thought, and that it would be a bad thing to code Eli. Why code Eli just to break his ribs and cause more pain and trauma when the outcome would be the same? Why do that to Eli?

Dr. Ardinger said we could to two things. Number one, we could keep Eli on the current treatment until he eventually went to 100 percent oxygen on his ventilator. From there, Eli would go downhill until cardiac arrest happened.

Number two, the medical staff could go in for a lung biopsy and Eli may die on the table, probably even die a few hours after surgery. They might find out what he has in his lungs, possibly treat it… but Eli may still die. Henry wouldn't help make a decision and so I did what I thought was best. I decided to leave the treatment as is and keep my baby boy as pain free as possible. Just when I thought I couldn't cry anymore, out poured more tears. I cried silently around Eli as my heart broke into a million pieces. When I thought my heart couldn't possibly break anymore, it just ripped open a whole new tear.

Finally, I went out to the phone to call Ardy and speak with her and Noah.

Eli received four more units of platelets this evening.

October 10, 1990 – Wednesday

After midnight last night, I had the EU police take me over to the Ronald McDonald House so I could sleep just a little and take a shower. I stayed in the basement with the TV on yet not watching it. Somehow, I felt less alone with the sounds of the TV to keep me company. At around 4 a.m., I phoned the hospital to check in on Eli—no change in condition. The PICU staff knew where to call me if there was any change in Eli's condition, good or bad. While the doctors were making their morning rounds, I did Eli's usual morning cares including his Hickman dressing change and entire range of motion exercises, while talking to him as I worked. I knew Eli could hear my voice. He always gave me a sign, such as a single tear, to let me know he knew I was with him. I tried to tell Eli stories I made up as I went along, and I knew he heard them. I was not sure if they were a comfort or not, but they did help put him to sleep.

Eli had more tachycardia episodes today, with the highest at 206 beats per minute. His oxygen was at 80 percent on the ventilator. How could Eli hang on like this? It felt like I was keeping him from crossing over into

Heaven, since I had not been ready for him to leave when he had wanted to go to Heaven prior to his lung surgery, so he was hanging on just for me. That wasn't the case; my only wish was for him to be pain-free and happy. My heart easily found new places to rip open and send forth more tears.

How can one cry so much and still have tears left to shed? Eli had a temperature spike of 102.5 F this afternoon, so we placed an ice blanket on him. The doctors had been talking about an anti-viral, Acyclovir, as well as Erythromycin to treat the possibility of Legionnaires Disease. I think they were grasping at straws at this point. But anything to help make Eli more comfortable was good to go. If Acyclovir could help bring down Eli's fever, I was all for it. Eli had a CT scan of his head and his abdomen done this evening and I went along, sad to see how they had to bag him throughout the whole procedure. It was vitally important to me that Eli knew I was with him all the way. I was able to talk to him and make him feel that he wasn't alone. It was late when I had the EU police take me over to the Ronald McDonald House.

October 11, 1990 – Thursday

At around 3 a.m., I phoned to see how Eli was doing and his temperature was 103.0 F, and he had more ice blankets in place. When I checked back an hour later, Eli was fever-free. That was good, as it meant he was more comfortable now. Henry just had to come down to the recreation room where I was resting, to harass me sexually. His words hurt and were so cruel, but I couldn't let him see a reaction from me. Eventually, he left me alone.

When I spoke with Dr. Ardinger this morning, he informed me the CT scans showed nothing. Eli's liver (the bilirubin) went from 2 to 8. His liver was failing. I knew I would see color changes in Eli's skin and in the whites of his eyes soon. Dr. Ardinger gave Eli a 2 percent chance of making it through this alive, and he asked me how I felt about codes. I told him, "If Eli has heart failure, don't do anything." I also said, "I want an autopsy done." I wanted to know what would eventually cause his death.

Henry showed up by 1 p.m. and Dr. Ardinger came to talk to both of us. Henry *did not* want to accept the inevitable – that Eli wouldn't live one more week. Henry was adamant that if Eli's heart stopped, he wanted medicines used to restart his heart. He was so adamant about this, and it broke my heart knowing all that would do to Eli is prolong his suffering for another minute or so. He would never have the life we wanted for him. Thankfully, he said that he didn't want Eli to have "chest pounding" (chest compressions). The doctor noted that down with Henry's signature, which was good. I didn't want the man to change his mind. Eli desperately needed comfort and peace.

Eli received packed red blood cells at noon, and his little body was still eating up all that was given to him. Henry left and I spoke with Kristy Patterson, RN, with Dr. Landon, and the EU social workers about Eli's condition, and what Henry wanted done in the event Eli's heart stopped. I told them I wanted an autopsy done and they understood where I was coming from. Dr. Benjamin came in to see Eli at around 4 p.m. He said they wouldn't be trying the Erythromycin because they didn't really think Eli had Legionella pneumonia in his lungs. However, Eli could have received this latest *bug* from his last transfusion before PICU.

Dr. Benjamin placed his hand on my shoulder in a gesture that told me Eli wasn't going to make it. I already knew this in my heart. Eli went into PICU twelve days ago with soft tissue in his lungs (normal) and two weeks later, his lung tissue had turned into cardboard-thick tissue, fully scarred. It was really impossible to ventilate with that much lung tissue damage; and lungs don't heal. The day-long wait to get Eli some platelets flown in from Winter Park was too long. I know the scarring in his lungs wouldn't improve. Eli opened his eyes three times thus far today, and each time, he looked at me. Each time, I told Eli, "I love you" and he nodded his head in agreement. I asked Eli if he was hurting and he shook his head no. I think Eli was trying to protect me yet again – this five-year-old little boy on a ventilator was telling me he didn't hurt when I knew damn well he had to be hurting. I was the mom – I was the protector – *not the other way around!* I went along with what Eli wanted me to believe. I asked Eli if it would be okay to squirt Dr. Benjamin with his little calculator water gun, and he shook his head yes. Eli had wanted to do this to him since before PICU, but never got the chance.

We started Acyclovir, tobramycin, and increased the dose on vancomycin. By 9 p.m., Eli had his worst blood gas since he had been confined. Eli had to go up to 85 percent oxygen on his ventilator, and there were only three more settings left. Eli opened his eyes at that and looked at me twice. I asked him if he was hurting anywhere, and again, he shook his head no. These brief moments of time with Eli awake was more precious than anything, but I didn't want him to hurt. As Eli fell asleep, Roni's mom, Carlye's mom and Mitch, RN, from 5D stopped by briefly to see him. After they left, Henry told me again that it was my entire fault as I didn't take Eli to the right doctor; and then he promptly left. He said that so loudly everyone in PICU, and maybe even Eli, heard him.

God—I will give anything, including my life, just so Eli can tear down the hall on his Batman three-wheeler, see him playing Nintendo at the Ronald McDonald House or riding his red bike with training wheels, or playing with his brother again.

October 12, 1990 – Friday

Eli was bumped up to 90 percent oxygen early this morning and by 8 a.m., he was at 95 percent. His saturations were dropping like crazy and he was back in the low 80s by 8:30 a.m. The moment we've been dreading has arrived - we went up to 100 percent! I left to call Henry at the Ronald McDonald House and tell him about Eli's condition, and then I went back to Eli.

Dr. Ardinger said we could increase the morphine and the Valium and let Eli sort of wake up from the Pavalon, the medicine that was keeping him paralyzed so he couldn't pull out the tubes attached to his body.

Eli looked at me and then he looked at his father. He squeezed our hands and shook his head "no" when asked if he was in pain. All of the 5D nurses took turns coming in to see Eli, as well as Kristy Davis (school teacher). I knew they had been keeping up with Eli's progress/lack of progress. The oximeter that monitored Eli's saturations was turned off at 2 p.m. His saturations were 88 percent at that time. Father Spencer came in and we prayed for Eli and he anointed my son with oil. I didn't care what Henry thought of this. I was way beyond his non-belief in God, and I had so many staff in PICU to stop him from doing anything to stop me. One extra mg of Valium was given to Eli because he let me know by shaking his head "yes" that he was "still scared, very scared." Fifteen minutes later, Pavalon was given to Eli for the first time since midmorning—a full five hours had passed.

Dr. Benjamin thought Eli was doing just great; a real trooper. He said this so that Eli could hear him before the Pavalon took effect. Father Spencer came back and he lifted up to God two more prayers for Eli. Throughout the evening and the night, Eli turned a little yellowish and his oxygen via arterial blood gas was 43 percent. Eli was putting up such a fight, even though he knew he would be going to Heaven soon.

In my heart, I believed Eli was hanging on because I loved him so much and didn't want to lose him. As Eli fell asleep, I was still telling him that *everything would be okay.* I wanted Eli to be at peace, yet my heart was aching so badly.

October 13, 1990 – Saturday

Eli's platelets were down to 19,000 early this morning. His body was still using them up faster than we could give it to him. Eight more units of platelets were infused this morning, and Eli had bleeding ulcers in his mouth. I tried to soothe his pains as much as possible, since he needed his intubation tube. Another mg of Pavalon was added as Eli started moving around way too much in bed and he was crying so hard. I knew he hurt. I knew he was scared. I did my best to give him comfort and reassurance. My heart ached to see him crying so hard and so much. I spoke for a long time this morning with Dr. Goertz. He said that unless other complications occurred (such as a pneumothorax, etc.), Eli may hang on a few more days. Then he said, "When Eli's oxygen hits around 30 percent or lower, Eli would have an event." That meant his heart would cease beating.

Looking back, I was glad Eli got to wear his Batman outfit a few times and enjoy playing with the costume. My little "Halloween Batman" would never again wear his costume... not this year, not ever.

But I could have it placed with Eli before he is buried. Unfortunately, I never had the chance to buy film and take pictures of Eli in the costume, having fun like little boys do. This made me sad. I wanted special things placed in his casket with him, such as his costume, his baseball, Mickey Mouse and Donald Duck, his toy light saber sword, his favorite baby blanket, his autographed photo of George, his bear Precious, and a few more things.

Eli's labs dropped again right before noon. I sat at Eli's bedside as much as I could. Dr. Benjamin came by as usual this afternoon and I told him that Eli wanted him to try out his new calculator gun. He did and received a tiny squirt, and we both told Eli that Dr. Benjamin got wet from it. Eli opened his eyes and he saw Dr. Benjamin and I and his calculator squirt gun. He seemed satisfied with that knowledge. Musingly, I remembered that Eli also wanted to be a witch for Halloween with a real broom he could fly on. Eli also wanted to be a Ninja Turtle, Donatello. These musings, memories, and photos were all I had left of Eli, and I kept them safely in my heart.

Eli started spilling bile in his urine this afternoon, and when his nurse and I turned him to his left side, I noted the increased swelling in the area of his original tumor (right side neck and head). Eli had serious pitting edema throughout. He had an egg shell mattress, and even though we turned him every two hours, it was not enough. Eli's favorite nurse, Rita, stopped by to see him three times today and we talked for a while. His blood gas was worse this evening; oxygen at 37 percent. All I could do was pray for Eli and offer him mama comforts.

October 14, 1990 – Sunday

Eli was being a real trooper, hanging on for so long—*tough to the finish!* Blood gas at 4 a.m. remained the same, but his HGB and HCT dropped. Dr. Goertz made rounds after I did Eli's morning cares, medicine, and range of motion exercises. He took a culture from Eli's ear drainage, but I was not so sure Eli would be here when the culture came back. Midmorning labs found Eli's oxygen at 32 percent. Eli and his heart were tough to the end.

I spoke for a bit with Casey when she stopped by to deliver medications to PICU. I told her that it wouldn't be long now, and that Eli would be gone soon. She said she was happy to hear that and it would be good for him to be back on 5D. She thought Eli was going back to the pediatric floor. She didn't know. I explained what I meant and I saw her face fall. I didn't mean to break the news to her the way I did, but she needed to know the truth. We spoke a bit longer and then she left to deliver medication to the other units. With Eli's blood gases the way they were this morning, I knew that his saturations would be in the 60s venous. Even now, not a day went by without Henry letting me know that Eli dying was my fault.

Casey stopped by PICU again and we talked of Eli's antics at EU. We spoke of Eli hiding under a gurney and squirting water at everybody, to his sneaking around the desk by 5D step down so he could surprise the nursing staff. Eli wanting to take the newborn babies home with him, his love of the swimming pool back home, and his blond hair kissed by the sun. How Eli hated not being able to get into a bathtub because of his Hickman, and much more. These were precious memories for sure.

Eli woke up for a short while this evening, and it was so precious to have a few minutes to talk with him before he went back to sleep. Then, I phoned Ardy to give her updates on Eli and to speak with Noah. Noah was excited as he got to ride on a fire truck and he received a red fireman's hat during Fire Prevention Week activities. After they had arrived back to Ardy's home, Noah said, "We forgot to get Eli a hat." Ardy told him that maybe he had to ride the truck in order to get one, and Noah was content with that answer. I was so happy to hear his voice on the phone, and Ardy was the best ever to take care of him while I was gone. She went above and beyond for Noah.

Eli's 10 p.m. blood gas numbers were worse this evening. His heart would not be able to hang on much longer. I was left with nothing to do but cry and pray.

When I passed the phone outside of PICU, I heard Henry on the phone and I could tell he was talking with my mother. Henry was trying to say that I would want a big funeral for Eli, and that he didn't have the money for it. All I could think of was; here he was talking about money and what he thought I wanted, when he didn't have a clue. All I wanted was to have an autopsy, and know what happened to Eli, and maybe keep this from happening to another child down the road. To place his favorite things in his casket and have a simple graveside service. I knew the life insurance company would cover what I wanted, but I didn't feel like getting into that with Henry at this time. I spent my time going from Eli's bedside to the waiting room for chair naps, and then back to his side the rest of the night, while Henry went to the Ronald McDonald House and slept on a real bed.

October 15, 1990 – Monday

Eli was wide awake for half an hour at around 2:30 a.m. I just talked with him and peppered him with tons of mommy kisses on his face and forehead. I treasured this time together as I knew it was limited. I continued my usual routine with Eli and talked to him as I worked. At one point I thought, "Why am I doing range of motion when he would no longer benefit from it?" Then I realized, maybe his joints and muscles will no longer benefit, but Eli received the comfort of knowing his mom was there to massage him and talk to him. And this would always be enough.

Dr. Hansen wanted to talk with Henry and me so I called for him to come over to PICU. We met with him in the Family Consultation Room to talk and he gave us three proposals. One, leave Eli's treatment as it was and he might live one more day. Two, slowly decrease the ventilator settings, wean Eli off the ventilator, extubate him and allow Eli to die. Three, since Eli was tough, (and his heart refused to give out – no one thought he would make it through the weekend), we could give the germs hell and get back at them. To "grab at straws" in one last effort to save Eli and keep him alive.

Henry chose to "grab at straws" and I said I wanted Eli to have "no pain." By 3 p.m., we were giving Eli's germs all the hell we could; new antibiotics, new narcotic drug for pain relief, and increasing the pressure settings on his ventilator. Dr. Benjamin was in agreement; however, I think he would have agreed with anything we chose at this point. Then,

Dr. Benjamin said that sometimes it takes others longer to come around to reality—meaning Henry not believing Eli was actually dying.

Thirty minutes later, Eli woke up enough for his father and me to look into his eyes and for him to look at our faces. We asked Eli if he wanted to try the new medications in order to get better. If yes, he was to open his eyes wide. He did open them wide. *Eli wanted one last ditch fight so we went for it!* My eyes became wet with tears yet again for the courage that was burning inside my dear Eli's heart.

More new medications at 4 p.m., ventilator pressure settings increased and a pulse oximeter placed back on Eli. Eli's venous saturations were only 20 percent and wavered from 20 percent to 40 percent with his blood pressure steadily falling. It was up and down, up and down, up and down. I was afraid to use the restroom as I just knew Eli's time left on Earth was in minutes.

At 11:20 p.m., all hell broke loose and Eli crashed. His blood pressure and heart rate dropped so low… before his heart stopped. IV medicine to restart his heart was given like Henry wanted. Eli's heart stopped again and IV medicine was given yet again to restart his heart.

Then, Eli's heart stopped for the third time.

I looked at Henry and begged him through my tears to, "Let him go." He finally nodded yes, and Dr. Goertz pulled the plug at 11:35 p.m.

During the last fifteen minutes of Eli's life, I held his left hand with my left hand, while my right hand and arm encircled his head and shoulders. I was beside him and wasn't about to let him do this alone. I kept kissing his face and talking into his left ear, telling him it would be okay and that I loved him.

It was painful to know that love could only do so much.

October 16, 1990 – Tuesday

After the nurses pulled all the tubes from Eli, I held him in my arms and rocked him for about twenty minutes. Then, I told Henry he could hold him and he did. I went out and phoned my mother to let her know. Then, I phoned Ardy to update her with the sad news. I wanted her to keep Noah from school in the morning. I wanted to try and explain Eli's death to him myself, rather than hear things from the school. Eli's body was taken down to autopsy and the morgue. I left Henry in Denver to wait for my mother's arrival. She planned to bring Eli's body home in the back of her truck where his casket could fit.

I left for Durango and during the entire drive, I couldn't breathe. Even breathing hurt so much. Sobs and trying to breathe was all I remembered of the drive.

At 6:30 a.m., I arrived at Ardy's and I did my best to explain things to Noah, but he couldn't understand at first. When he did figure out what I was trying to tell him, he just cried. I lay down on Ardy's couch with my arm around Noah, giving him comfort. As I dozed off, I heard Ardy calling the school and saying, "Little Eli died last night." Two hours later, Noah and I went to Parson's funeral home and I made the arrangements. When we returned home, I tried explaining to him again that Eli was now in Heaven. He finally completely understood, and my heart broke with his as we cried together for more than half an hour. Our evening was a quiet one and Parson's called to tell me that Eli's body had arrived.

October 17, 1990 – Wednesday

Noah and I went to the bank and took out Eli's life insurance policy. Then, we went to Parson's and I gave them the policy and we ordered flowers for Eli.

Eli wore his Mickey Mouse T-shirt and jogging pants. We placed his EU Jayhawk cap with him, and tucked his favorite squirt gun in his little right hand, along with his "trick" calculator, his nylon Batman playsuit, and his He Man power sword at his right side. We added his Donatello Ninja Turtle, his favorite "witch" pin with roving eyes, a basket of M&M's from Delano, Eli's packet of stickers, his autographed picture of George along with his Royals baseball, his stuffed Panda bear, Mickey Mouse, and Donald Duck, a colorful Snoopy band aid, and Noah wanted him to have his "baby pillow," blanket and stuffed Garfield.

Noah touched Eli and he also kissed his hand. I kissed my baby many times. Then we watched as the casket was sealed. Afterwards, I caught hell from Henry and my mother for having the *Batman* costume in with Eli and that I was promoting the devil.

October 18, 1990 – Thursday

We buried Eli today at Bow Mar Cemetery. It was a long, long sad day. So many staff from the 5D nursing unit at EU drove miles for Eli's service. Eli meant that much to the nursing staff.

The Report

The days went by slowly and I could still feel Eli's presence. Every day, I still got up at 6 a.m. automatically, as though my son still needed me to care for him. The Hickman, the slow buzzing of the machines that surrounded Eli in his last days… I could almost see and hear them. And sometimes, I wondered if I missed having them around. At least I knew they co-existed with my Eli.

The autopsy result came in and much to my surprise, it revealed that Eli was free of cancer. ELI WAS FREE OF CANCER! But, how could that be? And if that was the case, what happened? Why did my son have to go?

I was confused and utterly heart-broken, but that was what the results showed. Too late though to save my son. It was just ironic that there was no germ found in my son's body, and that his death could probably be due to the total organ failure caused by chemotherapy.

This, in a way, meant that Eli was somehow victorious. He had won his battle against cancer, but his immune system had already been compromised. My son died of Adult Respiratory Distress Syndrome, secondary to depleted immune system, secondary to multi-system failure due to effects of chemotherapy.

I pray for people with cancer. I pray for the treatment plans and hope they could be improved, so that people with cancer do not die from what is supposed to be treating the disease. I pray that there be no more ironies between cancer and chemotherapy.

I pray…and I pray.

Part Four

The Days After

Words For Those Who Have Not Lost A Child/Children

It matters not the age of your child/children as child loss is the KING of loss.

The only way for me to try and help non-bereaved parents in understanding child loss is the following. What if you took a beautiful photo of your child not knowing it would be the last photo you ever took?

What if you gave your child a loving hug not knowing it would be the last hug?

What if you spoke with your child on the phone not knowing it would be the last time you heard their voice?

Does it get any easier after losing a child? Somewhat…

Is it possible for a parent to be happy their child/children are perfect in Heaven above… and feel peace with that? Sure… (It took me twenty-three years for Eli and somewhat less for Joshua.)

Can a parent ever "get over" losing a child? No. This is the KING of loss. We can be happy that they are perfect in Heaven and sad at times when we miss them the most.

Bereaved parents are continually re-writing each day, as they try to cope with their new "normal." This won't change. We will think of our loss when other children reach milestones such as their first tooth, first steps, first words, kindergarten, holidays, best friend, graduation, prom, falling in love, first kiss, learning to drive, getting married… the list is endless. There will always be reminders of our loss. It is possible for a parent who lost a grown-up child to derive a tiny, and I mean TINY, bit of happiness in knowing their child was able to experience school, graduation, prom, falling in love, first kiss, learning to drive, getting married, and having a child of their own. But truly this is miniscule.

The WORST things you can ever say to a parent who has suffered the KING of loss, even after one, ten, twenty, or more years? "You should be over it by now," or "Move on with life." You see, we are moving on with life. We just do it one hour… one day at a time… re-writing life as we go along.

~M. Schmidt, February 2018

Chapter Twenty-One

Losing Eli

In 1990 - Eli the angel flew...

After my little son passed away, I would curl up in bed and wait for his face to appear in the darkness that cloaked my room. I told my son in prayer, that I wouldn't be scared if he would appear before me, and he should therefore make himself manifest. I missed him so badly and just needed to know he was safe in Heaven. The mommy in me needed this. When I felt so weak because I could no longer eat, and sleep came by in small doses which does not alleviate the body's suffering, I would find myself hallucinating that he was floating just above me, smiling at his Mommy. I would jerk up in bed to catch him, but he would disappear. My dear little son, Eli had found a new and better comfort in God's lap.

Tears would roll down my cheeks, and they never ran dry. I was literally crying buckets of tears.

I stood up, remembering Ethel as she taunted me with the cassette tapes—recordings of Eli's voice whenever she spoke to my son.

I begged Mother a thousand times to let me hear my son's voice again. She never relented.

In the night, when I lay awake thinking about my relationship with my mother, I searched my heart for forgiveness. It was difficult, for she was a horrible mother.

Other times, I would dream that I was inside Ethel's house, and my hands would search frantically inside her dressers, in the bookshelves, anywhere she could have kept Eli's voice tapes—but the moment my hands closed upon them, Ethel would come barging in, slap me in the face, grab my hair, and drag me out of the house.

I would wake up drenched in sweat with my heart beating rapidly. Then, upon realizing that it was all a bad dream, I would curl up like a fetus and sob, missing my son's voice all the more.

I was afraid that no matter how vividly I engraved my little Eli's voice in my heart, old age would get me soon. It might become a struggle to remember my name; how much more my son's voice?

But days, no matter how dragging they were, lolled like an unwelcome guest, and soon a year had passed since my son's untimely demise. I could hardly believe it. The anniversary of the day Eli flew to become an angel of God was coming, and yet, in my heart, I still remembered his last months with me clearly.

I looked outside and noticed the gray skies as though they were grieving with me. Tears fell from my eyes because I was afraid of so many things. What if I forgot how he used to smile at me? What if the many memories we had started fading? What if there was to come a time when I would no longer remember the feel of his silken hair against my lips, the way his body used to curl against mine in comfort, and how he would stare me right in the eye and grin at me with such affection?

Somehow, I knew that as a mother, forgetting would be impossible. But old age would come, and memories would blur no matter how much I would try to keep them safely tucked in my head. So, I pulled out a notepad and poured out my heart. I started remembering the face of my angel—his blue eyes, his blond silky hair, and his angelic face. I remembered how each time I would look at Noah or Eli, I would feel God's promise of a better life. Eli was one of the good things He had given me.

I shut my eyes tightly and tried to fight back the tears. I had to be serene when I wrote Eli a letter; a confession that throughout the year, he had never left my mind.

I looked at the calendar on the side desk in my room. It was October 13, two days before the anniversary of Eli's death.

With trembling hands, I bent down and opened the bottom drawer of the table and pulled out the old typewriter I used when I was still in college. The clean sheets of paper were atop the desk. I took one and fed it into the typewriter.

I stared at the blank paper for a long time. How would I start? Did I even have the courage to put down into words my feelings? And yet, when my fingers started hitting the keys, they danced as though they were alive. I wrote down my thoughts—opening my soul to write as honestly as I could—and yet keeping a lid on my emotions, so I wouldn't bawl as I told my son how badly-sadly he was being missed.

It was still two days before the anniversary of when Eli had gone to Heaven. But the words in my heart couldn't wait anymore. The emotions started pouring out on paper, amusing me how the five years we were together had held so many beautiful images.

Like a moving-picture, the images fluttered in my head. And my pen started to transcribe all that I was bottling inside my heart.

October 13, 1991

My Dearest Eli,

Yet again, tonight, I went to bed crying for you, Eli. Heart wrenching sobs escaped from me and in between them I relived your short life with such clarity.

I knew you were very special, Eli, from the day you were born. And now, with the first anniversary of your death upon us, I realize fully just how special you really were and still are. You affected so many people in your short life.

Even now, I have moments when it is hard to believe that you are really gone. Or are you? You're in my heart now and forever.

Will it ever get easier, Eli? Sometimes, I am very happy for you. Those times are when I know you are pain free and happy. Heaven must be such a wonderful place.

Then, there are times when my heart aches and aches for you, Honey. Those are the times when I relive moments of your childhood before the doctor diagnosed you with cancer, and also moments after being diagnosed.

I remember vividly the day you were brought home from the hospital after your birth. Your brother, Noah, only one-year-old, took to you instantly. Throughout your short life, the two of you were inseparable. Best playmates you two were. But you were the most daring, Eli. You had such a zest for life.

I remember the day you and Noah were on your 3-wheelers and racing around in and out of the garage. Noah came running into the house to tell me you had a snake cornered in the garage. Upon investigation, there you were, laughing with delight, and riding your 3-wheeler in circles, closer and closer, to a coiled king size bull snake.

Sometimes, when I wake in the morning Eli, I start to think about what I'm going to make my "boys" for breakfast. And then I remember.

And sometimes in the evening, when Noah is taking his bath, I remember how it always was two boys in the bathtub and not one.

My precious Eli, oh, how I miss you. I miss your sweet smile, shining blue eyes and pale blond hair.

You had to grow up so fast, Eli. It was such a shock to learn that you had cancer, one month before your fifth birthday. In a flash, I would have traded places with you.

You went from being a happy little boy into a world of doctors and nurses, needles and IVs, catheters and spinal taps.

I was selfish, Eli. I loved you too much to let you die. And so, you suffered. You went through head and neck, and open chest surgeries. How my heart ached for you, Eli, when, four hours after surgery on your lungs, I helped a nurse stand you up in bed. How you hated ICU.

Because I loved you too much to let you go, you suffered such horrible radiation burns on your sweet head and neck. The chemotherapy made you so very sick. Even under sedation, you were sick. But you knew the "good guys" were out to get the "bad guys". At four years old, you knew you would die without treatment.

It hurt me so bad that you were unable to eat for seven and a half months. Your only nutrition was IV. You always ate so well before. You had always relished the sheer taste of food. It was unfair of me to bring food into your room in the hopes that you would eat something. Sometimes you tried. I remember when you woke during the night once and asked for watermelon. I drove through half of Denver to get it for you. You only ate a couple of bites, but it was worth it.

I remember the long days and nights in the hospital those seven and a half months. I was able to take you home only four different weekends. I remember the isolation in times of high fever and the ice blankets, lots of oxygen and machines everywhere.

How I cried Eli, on the morning that we woke up and found all your hair lying in your bed and not on your head. You were too proud to wear a hat.

I also remember good times, like when the group came from the Denver baseball team and you received an autographed photo of George and a Royals' baseball. Or I would be wheeling you around, outside the medical center, and you would point out cars and ask me if they were "race cars." How we would talk about the race car we would have someday and how much it would be worth.

Having lived two hundred and thirty miles away, you were awestruck by the freeways in and out of Denver. You thought they looked like race tracks.

And how about the time I was able to take you to the Denver Zoo? You did not mind that I had to push you, a boy at five years of age, in a stroller, up and down the hills. You were so weak. You did not care; you only wanted to see the animals.

And on good days, I also remember how you would hide under a gurney in the hall and wait for a person to pass by, only to give them a good dose of water from your squirt gun. It did not matter to you whether or not you knew the person you squirted. Sometimes, you would sneak around the nurses' station and into the medication room, fully loaded with water, and let loose. No doctor, nurse, or visitor was safe from you.

Or how about the times an IV would complete and I would unhook you. You headed straight for your three-wheeler and down the hall you zipped. Everyone stayed out of your way and laughed. Such sport you had.

Other times, when you had to stay in bed, you made me chase down a VCR so you could watch Superman or Ghostbusters. You never tired of those two movies. You knew them by heart and delighted in telling anyone who would listen what would happen next.

I remember the times when you would have to undergo yet another series of X-rays, CT scans, or MRI and I would stay by your side throughout them, telling you stories and keeping you from moving.

I'm sorry, Eli, that I was not able to make you well. I think that you went through all that you did, those seven and a half months, simply because of how much I loved you and did not want to let you go.

I remember the times that I would feel down and you would come up to me. You would put your arms around me and say, "I'm sorry, Mom."

I remember when we were together, waiting in the OR before your lung surgery. You were feeling well and you looked at me and said, "I want to go to Heaven, Mom." I was speechless. And then I told you that sometimes we don't get what we want and that you might have to come back to me.

And yet, I remember so well how after your last chemo, you picked up yet another "bug" and ended up on a respirator; just how much you fought for life as we knew it, those last fifteen days.

Most of all, Eli, I remember how I cradled you in my arms, and whispered into your ear that soon you would not have any more pain and it would be okay, as your heart stopped for the third and last time, and you died in my arms.

Thank you, Eli, for going through what you did because I loved you and did not want to let you go.

I'll always love you.
Mama

I had so much to say. I didn't think that I was prolific, and yet, when it came to you, Eli, I wrote down pages. The pages were bleeding, not with blood, but with ink that blotched with my tears. I had no courage before today to write down these words because doing so would make it so real… that you would never come back to me.

As I read the letter once again, I broke into sobs. Up until now, I still couldn't let you go, Eli. What every parent said was true—that it was wrong to have to bury your child. I never really understood the depth of those words before, *until my turn came to bury you.* It was so wrong to have to see you go away, Eli. But like the angel that I knew you were, you flew. Far away, another angel awaited you as I was sure that your brother Joshua would have been delighted to finally meet you. And this time around, with two angels watching over my shoulders, the burden of losing two of my children may somehow be more tolerable.

But who was I kidding? No amount of words would comfort me now. Not yet, because I was still grieving. Another year would pass by, and another, and another— and maybe then, I would get accustomed to having only one son here on earth with me instead of three.

I love you, Eli, I whisper repeatedly. *I love you.*
Always and forever, Mama.

Epilogue

When Angels Fly

When Eli passed away, many of his things were given to Henry: clothes, photos, toys, painted pictures, and things they both made at school. I regretted not having kept at least one of Eli's shirts. Something to remember him by with his scent.

Eli's burial service cost $1908.34. Aside from that there were other expenses such as the stone for him, and Joshua as well. Overall, the total amounted to $2908.34.

A vault was selected, but I couldn't afford a steel one and neither Henry nor my mother wanted to pitch in and help. Apart from that, I also chose the service. I had life insurance on both my boys and that's how I was able to do this. My mother wasn't aware of the insurance, and she went on and on about the cost, yet I paid for all of it. Henry carried on about the cost as well, but then he wanted some of the insurance money, which he never received from me. This had to be accounted for to SRS, and it would have hurt Noah and I had I given him any money. Besides, he never paid the life insurance premiums anyway.

In January of 1991, shortly after Eli's demise, Dr. Brown and the Ear, Nose and Throat Specialist, Dr. Noonan, left their practice. I will always believe Eli did not have to die. I still think Eli could have been saved if it wasn't for incompetent doctors and radiologists. Dr. Brown went into the insurance side of practice, and Dr. Noonan moved to Arkansas.

In 1991, my petition for divorce was granted. I felt relieved that there were no more legal ties holding me to Henry. A connection severed to give way to something wonderful.

I wanted to marry Matt in the Catholic Church. So, working with Father Barry, I was allowed to have an annulment, and for that I was grateful.

While my life started to have some color once again, with Matt in my life, the moments of pain still came incessantly. It came in various forms, and one that scarred me so badly was when my mother repeatedly told me that she had Eli's voice on tape and that I would never get to listen to his voice as she would never allow it. She would call me and taunt me about it, and no amount of pleading would make her heart grow softer. I was begging her not just as her daughter, but as another mother who knew all too well the pain of losing a child. And so, I hoped she would understand. But she never did, for how can I expect someone so heartless to feel for me? My mother said she recorded everything. My siblings did my mother's bidding, but only when there was something in it for them.

I remembered when Eli was taken off the muscle relaxer, Propofol. Eli cried on and on, but when asked if he was scared a lot, Eli shook his head no. When asked if he was just a little scared, he nodded yes. I told the doctor I wanted Eli to have an autopsy. Casey came to see me in PICU. Then the jerk Henry worried about the cost of bringing Eli's body home. He went on and on about the cost. While I was meddling with my emotions, the jerk was worrying about the bills. It would have been all right if his intention was to provide for us. What became transparent was that he did not care about Eli.

I remembered the last moments of Eli's life and they still tear at me. Eli had been put on 100 percent ventilator. EU had not been a good place for Noah then, even though it meant him not seeing his brother alive again. Henry had not wanted Gavin to come to EU as well, as Eli wouldn't make it through the night and Gavin gets too emotional about things, according to Henry. Eli's heart rate was up to 178 and his saturations were hanging at 88 – 89 percent. Eli had opened his eyes and looked around; and before he started fighting the ventilator they had to give him

Propofol again, so Eli would not pull at his tubes. Eli had known he was going to Heaven just like he had wanted to do before the surgery on his lungs. Riley had picked up Noah for a visit, and Gavin had taken him back to Ardy. Eli's blood pressure had been normal, but his heart rate would go down. His heart rate had lowered to 30 beats a minute; and I had wondered how long Eli could hold out.

Henry had been really upset about social workers being around him now, especially because they had not been getting along well. He had hated Frida Bales the most. He said that he did not want Gavin down in Denver and that Gavin had displayed anger and had thrown his fist into Eli's wall, the elevator, and that he had cried when talking to the nurses. Henry had not wanted me to hear this, and he most definitely did not want Gavin's seizures and his issues to come out in court. Henry and Gavin were alike in many ways.

Henry thought he would win custody of Noah, but he would not. I loved my son too much to let him suffer at his father's and grandmother's hands. Henry had been threatening to file a lawsuit on the social workers at EU. He also made an allegation that I kept him from seeing Eli. Sadly, Henry had no leg to stand on. The social workers had seen Henry in action and they had known what he was capable of. Henry said it was not right that family (meaning Gavin who refused to wash his hands and punched out at walls) could not go into Eli's room, but that my friends (Anna, Lucy, Matt) and drug dealers (no dealers, no one on drugs) could.

But Henry was just being a royal bastard, as he well knew that Gavin had been having more seizures lately, even wrecking his car when he had a seizure after leaving work one time, and his visiting Eli would only pose danger to both Eli and Gavin.

On the other hand, Riley's voice had been light and she had seemed happy that Eli was dying. While Eli laid there and his life slowly ebbing away, my mother—this for the love of God I could not understand—had wanted to be the center of attention. That was vanity at its finest.

On December 9, 2013, which was a Monday, I finally managed to get my hands on the cassette tapes. I ran one on a player and I didn't know if listening to it was a mistake. I should have left the tape alone. Instead, I ended up bawling so badly.

The words I listened to were those of Eli begging his grandmother to leave. It was back in March, a Wednesday, at the Frisco Hospital in Silverthorne, Colorado. My mother came to Eli's room when my boy was not feeling well after the biopsy on his neck the day before, and she would not leave until making Eli and I upset. Eli kept saying to me, "Make her go away. Make her go away. Make her go away."

My tears welled down as my son's voice filled my ears. I remember the incident distinctly. My mother didn't budge until police came upon the summons of the nursing staff. Picture this—Eli was in so much pain and he had wanted (to the point of begging) his grandma to leave.

It is true, I had wanted all this time to hear my son's voice again, but not like this. Not the agony nor the begging; none of this. And yet, that was what I got—Eli begging me to make his grandmother leave. The police did make my mother leave, eventually. Eli just wanted his brother and me with him at the hospital. More than twenty-three years later, I finally heard my precious Eli's voice, only to hear him just wanting my mother to leave his hospital room.

On December 14, 2013, a Saturday, a friend of mine came to me who had been key in renewing my faith. After the things that I went through, I reasoned that my hate-love relationship with God was only fitting. I could count numerous reasons for hating Him: Eli's suffering, my mother's torture, my rough childhood, my marriage to Henry, abuse of Noah. And then the vicious cycle when things would start to turn out right, and yet again, I would battle challenge after challenge like Noah's cancer scare.

Each Christmas season, I confessed my sin for hating God at times. I cried each time I heard Eli's favorite song, Silent Night. This year, the tears would be joyful as it dawned on me that Heaven was where Eli wanted to be, that he was with his brother, Joshua, and they both sat on Jesus' lap.

At age five years, Eli wanted to go to Heaven. He knew of Heaven already, but my grief had overwhelmed me so much at times I just could not embrace this fully in my heart. Michelle made me realize that yes, Eli did want to go. Eli knew Heaven. Eli was not afraid to go, and I was the one holding him back.

Now, Eli flies with his brother Joshua and the other angels. It is with quiet acceptance that I conjure their images inside my head—that they are looking over their brother Noah.

Thank you, Michelle, for opening my eyes and allowing me to fully see the peace that came with knowing Eli and Joshua are in Heaven. Thank you, God, for giving me the peace I have been seeking for quite a long time.

Let the hate go; follow the Lord; He doesn't forsake any of us.

Not even when it was two of my angels that flew.

A Beautiful Day

On July 25, 1992 – Marriage to Matthew

Wearing smiles and the beautiful white, lacy dress, I committed myself to be the partner of the man who would stay with me forever, holding my hand. I knew this with certainty.

He smiled at me and his eyes shone with so much love and warmth.

It was wrong for me to remember Ethel at the moment that I felt my happiest, but her face just popped inside my head.

She's my mother, and she was married six times. Her first marriage lasted for twenty-one years, and then she started seeing younger men in the next county, followed by seeing married men in the same county. She divorced my dad when I was age fourteen and I was old enough to choose who I wanted to live with, and I chose my dad, Howard. Dad remarried to a wonderful woman but she died first. Dad died at age 82 of colon cancer.

Ethel's second husband though was taken away from her shortly after they married [six weeks married – George – awesome step-dad, buried on my mentally ill sister's birthday - April 21]. He had a heart attack. Then, there was Paul whose death earned mother the nickname "Black Widow." Lastly came Randy, and he died of a stroke, then she died many years later in November 2012 after having a brain hemorrhage stroke. My mother left my father after she started working on the evening shift at Ell-Kan in Durango. She had started to party with the young men on that shift, in the parking lot of Ell-Kan. She would arrive home drunk at times. My father worked nights and he had no clue when she presented him with divorce papers. After dating younger men, she married George. After he died, she then went after only the married men in Durango County, as though being married was a measure of a man's goodness.

My mother was always looking out for herself. She broke up one marriage and almost broke up two others. I was so uncomfortable with her behavior. Then, she went after the brother of a man whose marriage she broke, and they had a relationship of sorts. It was so embarrassing to be sitting outside his home, waiting in the car, for her to complete her sex act with him. Mother would come out of the house and join me in the car, and have my older sister, Blake, or I drive her home.

But enough of my mother's affairs; she had to answer to God.

Now, here I was about to take the vow for a second time. The first one I took with Henry ended in a sour divorce in 1991. And a year after that, I was to be married again. I shivered and felt cold. Was I doing the right thing?

Then my mother's face invaded my head again and it scared me, because I never wanted to be like her.

But I looked at Matt and he was smiling at me so warmly. This man was my best friend. He was holding my hand so tightly. Standing before him, a realization came to me. Even though I had my mother's genes in me, there was no doubt that I would become—what I hoped I would be—a better wife and mother.

Because the second time I married was because of love.

I put on his finger the ring that would bind me to him; and he did the same. In that essence, we were one.

Life would be beautiful this time.

And for a while, I forgot the pain I endured when angels fly.

Other Days Gone by and Some Family Background

Noah was sick, very sick in March 1994. He was ten years old and on medicine for a sinus infection. All of a sudden his temperature shot up and he developed a large swelling on his right neck, near his brain stem. I rushed him to Silverthorne and they were too afraid to do anything, so they said to go to EU (Silverthorne staff thought the mass was cancer). We rushed him to EU, and once the pediatric nurses saw him, they all came over - the ones who cared for Eli. Noah asked me if he was going to die like Eli did and it broke my heart. After scans were done, he went into surgery and they found that one tonsil was enlarged, blocking the area behind it. The area on my son's neck was drained of serious infection. It wasn't cancer, but a large mass of infection, and they got it out in time to keep it from going through the blood/brain barrier. Four weeks later, his tonsils were removed. This was very scary for Noah, and I was so worried. Two days post op, I was able to take him home with a large bandage and drain tube (Penrose) in one opening in his incision to allow the rest to drain out.

Today is twenty-three years (at 10:35 p.m. Central Time) since our little five-year-old Eli passed away with my arms around him. After his little heart stopped for the third and last time, I begged Henry to just let him go to Heaven. He finally consented. Then I rocked Eli for twenty minutes in a rocking chair before leaving pediatric ICU and EU and headed for home. My breath was just beaten out of me; it was so draining. But I knew Eli's body would be brought back by family after the autopsy. I only wanted to get home to my only living son.

I saw Matt at 5:45 a.m. and told him, and we prayed together. Then, I headed to Ardy's house as I knew Noah would be awake by then. I arrived at Ardy's house by 6:30 a.m. I told my son in person that Eli had died and gone to Heaven, hugging him as I broke the news. I had to be certain I was the one to break the news to him.

I kept on remembering this inside my head.

Tears would yet again spring from my eyes, which were now riddled with faint lines. Surely, the years had not made the pain subside. It ebbed and flowed.

Family Dysfunction, My Siblings

Now it seemed that many of my siblings were siding with my mother but what they were really doing was they didn't want her to cut off the money she dangled in front of them like a carrot on a stick. Some of my siblings feared my mother, but it was not that way with all my siblings.

My older brother, Caleb, hated conflict of any sort. When his sons were younger, he would bring his family to Durango near the holidays. When the boys became older, Caleb stopped doing this and discontinued visiting my mother. Years would go by without a visit and Caleb was happier that way. Caleb was an *only child* for seven years and he raised his children in Harwood, Colorado.

He saw my mother once, very briefly, in November 2012, in the hospital in Winter Park, Colorado, after she had a stroke.

My older sister, Blake, at one point in time, was a driver for my mother, after she finished with whatever man she was currently seeing and having sexual relations with. Blake became pregnant at age seventeen, married in May 1977, and had her first son on Thanksgiving Day of 1977. She had two more children, and what else was notable was the fact that Blake had to have my mother thrown off the premises where she, her husband, and three children lived. My mother had taken her to task as my mother decided Blake was insane. Of course, Blake was not insane.

Blake had a *Protection from Abuse* order placed on my mother for many years. Blake and her family moved to a different town in Durango County, and my mother would drive by their rural home on occasion and so Blake and her family moved to Juno, Colorado, for many years. My mother would drive by her place there as well, and finally Blake and her family moved to Gaylord, Colorado, where they stayed. By then my mother had other "fish to fry," other children she could harass to see things her way and *only her way*.

I would be remiss if I did not mention that Blake, one year older than me, also went to the sheriff of Durango County, and gave him her views regarding the death of my step-father Paul. Blake had not seen or had contact with my mother for decades, but she did go to Winter Park, Colorado, to see my mother once after her stroke. I really was not sure if Blake wanted to see my mother, or if she had only wanted to meet her great nephews.

I was born next and we know where we are now in my story. As a nurse, as a person, I did go to see my mother in the hospital in Winter Park, Colorado, but I went to make sure my son was okay, and I wanted the nursing staff to make sure my mother received morphine IV for pain and Ativan IV for restlessness. They assured me they would do this and so I left. My mother did open her eyes and she did hear exactly what the nurse and I discussed. I had no idea what went through my mother's head at the time regarding my visit, and I did not really care. She knew I had been there and she was able to communicate by shaking her head yes or no. I never cried over her in the hospital nor have I ever up to this very day.

I was not present when her urn of ashes was buried.

Younger brother Gavin came along two years after I was born. Gavin had a brain tumor found when he was a teenager, it was not cancerous, but it did cause seizures, and he was an emotional person due to the tumor's location in his brain. He cried easily all the time. He became estranged from my mother not long after Eli died. Gavin liked having the money she gave him to get any little bit of information on me that she could twist and turn to her advantage. After Gavin became estranged, he never saw my mother again to my knowledge, nor did he go to Winter Park, Colorado, to see her before she died.

Then Riley followed after Gavin one year later. She loved living rent-free in a trailer provided by my mother. Riley did most anything my mother wanted her to do, but only if she was able to benefit in some way financially or otherwise. What was most interesting was the fact that Ella's girls, Ava and Emily, were so scared of Grandma that they moved most of their things into Riley's trailer one night as Ella slept. The next night, as Ella slept, Matt and I, along with Lily, her husband and three sons, helped them move with Riley to a different house in a different town. Then things were set in motion legally. Ava was a senior in high school and Emily a sophomore. Ava is on her second marriage and Emily is not far behind her. Both left Colorado after turning eighteen.

Ella was born a year later. She had been plagued by mental illness for most of her life starting with the abuse she received from a neighbor. She was so afraid of her shadow for many, many years afterward. She always felt that her shadow was chasing her.

Ella has been dependent on Social Security and my mother all her life even though my mother did brainwash her and treat her with physical, emotional, and mental abuse.

Two years later, Lily entered our lives. She was the baby for so many years until Gabriel joined the family. She was not the last to be estranged from my mother, but she had to have my mother thrown off her property with the aid of her husband, Morgan, and my mother never got to see her or Lily's children again until she had the stroke and was dying.

My mother would drive by and harass Lily's children when they were working on a roof of a home in Kiowa. When her youngest was around six years old, they had become estranged.

In 1978 – Innocent Gabriel was born with Down syndrome.

Caleb saw mother at the hospital once for a bit before she died; he chose not to see her urn buried. Blake went to the hospital in Winter Park once, too. She gave my mother one look, smiled at her in a malicious manner, and then she decided that Adam and Noah were who she wanted to see more of so she never went back. She chose not to see the urn buried.

Then I went, too. Gavin never once went to see my mother as she lay dying and he chose to not go for the urn burial. Riley saw mother once before she died, but she did not go to the urn burial, and Ella, well, you know that one. Lily went to see her once, and then Lily decided she just could not scatter her ashes over my stepdad Paul's ashes at Bow Mar, so she decided to have the urn burial at Bow Mar Cemetery.

Lily was the only one present for that. They all liked the stone I bought for Gabriel although none of my siblings offered to provide money for the stone. I knew that none would offer, and I liked the fact it was I and I alone that did that for my baby brother.

I spoke to Caleb and his wife, sometimes with Blake. Gavin was out on occasion in Silverthorne and I see him; I do not see Riley anymore but we did practice nursing together in Silverthorne. Lily is a drill sergeant with questions; I try to avoid her.

As it turned out later in life, Mother promised the house to Noah, yet she died "intestate" November 2012. The estate remains unsettled as of November 30, 2013, as I am contesting the legality of the adoption of Ava, who was born of my younger sister Ella, who had mental health issues. My mother had forced Ella to allow her to adopt Ava, while she was in a mental hospital.

Ava is not happy with me right now, but eventually karma runs its feisty hand and now it is Ava in the hot seat. She knows her adoption was never truly legal. Almost all accounts were in her name and so all the oil money and such are completely under her control.

As you can see, none among us were brought up in a home where love and hugs thrived.

On Matt's side though, I do have some of his siblings who consider me their sister and I feel the same way. To have a man who truly loves you is most precious. I am thankful that Matt is in my life, I am thankful to have had my boys on Earth for the time the Lord let me have them; I am most thankful for Noah – the one who kept me going all those long months – the ones who I fought hard to save and keep from my mothers and Henry's grasp, and I am thankful for Matt's sister, Jolana, as she has shown me what being sisters really mean.

After everything, I am simply—thankful.

About S. Jackson & A. Raymond

S. Jackson aka Mary L. Schmidt is a retired registered nurse who has won numerous awards, including the coveted Leora B. Stroup award in nursing excellence and community involvement. She is a lifetime member of Sigma Theta Tau International, the largest international nursing organization. Mary is a member of the Catholic Church, and has taught kindergarten Catechism. She has worked in various capacities for The American Cancer Society, March of Dimes, Cub and Boy Scouts, (son Gene is an Eagle Scout), and sponsored trips for high-school music children to Washington, DC. Mary loves all forms of art, but mostly focuses on the visual arts, such as amateur photography, traditional, and graphic art as her disabilities allow. Recently, she has begun writing poetry. Mary loves being a wife to Michael, mother to Gene, and grandma to Austin and Emma. Contact her at ShaneGeneSamuel@gmail.com.

A Raymond aka Michael Schmidt is a member of the Catholic Church and has helped his wife with The American Cancer Society, March of Dimes, Cub and Boy Scouts, and sponsored children alongside his wife on music trips to Washington, DC. He devotes his spare time to fishing, reading, playing poker, Jeeping, travel adventures with his wife, and spending time with grandson, Austin, and granddaughter, Emma.

Please leave a review wherever this book was purchased.

Thank you.

Fresh Ink Group

Independent Publisher

&

Hardcovers
Softcovers
All Ebook Platforms
Worldwide Distribution

&

Indie Author Services
Book Development, Editing, Proofing
Graphic/Cover Design
Video/Trailer Production
Website Creation
Social Media Management
Writing Contests
Writers' Blogs
Podcasts

&

Authors
Editors
Artists
Experts
Professionals

&

FreshInkGroup.com
Email: info@FreshInkGroup.com
Twitter: @FreshInkGroup
Facebook.com/FreshInkGroup
LinkedIn: Fresh Ink Group

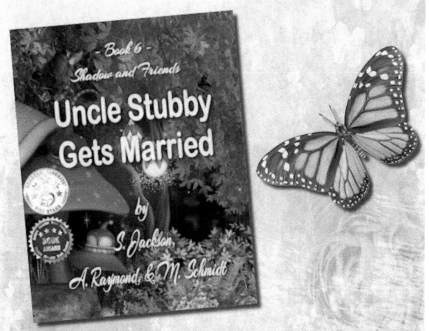

Believe in Valentine Fairy Forests and tap into the flavor of a whimsical wedding and celebrate the love of two squirrels!

@MaryLSchmidt writes under the pen names S. Jackson and A. Raymond. She writes, Illustrates, and edits books for all ages. She believes that children should have books, and be read to, so children can explore their imaginations without limits.